Gordon Bowker is Principal Lecturer in Sociology at the University of London Goldsmiths' College. He was born in 1934 and educated at King Edward's Grammar School, Camp Hill in Birmingham, Nottingham University and the University of London. At sixteen he went alone to Australia and worked on sheep farms, then spent three years in the RAF, mostly in Egypt and Cyprus. He spent two years as Visiting Professor in Canada, in New Brunswick and Alberta, and in 1983 went to Mexico to cover the filming of John Huston's version of *Under the Volcano* for *The Observer*. He wrote and presented a radio programme on Lowry, *The Lighthouse Invites the Storm*, which was broadcast as a tribute on the novelist's birthday, in July 1984.

He has edited three books, *Under Twenty, Freedom: Reason Or Revolution?* and *Race And Ethnic Relations*, and is the author of a book about immigrants. He is currently working in the field of biographical studies, with special reference to literary biography.

· GORDON BOWKER ·

MALCOLM LOWRY
Remembered

ARIEL BOOKS

BRITISH BROADCASTING CORPORATION

Acknowledgements

The publishers, and Gordon Bowker, wish to thank the many contributors and their relatives listed here who have allowed us to use their material for this book. (In spite of all efforts we have been unable to trace: Charlotte Haldane, Edwina Mason, Joseph Warden.)

Dr Earle Birney, Harvey Burt and Dorothy Templeton Burt, Dr Ralph Case and Adrienne Case, Roger Davenport, Laura M. Deck, Robert Duncan and the National Film Board of Canada for permission to print the following people's extracts: Hugh Sykes Davies, Albert Erskine, Jan Gabrial, Dr Michael Raymond, John Stirland; Eric Estorick, Elaine Greene Ltd for Arthur Calder-Marshall's interviews, James Hepburn, Ronnie Hill, Clarissa Lorenz Aiken, Russell Lowry, William C. McConnell, Dr C. G. McNeill, David Markson, Gerald Noxon, Mrs Trekkie Parsons, John Sommerfield, James Stern.

We also thank the following for giving permission to quote from published material in copyright.

George Allen & Unwin, extract from *The Land Unknown* (originally published by Hamish Hamilton) by Kathleen Raine; *Les Lettres Nouvelles*, extract from an article by Clarisse Francillon, translated by Suzanne Kim; Literistic Ltd, extract from *Malcolm Lowry: Psalms and Songs*, published by New American Library 1975, by Norman Matson; *The Paris Review*, Volume 42 (Spring–Summer 1968) and Viking/Penguin's series *Writers at Work Volume 4* and Secker & Warburg Ltd for the extract from an interview by Robert Hunter Wilbur with Conrad Aiken.

First published 1985

Published by the British Broadcasting Corporation
35 Marylebone High Street, London W1M 4AA

Typeset by Phoenix Photosetting, Chatham
Printed and bound in Great Britain by
Mackays of Chatham Limited

ISBN 0 563 20374 9

Contents

Preface

It was while gathering material for the BBC radio programme, *The Lighthouse Invites the Storm*, to mark 28 July 1984, when Malcolm Lowry would have been seventy-five, that the idea for this book emerged. Audrey Coppard and Bernard Crick had already compiled an excellent collection of reminiscences about George Orwell, *Orwell Remembered*, based on published memoirs, unpublished letters and material gathered for several BBC radio and television programmes. The Corporation had produced two previous documentaries on Lowry: *Rough Passage*, made for BBC TV by Tristram Powell and Melvyn Bragg in 1967, and, in the same year, a radio programme, *A Portrait of Malcolm Lowry*, written and narrated by Arthur Calder-Marshall. Numerous memoirs had also appeared since his death in June 1957, but had never been brought together in any systematic way to show this unusual writer's life from a variety of points of view.

There seemed also to be another important reason for producing this collection. Two biographies of Lowry were published almost simultaneously in Britain in 1974: Muriel Bradbrook's *Malcolm Lowry: His Art and Early Life* and Douglas Day's *Malcolm Lowry: A Biography*. Bradbrook's work is much to be preferred, although it is shorter. In spite of the fact that it is often referred to as 'the definitive biography', Day's book suffers from a number of weaknesses. It contains, in the first place, a number of factual errors which even the recently published paperback edition 'with corrections' does not correct. Then there are gaps in the narrative, due to Day's failure fully to consult the Lowry family about Malcolm's childhood and to trace Jan Gabrial, his first wife. Finally, the psychoanalytic interpretation which he places on the life is not only tedious but imposes a reading which is virtually closed to any alternative understanding. This collection of reminiscences attempts to make amends for these biographical shortcomings.

A number of people have offered generous encouragement and advice in the preparation of this volume. I would like especially to mention Russell Lowry, Dr Ronald Binns, Professor Muriel Bradbrook, Dr Paul Tiessen, Dr Sherrill Grace, Professor Richard Hauer Costa, Julian Trevelyan, Wieland Schulz-Keil, Robert Duncan and the National Film Board of Canada, and Mr C. G. Houghton of The Leys School. My thanks are also due to Alan Wilding, Chief Producer, Continuing Education Radio, for commissioning *The Lighthouse Invites the Storm*, and Michel Petheram for the actual production, and to all those acquaintances of Lowry who kindly allowed themselves to be interviewed both for the programme and for the book.

Gordon Bowker, London, April 1985

Introduction

The Canadian writer and critic George Woodcock once predicted, with good reason, that Malcolm Lowry would be the despair of his biographer. The reason is not hard to find. Lowry was a contriver of fictions and one of his finest fictional contrivances, it sometimes seems, was his own life.

From the moment he embarked on a serious writing career, he centred all of his imaginative effort around himself. He sought experience and then turned these experiences into fiction, with the result that his novels and short stories are intensely autobiographical and his central characters are all Malcolm Lowry in one guise or another. Even when he was not writing he romanticised his past life and, like the Ancient Mariner, had the power to convince those on whom he fixed his glittering eye that the myths he established were indeed the truth. This was the power which enabled him to create one of the most gripping and complex masterpieces produced by an English writer this century, *Under the Volcano*. But it also generated the legend of Malcolm Lowry, a labyrinth fascinating to explore, but more than usually difficult to navigate.

The picture is further complicated because significant portions of his life went unrecorded. From an early age he adopted the role of a drunken Bohemian poet, exiled, alienated and condemned to suffer for his art's sake. He came to hate polite literary society, preferring a marginal existence as an alcoholic in Paris, New York and Mexico, and the remote obscurity of the forest shores of British Columbia, so that most of his English friends lost touch with him. Even while married, he would disappear for days on drinking sprees which he was unable to recall. He died, almost unnoticed, in a small Sussex village a month short of his forty-eighth birthday.

The task of his biographer is, therefore, twofold – to try to make good the omissions left by previous biographical accounts of Lowry's life, and to attempt to separate the myth from the man.

This volume does go some way towards filling in the empty spaces, with new material from his family, from one of the men who sailed with him on his first sea trip and, most importantly, from his first wife. But the myth and the man remain difficult to disentangle for, as one of his friends from Cambridge puts it, Lowry was mytho-genic – not only could he make the tallest stories about himself believable, but others were always ready and willing to add their own embellishments to the legend. It is not surprising that he appears, thinly disguised, in numerous works of fiction by those who knew him as well as by those who did not.

Memory, of course, is a fickle jade and time can distort events. Yet distance can also help to clarify the past, especially when new evidence or fresh witnesses appear to deny or confirm long-held impressions. We must remember, of course, that all remini-scences of persons and events are offered from particular points of view and several witnesses of the same event can come up with as many versions of what occurred, as is evident every day in the courts. All memories are selective, we might say, but some memo-ries are more selective than others. And, while memory can fade over time, it can also be brought vividly alight by old associations – a picture, a song, a smell or even a taste, an experience out of which Marcel Proust was able to create his monumental novel *Remembrance of Things Past*.

So reminiscences cannot be relied upon to provide us with a definitive biography, whatever that may mean, for it is Lowry's audience from which we will be hearing. And if, as Shakespeare tells us in *Macbeth*:

Life's but a walking shadow; a poor player,
That struts and frets his hour upon the stage. . .

then the life of Malcolm Lowry is more than usually full of darks and shades. At times the shadow is very blurred, at times it dissol-ves into darkness. But, viewed from many angles, perhaps the shadow can be brought just a little more into focus, and possibly, where it had seemed to have disappeared, the shade can be con-jured back towards the limelight. Or if we prefer to see his life as a tangled forest, strewn with false trails, maybe, with the help of others, we can discover a way through it.

As for the man himself, he was undoubtedly a man of many parts, as his friend John Davenport points out. He wore different masks to impress different people. The poet Conrad Aiken thought that, even as a writer, he felt he had no identity of his own and could only exist by adopting the identities of others. But despite the many faces of the man to be glimpsed in the following pages – the tough, the vulnerable, the witty, the self-destructive, the gentle, the boorish, the self-mocking, the drink-sodden, the unacademic, the brilliant – some continuities emerge. He was a man obsessed – obsessed by the pen, obsessed by the bottle, obsessed by private terrors. He was also endearing, and rarely recalled with bitterness. He believed that we are all writers involved in creating the fictions of our own lives, and so perhaps this book is best read as a Lowry novel, a story with many possible readings, and perhaps it is only in its contradictions and complexity that the real meaning of his life is to be found. But maybe that is true of any life. In the end, of course, it is for you, the jury, having listened to all the witnesses, to decide for yourselves what sort of man Malcolm Lowry might have been. One thing is certain: this is by no means the end of the story.

Some of the interviewees were more fluent than others, some of the reminiscences were well rehearsed through frequent repetition, while others were dredged up hesitantly from a half-forgotten past. Where it was thought helpful for the reader, some of the interview transcripts have been reordered and some hesitations, repetitions and deviations have been excluded. Where cuts have been made they are indicated by dots.

Lowry's life is here divided into eight parts, each of which is preceded by a short biographical link to set the context and to help the reader understand certain references which might otherwise seem obscure.

1 Childhood and Schooldays, 1909–29

Clarence Malcolm Lowry, as he was christened, was born at Warren Crest, North Drive, New Brighton, Cheshire, on 28 July 1909. His father, Arthur Osborne Lowry, was a successful Liverpool cotton broker; his mother, Evelyn Boden Lowry, was the daughter of a sea captain. There were three older brothers: Stuart, born in 1895, Wilfrid, born in 1900, and Russell, born in 1905. In 1911 the family moved to a new home, Inglewood, at Caldy, close to Hoylake, on the River Dee.

Lowry senior, it seems, was a typical turn-of-the-century parent, a strict and humourless man who kept his sons distinctly short of money. Nevertheless, he seems to have been caring and kind in his own remote way and always willing to forget the indiscretions of his children. He was a Wesleyan by upbringing and the boys were all sent to a Wesleyan school, The Leys, in Cambridge. Mr Lowry was a keen swimmer and physical culture enthusiast, and the boys, in turn, all became keen sportsmen. Malcolm is said to have both feared and respected his father and later to have become terror-stricken and paranoid when faced with figures in authority.

Mrs Lowry is a rather more shadowy character, rarely spoken about by the family. According to Douglas Day,[1] she was an obedient Victorian wife, very much under the thumb of her autocratic husband. John Davenport, a friend from Lowry's university days, claimed that he spoke of her 'only with hatred', and that she would have preferred her last child to have been a daughter. But Stuart Lowry told an earlier biographer[2] that Malcolm was much loved and cherished, and entirely over-dramatised his parents. Certainly their correspondence reveals considerable tenderness, and Lowry is said to have been greatly upset by her death in 1950.

But the picture he painted of his childhood was a grim one – a

---

1 *Malcolm Lowry: A Biography.*
2 Conrad Knickerbocker, 'Swinging the Paradise Street Blues'.

sad tale of neglected eye-trouble resulting in near blindness, chronic constipation, intolerable discipline and brutal treatment from cruel nurses. Russell Lowry discounts his younger brother's version of life at Inglewood. The eye condition was expensively treated, the 'guilty' nurse wrote him sweetly loving letters. The story that at the age of six he was taken by Stuart to a syphilis museum in Liverpool is also refuted. But these woeful accounts of a tormented childhood contributed to the doomed image he wanted to project and were later fed into his highly autobiographical fiction. And some of the stories have stuck, as is evident in the following pages.

In 1917 Lowry went to Caldicott preparatory school in Hertfordshire, where he acquired the nickname 'Lobs' because of the way he would colour up like a lobster when angry. In 1919 Stuart, who had been disabled during the First World War, married and emigrated to Texas, and in 1920 Wilfrid was capped for England at rugby. Malcolm swam, played hockey at school and golf on a putting green in the garden at Inglewood.

The house commanded breathtaking views of the Welsh mountains to the west and offered the impressive sight of ships sailing to and from the Mersey across Liverpool Bay to the north. The theme of the sea recurs often in Lowry's poems and stories, and that of the voyage became the overriding design of his creative fiction. The natural beauty surrounding him at Caldy contrasted sharply with the stark industrial landscape across the Mersey, and provided him with images of heaven and hell which were to haunt his later writing.

In 1923 he entered The Leys. It was the school on which an earlier pupil, James Hilton, had based his novel *Goodbye, Mr Chips*. 'Chips' was modelled in part on Lowry's housemaster, William Balgarnie, who also edited the school magazine, *The Leys Fortnightly*. Lowry wrote his first published stories for *The Fortnightly*, became its controversial hockey reporter, dressed eccentrically and took up the ukulele, which mysteriously he called a 'taropatch'. He also became hooked on the jazz music of Bix Beiderbecke, Frankie Trumbauer and Eddie Lang. Late in 1926 he met a younger boy called Ronnie Hill and together they composed 'hot' dance tunes, two of which their parents paid to have published. They played to great acclaim at the end-of-term concert, according to Hill, and Lowry also received good reviews in *The Leys Fortnightly* for acting. Performing to an audience was something at which he was clearly becoming adept.

Back at Caldy he had shown a talent for golf, winning medals for his age group at Hoylake in 1923 and 1925. He went to London to compete in a schoolboy championship, but failed to take part, having got himself incapably drunk the night before. (He later claimed to have won the competition.) Already gripped by the pen, he had now succumbed to the bottle. He managed to conceal his drinking from his family, but not a more obvious obsession, recalled by Russell – that of memorising and noting down strange names, tune titles, public notices and coincidences.

He had become engrossed in the plays of Eugene O'Neill and the sea novels of Herman Melville,[3] Joseph Conrad and Jack London. In the spring of 1927, prompted by a desire to experience life in the raw, he announced his intention to go to sea. After the Easter holidays he did not return to The Leys, and Ronnie Hill was surprised and impressed to learn that 'Lobs' had sailed to the China Seas as a deckhand on a Liverpool freighter.

A Letter from 'Bey'
Miss Bell

Miss Bell was employed by the Lowry family as nursemaid to Malcolm in 1910, the year following his birth. A local girl from New Brighton, a residential district of Wallasey, she was then in her early twenties. She stayed with the family until Malcolm entered the local day school in 1915, and later ran a village shop and post office in North Wales, after which all trace of her disappears.

The following letter was written to Malcolm on his third birthday while she was a temporary stewardess on a liner. By this time the Lowrys had moved to Caldy. The letter is offered by Malcolm's brother Russell as evidence against his later claims to have been put into the hands of cruel and uncaring nurses. It gives an idea of his quite early attachment to the sea, referred to by a number of contributors to this book. The reference to 'Tynwaldi-tis' is to the *Tynwald*, the Isle of Man ferry on which Miss Bell had once been seasick.

On Board RMS *Teutonic* 27 July 1912

Bey's own little Blessing.

This is a letter to wish you many happy returns of your birthday. Fancy, the dear little baby with a brown face and

3 There is some discussion about whether Lowry read Melville as a schoolboy. Douglas Day suggests that he did, but in *Under the Volcano*, Hugh, supposedly based on the young Lowry, reflects that when he went to sea he had not read Melville.

blue eyes being 1.2.3. I wonder if you have started to be Admiral of the British Fleet yet, because by the time you are big enough the Admiral they have now will be getting rather too old. So please don't forget and be something else. I was showing your photograph to the captain of 'my' ship and he says you just look like a sailor bold especially as you have blue eyes.

Bey likes going in big boats *very much* (tho sometimes I feel very 'Caldy sick'). This is something like 'Tynwalditis' tho not quite the same.

When we were coming in last Wednesday we passed close to the Isle of Man boat going out, the *Empress Queen* I think it was. We could hear them cheering quite plainly. Two or three days before I saw quite a lot of 'flying fish' – it did look quaint to see them spring up suddenly out of the water, fly along with finny wings for a while then drop down and disappear into the deep blue sea.

One night, when I was up on deck getting some lovely salty air, and looking at the stars, I was thinking of a little boy I used to know who used to sing 'Twinkle, Twinkle little star', and do you know, I thought so hard that I nearly heard him. The stars at sea don't look quite like the stars on land. They look just as if they had been hung up like lamps and once or twice I saw little bits of stars shining deep in the water.

Well honey, I must stop this long letter or you won't get any breakfast. Please give my love to dear little Russell and tell him I will write to him next and to Wilfrid and wish him many returns of his birthday (tho rather late) and kindest regards to Mother and Daddy.

If you look on the bottom left hand corner of the inside of this paper you will see a little red blob. That is a kiss for my little Blessing from your own

Bey.

Please remember me to May and Minni, and also to the flowers in the garden and 'my' rose tree and to the herbaceous border, and please don't forget the swallows. Have they come back yet?

B.

Brother Malcolm
Russell Lowry

Russell Lowry (b. 1905), third of the four sons, remembers enjoying a close relationship with his younger brother while they were together at Inglewood. He has gone to great pains, especially since the publication in 1973 of Douglas Day's *Malcolm Lowry: A Biography*, to refute stories which his brother spread about the family and his childhood years at Inglewood and which tend to have gone unchallenged. He recalls their shared interest in golf and the ukulele, Malcolm's photographic memory and his obsession with collecting odd scraps of information, and gives an idea of when he first began to drink. They were later to have a fight from which their relationship never recovered. Russell went into the family business while his younger brother chose to live as a prodigal in exile at his father's expense.

This is an extract from an interview he gave me on 2 September 1983.

How different were each of your brothers in character?
Wilfrid was, shall we say, the pure-souled, 'high-minded' type and the muscular athlete. A very nice chap indeed. Stuart was dark and shortish, whereas Wilfrid was fair-haired and moderately tall. Stuart didn't complete his schooldays; he was a bit of a rebel. He joined the Army in August 1914 and after the War he went off to America where he widened his own education. He had a wide-ranging mind. Stuart was a very strong man and during the period after the War, when he was crippled in one foot, he made up for it by physical jerks and things. They had very good facilities in the YMCA in Dallas where he went to live.

Can you remember Malcolm from those very young days?
Yes, very well. The first thing I remember about him was his extraordinary bad temper. He would flare up in a rage at the slightest provocation. I've no idea why, but he did. He was a very bad-tempered little boy.

And were you often having rows together?
No, no. The rows were not between us. The rows were with whoever happened to be in authority, and therefore it wasn't with me, though the odd incident did occur.

He got annoyed, didn't he, about his name? He dropped 'Clarence'. Was he called Clarence at home?
The name was never used, but, curiously enough, was included on the insistence of brother Stuart. Why, I don't know, except that

Stuart had a great chum whose name was Clarence Jones . . . and I
dare say he persuaded Father to include Clarence in Malcolm's
name.

Tell me about your parents.

Oh well, the parents have been much maligned. They were typical
Victorian parents. Father was a strict man, quite convinced about
his own rectitude in all things. He was a successful businessman.
Mother was – I'd rather not talk about Mother. A complicated but
blank relationship which only seemed to get worse.

Was she just a bit remote, do you think?

As I said, I'd rather not talk about her except to say that the idea
that she over-protected us, or fondled us, or anything of that kind,
is sheer, absolute nonsense. We saw very little of her.

How did your father get on with the four boys?

I can only say that he never made a friend of us – and this, to me,
was an enormous pity. He always said he had 'plans for all his
boys', but he never told us what the plans were! He had no sense of
humour himself, and he couldn't understand that we tended to
take a light-hearted view of life. He was a disciplinarian, but he
was very kind. He kept us ridiculously short of money, but on the
other hand . . . if you had a real problem Father would step in and
sort it out, and he would never make capital out of it afterwards.
He was essentially a very kind man. I think he thought that kind-
ness was weak, and he didn't want to show weakness.

He was a man of strong religious principles, wasn't he?

I suppose the answer to that is 'Yes'. He was brought up as a Wesleyan. We were sent to a Wesleyan school. But he defected, if
that's the word, to the Church of England, because it was nearer to
walk to. We all walked to church on Sunday mornings.

*Were the four of you influenced in any way by his religious beliefs, do you
think?*

No, not at all. I must say this for Father – among his many kind-
nesses he didn't endeavour to impose his opinions on us, either
politically or religiously. I never, in fact, knew what his politics
were, if he had any.

But he encouraged you in your sporting activities, did he not?

Encouraged? No, 'encouraged' is the wrong word. We encouraged each other. He was prepared to help in so far as help might
be necessary. But if, for instance, we needed a new golf club, we
had to engage in all sorts of curious conspiracies to persuade
Father to part with five bob to buy it.

Was he a sportsman himself?

It depends on how you define a sportsman. He was not athletically inclined. He played golf with the utmost monotony; he played the ball straight down the course. But no, I wouldn't say that he engaged much in sport. Swimming was his favourite activity. He was a very keen swimmer indeed.

Malcolm has told some extraordinary stories about being blind as a child. What is the truth about those early events?

There is always a grain of truth upon which Malcolm's stories are based, but it's a very small grain with a very large building put on it. He was supposed to be blind. I have photographs of him beaming all over his face, on holiday with the family in the Channel Islands, when in fact, according to himself, he was bandaged, blind and not allowed home because Mother would be upset by the bandages. It is absolute nonsense. But he did have trouble with his eyes. He had corneal ulcers which, according to Malcolm, were neglected to the point of blindness. This simply is not true. He was taken to such local people as there were, who applied whatever remedies seemed appropriate – drops and things like that. When these didn't work, he was taken up to London to Harley Street's leading eye man, who scraped his eyeballs. There was absolutely no trouble thereafter. So there were no bandages, except possibly after the scraping. I have a letter here from Malcolm during that time, from school, saying that he can do absolutely anything, and there's no conjunctivitis left at all in his eyes. The story is nonsense.

When you and Malcolm were young men at home together, how did you entertain yourselves?

Our field of entertainment was very limited. But we had a large garden and the countryside was there to knock about in. Golf was our chief entertainment. We were free to use the local golf course, which was an unassuming one, a nine-hole course . . . we were issued a cut-down brassie apiece, and off we went to play golf. We also played golf in the garden on a small scale – putting golf, which was a conversion of croquet to golf. Eventually we rode our bicycles around the place, and still more eventually we went to the cinema, when we could raise the price, which was sixpence – and that was very seldom.

Tell me about Malcolm Lowry, the boy golf champion.

Well, he didn't exist. Malcolm was a very good golfer, with a nice, natural, easy style. And we, as schoolboy sons of a member, were allowed to play at Hoylake. And there came a year when a tournament was arranged. . . . Malcolm did pretty well. And the following year he also did pretty well. He went round in, I think, about 90. As a boy of fifteen this wasn't bad. And the following year, or shortly thereafter, there was a schoolboys' championship played at, I think, Sunningdale ... certainly one of the London links. A party was arranged – Malcolm was one – to compete. He came back not actually having played, and the story went that it was something he'd eaten, and that he hadn't been very well. So he hadn't played and was very disappointed. . . . In point of fact, as I found out years later, he got so drunk – this was at the age of fifteen or sixteen – that he couldn't even get to the first tee. He seems to have corrected this in his own estimation by dressing himself up as a Schoolboy Golf Champion, which he never was. I have a letter from the Royal Liverpool Golf Club Secretary confirming that this event in which we took part was not in any sense a championship at all, and giving his scores. The letter reads:

> Your brother won the Boys' Medal for those under fifteen years of age in 1923 with a score of 95. In 1925 he won the Medal for Boys of fifteen to eighteen years of age, with a score of 88. Records show that in both cases they were purely Club events and not regarded as Schoolboy Championships outside the Club. There is nothing to suggest that in the process of winning these competitions he beat the course record, in fact scores lower than his 95 in 1923 and 88 in 1925 were recorded in previous years.

What sort of books did you read at home?

One of Malcolm's favourite authors was Edgar Rice Burroughs, rising to the enormous level of Tarzan and the Apes in many versions – that's the first one that comes to mind. Another was an author whom he affectionately knew as 'Tablet Baines Reed'. I think Tablet – Talbot – Baines Reed wrote *The Fifth Form at St Dominic's*. That was the sort of stuff that Malcolm read in the early days. And I think it is appropriate to remember that Malcolm, until very much later, didn't regard himself as literarily interested at all. Not until years later. His first burst to do anything at all was as a comic songwriter. And he 'played his ukulele as the ship went down'!

When did he first come across this famous ukulele?

Oh, *he* didn't – *I* did. There was a cult for the ukulele ... and friends of mine who were up at Cambridge got ukuleles, so I got one. So Malcolm played it and we both got ukuleles.

When you were at The Leys School together wasn't there a master who later on became 'Mr Chips' in James Hilton's book? What memories do you have of Mr Balgarnie?

Balgarnie was a very dried-up little man. He's been much over-romanticised in *Goodbye, Mr Chips*, and Mr Chips was actually a composite of three or four masters. Any contemporary at The Leys would recognise them. He was an interesting man, I suppose. He was our housemaster. I don't think Malcolm was influenced by him particularly because Malcolm was not a classicist, and Balgarnie took the sixth form in Latin and Greek.

It's said that Balgarnie encouraged Malcolm to write for The Leys Fortnightly, *the magazine for which he began to write sports reports.*

Oh yes, there are wonderful bits about protests 'pouring into *The Leys Fortnightly* offices'. Balgarnie put the magazine together and encouraged anybody who could write – probably James Hilton is the other most celebrated one – to write articles or accounts of matches for *The Fortnightly*. Malcolm dropped into the spot of writing the hockey ones and indeed did it very well. They were fairly rebellious articles, but this was rather fun. It's been said that they were much resented. In fact they weren't; they created a great deal of amusement.

You have written about his photographic memory. How did that manifest itself?

Malcolm would interest himself in some subject and would seem to collect everything about that subject and remember it. He knew all the local footpaths and the distances from here to there, and from everywhere else to everywhere else. He – for some reason or other – collected hymn tunes and knew the names of all the tunes that the hymns went to. He knew who'd written the hymn, he knew who'd written the tune. He wasn't really interested in the subject, but he just couldn't help collecting things. I've got a son who does the same.

What other qualities did he have? Was he a good linguist, for example?

No. Malcolm, curiously enough, was not a good linguist. He uses a lot of foreign language in his books and writings, but I think this is from his photographic memory. He collected amusing public notices and he collected coincidences and this kind of thing. He would write down and remember all sorts of details of that kind in foreign languages which he didn't necessarily understand, and, in due course, he would build them into his narrative as a piece of comic relief or to carry forward a coincidence. The *Orlac* film[4] is an example.

When do you think he began to drink?

This has been a matter of great surprise to me. He apparently began very early, as revealed by the golfing story. But as late as the 1930s he and I used to go out very naughtily and buy each other a

4 *The Hands of Orlac.* See p. 30.

pint of mild on a Sunday morning and think we were cutting a dash. And Malcolm showed no signs, in those fairly early days, of drinking at all. He must have done it very much on the quiet. Where he got the money from I don't know.

The Sophisticated Schoolboy
Ronnie Hill

Ronnie Hill (b. 1911), composer, pianist and ex-BBC radio producer, first met Malcolm Lowry at The Leys in 1926, at the beginning of what turned out to be Lowry's final year at the school. They composed foxtrots together and shared a common interest in jazz. Two years younger than his collaborator, and somewhat timid, Hill was greatly impressed by the tough-looking senior who swaggered around with his friend Michael Rennie, both of whom had adopted eccentric styles of dress. Rennie went on to achieve fame as a film actor, appearing in such post-war classics as *The Wicked Lady* and *The Robe*, and a television series based on *The Third Man*. Hill provides a vivid description of how Lowry changed into 'a noisy drunk' as a result of his voyage as a deckhand to the Far East in 1927, something that he appears to have managed to conceal, at least temporarily, from his family (see Russell Lowry, pp. 36–7).

This interview was given to me on 27 July 1984.

Can I ask you to tell me a little bit about The Leys School, where you first met Malcolm Lowry?
It was a minor public school . . . situated on the outskirts of Cambridge – a very well designed and built school. I suppose it was like most of those establishments of the time. There was strong discipline and, as far as I was concerned, what horrified me was a great emphasis on games. . . . The staff were extremely good and very helpful really, if one would let them be helpful. We also had among the staff that famous man Mr Balgarnie, who was the original 'Mr Chips'. . . . I remember one year I worked up to being able to sit at his table for meals, which was really wonderful, because there was this wonderful mind and he expected great coherence from all those who sat around him. . . .

I met Malcolm through my aversion to games, I suppose, because I used to take refuge in the music rooms underneath the main hall of the school. I was a bit of an outcast there because I was not interested in what I should have been interested in. I was much more interested in making my own music, making jazz. . . .

One day I was practising in the music rooms (at least if one can call it practising – I was playing jazz) and, quite unasked, this stocky figure sidled in. He didn't have his ukulele with him that day, and we got talking. . . . He was very well-built and very muscular and he seemed older than most of us – much more sophisticated and developed. And his close friend in school was a very impressive man, Michael Rennie, who later became a famous film star. I remember they had their sideburns cut in points and they always wore flannel trousers without turn-ups, which was unheard of. They would wander arm-in-arm . . . about the place looking very distinguished and very special. So anyway, I felt rather proud that this legendary figure should have come in. And then – I don't know how it happened – but I think we played and sang various well-known things together, and then we started to write. . . .

Was it understood from the start, that Malcolm wrote the words and you wrote the music? Or did you share?

I wouldn't allow anyone to do *all* the lyrics. No, I did bits of it – probably the odd line. I remember one very weird number we wrote called 'Dismal Swamp', full of extraordinary imagery, but very beautiful.

Do you remember that?

No, I don't remember a note or word of it. I'm afraid the main ones I remember are . . . 'Goodbye to Shanghai' and also that dreadful 'Three Little Dog-gone Mice' . . . and also the one that he used to fart in rhythm to called 'Hindu Babe'.

Hindu Babe [fart]

I love you [fart]

I love you [fart]

and that was a great achievement. Well, we went on writing and then somehow we read somewhere that a certain publisher, for a small fee, would print your music. We came down to London on a holiday and we had a wonderful reception from this publisher. . . .

What did the publisher charge you?

I can't remember. I should think about £100 . . . a lot of money in those days.

How did you manage to dig it up?

Well, I think our various fathers forked up, you know. . . .

Was 'Three Little Dog-gone Mice' played by Alfredo's Band, as it says on the songsheet cover?

I very much doubt it, because in those days people used to allow their picture to be published on a song copy for publicity purposes

... I really don't think he did. ... I would have thought it was highly unsuitable.[5]

How many songs did you and Malcolm have published?

Two. 'I've Said Goodbye to Shanghai', with nobody's picture on the cover, and 'Three Little Dog-gone Mice'. ... Anyway, we were accepted in the school as songwriters – strange people who weren't awfully good at games[6] and didn't really conform all that much, and we had the final accolade when we were invited to perform at the annual concert in the hall, which was usually given over to people who were giving recitals of Chopin or reciting some famous poem. We were suddenly given the closing spot of this thing and it was, as I remember, a sensation. It went very well indeed, a real breakthrough. ...

How old were you at that time?

I suppose about fourteen or fifteen and Malcolm was about seventeen.

Was Malcolm frowned upon by the school authorities?

I can't help thinking that he was. I don't know for certain, but I think that he was sufficiently nonconformist in the general sense to be under a certain amount of suspicion.

What did he look like?

Well, 'stocky' is the word that comes to my mind. He had funny legs and when he walked it was rather in a twenty-to-four position. You know what I mean? Always feet slightly turned out. He was thickset. He looked very tough.

Did he have a very good sense of humour?

Yes, but I think one had to adjust one's idea of a sense of humour to his. He would be very amused at certain things that he had thought. He had a quiet chuckle about something and you never found out what he was laughing about, and I'm afraid I always turned it to myself and I thought he was laughing at me. But then I think I grew to discover that he was not. It was some little fantasy of his own which he found amusing at that moment.

Did he have a reputation as a writer at the school?

Yes, he was quite well in with the man, whoever it was, who ran *The Leys Fortnightly* . . . and he wrote a lot for that under the name 'Camel'. . . . He also had a reputation as an actor. He was in *Oliver Cromwell* by Drinkwater, and he played a sort of military leader in that quite effectively. . . .

5 The story quoted in the *Liverpool Daily Echo* report on pp. 31–2 is probably another Malcolm Lowry story.
6 Though Lowry was a good sportsman, he seems not to have participated much in his later years at The Leys.

Did Malcolm's family come to the school?
I never met them. I never knew anything about them, although again he must have referred to his father in letters.
But your friendship was relatively short-lived, wasn't it?
He left the school . . . in order to go to sea, and the first I really knew about this was the headline in one of the rather tatty Sunday papers: 'No Silk Cushions for Me, Says Mersey Lad', or something like that. And off he went on this tramp steamer, which must have been a very tough life. . . . That was hot news at The Leys. Everyone was delighed. Then, while he was at sea, I had a number of – I suppose they were – marvellous letters describing what it was like, which, to my shame, I haven't kept. But they were wonderfully vivid and I almost envied him. I didn't really, but I thought what a wonderful thing to do – until he came back. And this was a very traumatic meeting. . . . I was shaken by it for days. . . .

I was sitting in my room one evening and somebody rushed to my door and said, '"Lobs" has come back and he's looking for you.' And lo and behold he found me, but it was quite obvious that 'Lobs' by that time had got himself good and high, and noisy with it. He was a noisy drunk. And I felt quite seriously that that whole part of my life had finished anyway. He'd gone away, although we had sort of planned, as schoolboys, to go to the same college in Cambridge. In those days one could do that. And I went eventually to the college that we had chosen jointly – Christ's – and he went instead to St Catharine's. But by that time I really didn't want to know any more. I was delighted that he was not at Christ's.
Did you see him at Cambridge?
As little as I could, because he was usually heralded by noise, and he'd be swaggering along entertaining his companions. He came to see me once . . . at my digs, and I must have made it known that he was not welcome and I think he may well have been hurt. But I felt he was a dangerous one.
Can you say a bit about that, about how you felt sometimes when he was around?
I'm not sure how much of this was real or how much of this was his talk, but I always had the feeling at the back of my mind that he could very well do a bit of quiet mugging, you know, if someone said something out of place. I'm quite sure he could have beaten one up – at least that was the fear that I had – particularly as I was not prepared to go along with a lot of his ideas.
What sort of ideas were they?
Well, I think probably the idea of this very heavy drinking. I considered then that that was a serious waste of time, but if you were a

friend of Malcolm's that's what you did, and it was not my idea of a good time.

So how did you spend your time?

I moved into the Footlights set. I was sure in my own mind that the Footlights would be my key to success, and I went in at a very dud time when there was really no talent and, in fact, the main activity there seemed to be racing cars, horse racing and booze. However, I persevered with my theatrical aspirations and I think Malcolm came into it later.

Oh, he got into the Footlights, did he?

He had connections with it. . . . It was after I'd gone down. I didn't stay the full course. . . . It was after that that Malcolm stepped into the Footlights. . . . He played in a sort of cabaret scene. He played the ukulele and sang some of his songs – could have been some of my songs, I don't know. . . . As a schoolboy he was very fixed on writing. He was always jotting things down – notes and things that he could use as a line in a song or a section of his book or his articles on hockey. He was also very fixed on jazz. . . . He really had a remarkable style of performing which I feel was remarkably close to the American style. . . . He was an enthusiastic player. I don't know about his technique, but it was certainly done with great – sort of – bravado.

'Son of Mr Chips' Remembers
John Stirland

John Stirland (1890–1983), a language teacher, first at Caldicott preparatory school and then at The Leys, knew and probably taught at least three of the Lowry boys, including Malcolm. Stirland was a colleague of William Balgarnie, the model for James Hilton's fictional schoolmaster in *Goodbye, Mr Chips*. After Balgarnie's death in 1951 John Stirland is said to have become a sort of 'Son of Mr Chips', and, as school archivist, took trouble to follow Malcolm's career along with those of all other old boys. His recollections confirm Lowry's academic weakness, the fact that he was coached for Cambridge by an ex-Leys master, and that strings were probably pulled to get him his place at what was then one of the most impoverished Cambridge colleges, St Catharine's, in 1929.

This 'school report' was taken from an interview conducted by Robert Duncan for the 1976 National Film Board of Canada documentary feature, *Volcano*.

How was he academically?

Academically he was average. He had no special ability. But he must have obviously read a great deal of literature. He was certainly encouraged to read outside the normal form reading, and it is quite clear that he read a good deal of English literature probably not normally read by the average schoolboy. How he obtained these books I don't know. I know that he was encouraged in his reading by his housemaster, Mr Balgarnie, that is, Mr Chips. And also by a young history master.

What sort of chap was he aside from his academic work?

Well, he was a very good-looking chap. All the Lowry boys were very good-looking. He didn't pay much attention to dress. In fact he probably tried to be as unusual as school regulations would allow. I particularly remember his wearing wide Oxford bags, as they were called in those days, and he tended rather to possibly slouch a little about the place. He really gave as little attention as possible to personal appearance and that may have been a quite deliberate attitude on his part. But he was very early recognised as being unusual.

Was he very active in sports?

He was interested in games, but he didn't seem to want to become a serious participator. It's on record that he won a golf tournament for boys under eighteen at Hoylake in 1925. His favourite school game was hockey.

Did he play hockey at The Leys?

Well, he was a member of his house but he wasn't a member of any school team as far as I remember. . . . Later he became a hockey reporter for the school magazine. And he produced in *The Fortnightly* some amazing reports which were extremely unconventional and frank. In fact they drew protests from some readers, especially the old boys who rather took exception to his treating a game like first eleven hockey as being rather trivial.

Did he take part in debates?

Yes, he took part in debates and sometimes he proposed motions or opposed them, but usually he was the speaker from the floor, so to speak, rather than the proposer of a motion. As you probably know, he was also a frequent contributor of short stories to *The Fortnightly*.

His entry into Cambridge was rather unusual, wasn't it?

Yes. . . . In those days you had merely to pass an examination which was equivalent to what we nowadays call school certificate. . . . But with the help of one of the masters who was a graduate of St Catharine's College, I think it was arranged that he should be able to go to that College. One of the difficulties might have been caused by the fact that he left school and there was a gap of a year or two before he went to university.

Was he popular with the other boys?

I wouldn't say exactly that he was popular in the sense that a boy might be popular who was, say, in the prefects or in the first eleven. But he was recognised as being unusual, and boys treated him with that kind of amused tolerance which boys show to somebody who is obviously a character.

2 To Sea and to Cambridge, 1927–31

Lowry set sail for the Far East on the Blue Funnel freighter *Pyrrhus* on 15 May 1927, a trip arranged for him by his father. Malcolm alerted the press, hoping to get publicity for his songwriting. 'Rich Boy as Deckhand' ran the headlines, and he was reported as saying, 'No silk-cushion youth for me, I want to see the world and rub shoulders with its oddities and get some experience of life.' He later claimed he was delivered to the dockside in the family Rolls, which put the ship's crew against him, but Russell Lowry dismisses his brother's version of the story as largely invention.

However, it is clear, from Joseph Ward's letter, that during the trip the 'superior' public-school boy was mocked, tormented and sexually humiliated. The story he told later, of having finally won the crew over, is obviously yet another Lowry myth. On his return, he admitted to the newspapers that 'once is quite enough' and that a deckhand was nothing but 'a domestic servant on a treadmill in Hades'. But there is no doubt that the hard work had toughened him, and now he had another story of travail to add to his catalogue of suffering, and a new role to play – the drunken sailor.

Soon after returning, he was sent to Blackheath in London to be crammed for Cambridge entrance by an ex-Leys master, but his mind was elsewhere. He had begun to write a book about his sea trip which he called *Ultramarine*, and was looking for a style that would enable him to capture the inner torment he had experienced. He found it in *Blue Voyage*, a sea novel by the American poet Conrad Aiken. When he wanted to visit Aiken, Mr Lowry told him he would have to find a place at Cambridge first. According to Russell, he was now becoming more morose and difficult and, after he had passed his examination, his father was quite content for him to remain in London on an allowance rather than returning to the family home.

Early in 1929 he spent eight weeks in Germany at the 'English College' in Bonn. He drank a great deal and was too undisciplined for the taste of his strict German teachers, but he acquired a passion for Expressionist movies, such as *The Cabinet of Dr Cali-gari* and *The Hands of Orlac,* whose images and visions he later embodied in his work.

Lowry was accepted to read English at St Catharine's College, Cambridge, in March 1929, and immediately wrote to Conrad Aiken inviting him to act in the meantime as his literary tutor, for which his father would pay six guineas a week. The impoverished poet accepted readily, and Lowry took ship for Boston, travelling via Barbados as a steerage passenger on a cargo boat. He arrived with little more than a suitcase, a draft of *Ultramarine*, and his ukulele. It was the beginning of a long and, some would say, fateful relationship. Aiken was a hard-drinking sensualist and only pro-vided Lowry with a pleasingly dissolute model to set against that of his sombre Victorian father. If Lowry imbibed something of Aiken the decadent he practically consumed Aiken the writer, his pecu-liarly Joycean style and his subjective approach to the novel. In rewriting *Ultramarine* he borrowed openly from *Blue Voyage*, though later he became intensely sensitive to the charge of pla-giarism.

By the time he returned to go up to Cambridge he had perfec-ted a series of new roles for himself: the tough ex-sailor, the experienced man of the world, the doomed genius, the shy writer and the serious jazz addict. He exercised with barbells and boxed with a new-found friend and fellow drinker, John Davenport. Davenport found him a man with many masks, each a true repre-sentation of himself, and each reserved for separate groups of his friends.

Through Davenport he entered the literary circle of Charlotte Haldane, wife of the physiologist J. B. S. Haldane. His perform-ance as wild, ukulele-playing poet clearly charmed her and she included him as a character in a novel. Stories of an affair between them are discounted by Arthur Calder-Marshall, who remembers Charlotte being 'so on-coming that she was completely off-putting', and Lowry's apparent fear of women also casts doubt on its credibility.

In his first term a friend, Paul Fitte, committed suicide, and later a remorseful Lowry claimed it had happened because he had callously rejected Fitte's homosexual advances. The inquest, however, revealed that Fitte was the victim of blackmail, yet the guilt-ridden version was the one Lowry chose to fictionalise in his novel *October Ferry to Gabriola* and to relive (see the interview with his psychiatrist, Dr Raymond, on p. 193).

He was now writing obsessively, drinking indiscriminately, and spending his summer vacations with Conrad Aiken at a house he had taken at Rye in Sussex. His reputation as a writer was confirmed when extracts from *Ultramarine* were published in the Cambridge literary magazine *Experiment*. He discovered another sailor-writer, the Norwegian, Nordahl Grieg, whose novel *The Ship Sails On* gave him the structure he needed for his own book. He made a journey to Oslo to meet Grieg, and the trip provided the material for his next novel, *In Ballast to the White Sea*, destroyed later in a fire in Canada.

In May 1932 he managed to scrape a third-class honours degree, due mainly to the fact that his tutor, T. R. Henn, arranged for a passage from *Ultramarine* to be submitted in place of an examination paper. Relations at Inglewood were becoming increasingly strained, and the final break with his family was not long to follow his graduation.

The Return of the *Pyrrhus*
Liverpool Daily Echo

In May 1927 Lowry, then seventeen, set sail for the China Seas as a deckhand aboard the freighter *Pyrrhus*. He was composing popular songs with his schoolfriend Ronnie Hill, and the trip was intended, in part, as a publicity stunt. The press were duly invited to cover the departure, and the headlines ran: 'Rich Boy as Deckhand. Prefers 50 Shillings a Month to "Silk-Cushion Life".' By the time he returned he had somewhat changed his mind about life as a deckhand, as the following report which appeared in the *Liverpool Daily Echo* on 30 September 1927 suggests. However, his first novel, *Ultramarine*, was based on the trip, and he also used the experience in Chapter 6 of *Under the Volcano*, where it became part of the history of Hugh Firmin, a character based largely on the young, innocent and still adventurous Lowry.

SEEING THE WORLD WITH A UKULELE

Liverpool Schoolboy's Trip to Sea

Armed only with a ukulele, a schoolboy-composer sailed away from Liverpool in a tramp steamer last May to search for inspiration and to gather experience. He was Malcolm Lowry, the eighteen-year-old son of a Liverpool cotton broker. He was paid off yesterday, and today he described some of his experiences to the *Echo*.

The vessel, which Lowry joined as a deckhand at £2 10s a month, was the Blue Funnel Line tramp steamer *Pyrrhus*, sailing to the Far East. The boy was fresh from Leys School, Cambridge, when he took his kit aboard, and in a short time he will enter Cambridge University. His musical compositions are of the lighter sort – dance tunes, one of which, 'Three Little Dog-gone Mice', has been published. It was played by Alfredo and his band when they came to Liverpool Hippodrome a little while ago. Two years ago Lowry won the Hoylake Boys' Golf Championship.

A Treadmill in Hades

He told the *Echo* he wasn't anxious to go to sea again. At least not as a deckhand, for a deckhand was 'a domestic servant on a treadmill in Hades'. Nevertheless, he had enjoyed the trip, and he had found the rest of the crew a fine lot of fellows to work with – or, more correctly, to work for.

'My day began at 5.30 a.m.,' Lowry said, 'and I was on the go until seven at night. I had to scrub out the mess-room and the galley, and get the whole of the foc'sle absolutely clean, and be up on deck by 10.30.

'At mealtimes I had to make tea and coffee for the crew, carrying food from the galley to the foc'sle – quite a long way – and then wash up. In the intervals I was scrubbing decks, polishing brasswork, and so on.

Atmosphere

'Of course I was supposed to work twelve hours a day; that was in my articles. But the ordinary day for a deckhand anywhere is fourteen hours. Yet I am extremely glad I took the trip. I went for "atmosphere", and I got it. I have seen the world, and been paid for doing it.'

Despite his fourteen-hour day, the young seeker after information found time to entertain the crew with his ukulele – 'I think it was the only instrument on board,' he said – and to think out and write some new dance tunes.

These helped in some way to solace him for some of the dirty work he had to do, such as painting the inside of a coal-bunker and chipping the paint off winches.

Lowry has been reported as saying that what could not be chipped off had to be removed with the aid of nails and teeth. He admitted that this was something of a hyperbole, but 'you have to use everything but your teeth,' he said.

'It's quite true you have to get off with your nails the paint the scrapers will not remove. The paint has to come off, whatever way you go about removing it.'

Letter from an Old Shipmate
Joseph Ward

Little is known about what happened to Lowry on his trip aboard *Pyrrhus*. In his novel *Ultramarine* he tells how the young adventurer, despite the initial hostility of the crew, wins them over by swaggering the dockside bars and brothels with the best of them, by standing up to the tough ship's cook and finally by being prepared to dive overboard to save a drowning bird.

The following letter, sent to the *Liverpool Daily Post* by one of the sailors who was on *Pyrrhus* with Lowry, casts a rather different light on events. Both he and the *Post* are of course wrong in saying that Lowry had died near Vancouver.

'The Nook',
Mostyn,
Flintshire.

14 April 1962

'Postman'
Daily Post
Liverpool

Dear Postman,
Friday's issue contained a sad reference to 'Lobs' Lowry, whom you stated died five years ago near Vancouver Harbour. 'No silk-cushion youth for me, I want to travel the world and rub shoulders with its oddities.' This was his expression as he signed on as a deck boy on the good ship *Pyrrhus* in 1927. Through his brother, W. M. Lowry, of Birkenhead Park and Cheshire, and capped once for England, I made contact with him aboard *Pyrrhus*. He was a lad lost, without much idea of the ordinary needs of cleanliness in his own body, and his job as 'Bosun's piggy' nearly lost the lives of several members of the crew. Incidentally, *Pyrrhus* was not a 'tramp' as such is known at sea. She was a regular Blue piper trading to the Far East, whose captain hailed from West Kirby, which is alongside Caldy. 'Lobs' decided that the best way to administer lime juice was to pour the strong essence into the filter as supplied in the mess-rooms. The resultant verdigris, when tasted, was the most horrible devil's brew, and the cleaning out [of the] filter job that 'Lobs' earned for himself was very little to pay for what may have been tragedy. How 'Lobs' ever managed to reside in China, Russia, etc. (as reported by 'Postman' in the earlier issue quoted) is beyond imagination, for the Chinese were described by 'Lobs' as 'slant-eyed B's', and he had inherited strange beliefs in the magic of being English. A song stanza that 'Lobs' composed was 'Marching down the Road to China, You will hear me singing this Song, Soon we'll be aboard an Ocean Liner sailing for Hong Kong, And when we've put these Yellow Faces in their proper places, We'll be home once more, and I'll take my Alice to the Crystal Palace at the end of the China War.'

He used to strum this on the ukulele with gusto, but, as I stated, he seemed a lost soul and his reproductive organ was certainly in the back row, it was a teeny-weeny object that disgusted a Japanese geisha girl to such an extent as to frustrate her into most impolite abuse. On one occasion he received the full contents of a Red Lead Drum, and everyone aboard did the whahoo Indian dance at the spectacle of about 14 days of 'Lobs' looking a real Indian brave. He had no real villainy in his make-up, other than the distinct belief that he was very superior to everyone on board, and he sorely disliked the old QM who could read him like a book. In fact he averred he would write an article on this man, but was told very forcibly that if he did so transgress, a similar article would be written against himself.

What a man he was! I remember upon one occasion one of our unbidden passengers was a dove. 'Lobs' was fond of it, as indeed were all [the] sailors, but in Port Swettenham the dove fell overboard and could not rise from the water. 'Lobs' decided he had lost the chance to prove himself a hero by not diving in after it, even though as we watched its struggles, there was a sudden skirmish in the water and the dove had become a meal for a hungry inhabitant. Yes 'Lobs' wanted very much to shine, but at the vital moment, or moment of truth, he just could not make it. Somewhere, within his depth, he must have had the urge to write, and it will be interesting to read his autobiographical story when published. . . .

I am, Dear Postman,
Yours faithfully,
Joseph Ward.

PS 'Lobs' *was* a silk-cushion youth, regardless of his desire to travel, etc. May the Almighty rest his soul, for he must only have attained about 47–8 years when he passed.
PPS The Captain of the *Pyrrhus* was named 'Elford'. He was twice married.

The Songwriter Goes to Sea
Russell Lowry

Malcolm's older brother continues his account of their early life together at Caldy in Cheshire. He takes up the story where Malcolm decided in 1927 to go to sea as a deckhand. He is particularly scornful of the version of his departure from Birkenhead which his brother later told – that of being driven down to the dockside in a Rolls-Royce by the family chauffeur, which put his shipmates on the SS *Pyrrhus* strongly against him. (The story is also referred to by John Sommerfield and Arthur Calder-Marshall on pp. 72 and 77.) He also recalls how Lowry's first novel began to be written, and how he gradually changed from being a warm, jolly companion into a morose rebel, increasingly alienated from the rest of the family.

This is a continuation of the interview he gave me on 2 September 1983.

When did he start talking about going to sea?
During his later years at The Leys, when I'd left . . . Malcolm came under the influence of, or became friendly with, various wild and woolly characters, one of whom was the son of the Australian High Commissioner in London, who was used to the outback, and seems successfully to have sold Malcolm the idea of 'roughing it'.
So he came home one day and announced that he was going to sign on as an ordinary seaman on a tramp steamer?
Oh no, no. You couldn't go and sign on as an ordinary seaman in those days. Certainly not, with the dockside full of unemployed seamen. It had to be arranged . . . and this is the sort of thing that Father would do. He must have sold Father the idea that it would be an improving exercise for him and widen his mind and do all sorts of things. But Malcolm would be quite incapable of *arranging* that. . . . He wanted me to go with him. My aim by then was to get married. . . . But he was very young and very enthusiastic. . . . We had books about the sea . . . I'd never been to sea myself – I'd no desire to go to sea.
When he left, his departure was given some publicity in the press which he later came to feel upset by. What's the story behind that?
The key to this situation is that Malcolm at that time fancied himself as a comic songwriter and so, from his point of view, there was no such thing as bad publicity. Malcolm could easily have got himself down to the docks by bus or on his two flat feet if he'd wanted to. However, stories appeared in the press, I remember, announcing, ' "No silk cushions for me," says wealthy cotton broker's son.' Well, we've all been wealthy cotton broker's sons in inverted commas ever since. It became a standing joke in the family. And (according to these stories) the chauffeur-driven car, which some biographers have turned into a Rolls-Royce, but which was only an old Minerva, supposedly went down to the docks and Malcolm went aboard. But any publicity of that kind would have been created by Malcolm.

Did he talk about writing a book about his voyage before he went?
No, no.

And when he got back was it obvious that he was writing a book?
When he got back Father and Mother were away, so Malcolm and I were alone at Inglewood being devotedly looked after by our dear friends Mary and Sarah,[1] so we spent many long hours discussing and chatting away. He told me his 'rollicking yarns' and the book began to be written and read aloud and criticised. We spent many hours together in the dining-room like this, with the table in between us and our ukuleles in the background. Here the book was born originally. In point of fact the title, *Ultramarine*, was my idea. He wanted to call it *Ultramarine Blues* – he was into songs, as the saying is these days. But it seemed to me that a very much more effective and still punning name would be simply *Ultramarine*. The alternative was *Penalty Goal*, because the *Pyrrhus* was known as a 'goalpost' ship, owing to the arrangement of her masts and derricks.

Of course it comes through, when one reads it in its published form today, as a very poetic, highly abstracted novel. What was it like when he first read it to you?
Just a straightforward account of what happened.

When he came back from the voyage had he changed in some ways? Physically he'd changed, hadn't he?
Oh yes, most noticeably. He was big-barrelled and heavy-chested. Certainly he'd expanded enormously because they worked him. They tried to work him to death, and I suppose he regarded this as a challenge, so he worked. He did his share of pulley-hauling and lots of it. And it changed him physically certainly.

Had it changed him in any other way? For example, did he use nautical jargon a lot? Did he see himself as a seaman?
No, he didn't . . . he didn't like it. He never wanted to go to sea again, and in fact his assumption of nautical jargon and 'I must go down to the sea again' type of thing had no part of him at that time. That was all built in, or acquired, afterwards.

By that time had any change come over your relationship with Malcolm from when you'd been so close at fifteen or sixteen?
I don't think so, no. I think that these were probably our closest years, because I had a few shillings and we could borrow Wilfrid's motorbike and we could go off to the pictures sometimes. We could play golf at Hoylake rather than just going down to Caldy. No, no – those years, I would say, were among our closest. This is

1 Maids at the Lowrys' home.

why it's all the more surprising to me to learn that he was already an alcoholic.

But some time shortly after this his generally friendly character did go through some sort of change, didn't it?

The actual dating is a bit obscure. At that time I wanted to keep a low profile with the parents because I wanted to get married, whereas Malcolm was getting more and more rebellious, so the ice was getting thinner as our paths diverged.

Not long after that he went to live in London for a while, and later he got in touch with the American poet Conrad Aiken. What did your father think about his going off like that?

Oh, well, Father was becoming frightened of going to his office because he didn't know when the telephone was going to ring to say Malcolm's just kicked Mother in the teeth. So Father was only too glad of any means really of getting Malcolm out of the house and away. He was sent down to London where he was put in digs with a retired master from The Leys called Jerry Kellet, and this was his Blackheath period. Well, I shouldn't think he'd stand much discipline from Jerry Kellet, so I imagine that he then wandered off into the back blocks or wherever it was, and this was his Bloomsbury period. But I don't know anything about that. He was on an allowance from Father. What else can I say about that?

Wasn't there one occasion when he upset the family when he said something rather unfortunate about his childhood?

This, as far as I can place it, was on his twenty-first birthday, which would be in July 1930. It wasn't a party, as it has been described – but it was his birthday and we were celebrating it in a glass of cider, I think. It was the usual family dinner, which consisted of Father and Mother sitting at opposite ends of the table and Malcolm and I in the middle. Dinner being over, Father, who was not a brilliant conversationalist, cleared his throat as he always did and said, 'And what is your earliest recollection, Malcolm, of your earliest birthday?'

So Malcolm looked at the ceiling and cleared *his* throat and said, 'As far as I can recall, my childhood was one of perpetual gloom. I was either blind, constipated or a cripple.' You can imagine the effect that made. The ice descended on the room. But the affair passed off, and was only remembered by me, long afterwards, with the spreading of stories of blindness and the rest, by Malcolm.

He doesn't seem to have done much serious academic work at Cambridge. Did the family get worried about that?

The family wouldn't know anything about it. 'No,' is the answer.

Did he bring any of his Cambridge friends home with him?
No, no, this was one criticism that has been levelled fairly justly at
Inglewood – that there were no real facilities for entertaining.
This is quite a large subject, I think, which is wrapped up in
Mother. But no, he didn't. *We* didn't. There was very little enter-
taining at Inglewood.

The Father Surrogate and Literary Mentor
Conrad Aiken

The American poet and novelist Conrad Aiken (1889–1973) was
educated at Harvard as a contemporary of T.S. Eliot and Edmund
Wilson. Lowry was deeply impressed by Aiken's writing and
invited him to act as his literary tutor at his father's expense, an
offer which the impoverished Aiken found impossible to refuse.
But Lowry learned his lessons possibly too well, taking over
Aiken's highly subjective style and even lifting lines from his work
as well as ideas on which he was working. In his highly wrought
experimental autobiography, *Ushant: An Essay* (New York 1971),
Aiken calls Lowry 'Hambo'. Doubtless this presents a picture of
how Aiken saw his protégé, but it contains accounts of events in
Lowry's life which have been strongly challenged, not least by Jan
Gabrial, Malcolm's first wife, who met them both in Spain in 1933.
Lowry thought highly of Aiken until the last, but others con-
sidered his influence on his young pupil to have been damaging.
(See Arthur Calder-Marshall, p. 157.)

The following is an extract from an interview conducted in
September 1963 by Robert Hunter Wilbur and published in *The
Paris Review Interviews* (fourth series, London 1977).

When did you first meet Malcolm Lowry?
In 1929. He came to Cambridge to work with me one summer on
Ultramarine.
How old was he then?
Barely nineteen, I think. He went back to matriculate at Cam-
bridge that autumn.
Later you moved back to England yourself?
Yes, the next year. Then it was that his father turned him over to
me *in loco parentis.*
To keep him out of trouble or to teach him poetry?
To take care of him and to work with him. So he spent all his holi-
days with us in Rye or went with us if we went abroad. During his

years at Cambridge, he was with me constantly.

What was he working on at this time?

He was finishing *Ultramarine*. I've still got about a third of one version of *Ultramarine*. An interesting specimen of his deliberate attempt to absorb me came to light because there was a page recounting the dream of eating the father's skeleton which comes into my own novel, *Great Circle*. He was going to put this in his book and it didn't seem to matter at all that *I'd* had the dream and written it out.

He doesn't put that in the final version?

No. I said, 'No, Malcolm, this is carrying it *too* far.'

What about Under the Volcano? *Did you work with him on that also?*

No. The first version was already finished when I arrived in Mexico in 1937. He'd been there two or three years.[2] The extraordinary thing is that it was not published for another ten years, during which time he was constantly revising and rewriting. He changed the end, I think entirely, from the version I saw. But the book was already finished and so was another novel called *In Ballast to the White Sea*, which was lost. I think it was in his shack that burnt down at Dollarton, Vancouver.

That was a remarkable thing, too, although very derivative. You could swim from one influence to another as you went from chapter to chapter. Kafka and Dostoevsky and God knows what all. But it was a brilliant thing, had some wonderful stuff in it, including, I remember, a description of a drunken steamboat ride up the Manchester Canal from Liverpool to Manchester.

He lived through a lot that he was able to use very effectively.

Oh, he didn't miss a trick. He was a born observer.

Was Lowry a disciplined writer? His life seems to have been so undisciplined.

Yes, when it came to writing, Malcolm was as obsessed with style as any Flaubert and read enormously to *feed* himself. As I mentioned, he wrote and rewrote *Volcano* for ten years. He once chided me for not taking more pains to 'decorate the page'.

Do you think writers – fiction writers, particularly – should try deliberately to get out and live through the sort of thing he did? Search for experience? I doubt if he did it quite so consciously, but he lived a very active and varied life.

No, I don't think that was the intention, or not wholly the intention in his case. He really had a yen for the sea. And he came by it naturally; I think his mother's father had something to do with the

2 In fact Lowry had been in Mexico for just six months when Aiken arrived.

sea. Of course, that's how we met, through his reading *Blue Voyage*. And he always assumed that in some mystic way the fact I had dedicated *Blue Voyage* to C. M. L. was a dedication to him. Those are his initials. Actually these were the initials of my second wife. But he always thought this was the finger pointing.

The very first night he arrived in Hampton Hall, on Plympton Street where I was living, next door to the Crimson Building, he and I and my youngest brother Robert had a sort of impromptu wrestling match. In the course of this I suggested we use the lid of the w.c. tank and each take hold of one end of it and wrestle for possession of this thing. So I got it all right; I got it away from Malcolm but fell right over backward into the fireplace and went out like a light; and when I came to, all I could see was red. I was stripped to the waist and lying in bed by myself. They'd disappeared of course – we'd been imbibing a little bit – and I galloped down the hall to the elevator not knowing what to do. I thought I'd better get a doctor because blood was pouring down my face. It turned out I had a fracture of the skull, and I was in bed for the next two or three weeks. Malcolm would sometimes remember to bring me a bottle of milk, and sometimes not. And during all this we were working on *Ultramarine*. That was the day's work, always.

'He Was Different from the Rest of Us'
Hugh Sykes Davies

Hugh Sykes Davies (1909–84), Fellow of St John's College, Cambridge, was joint editor of the Cambridge undergraduate literary magazine, *Experiment*, together with Jacob Bronowski and William Empson, when Lowry arrived in Cambridge in October 1929. Two of Lowry's short stories, 'Port Swettenham' and 'Punctum Indifferens Skibet Gaar Videre', were published in *Experiment* and were later included as chapters in his first novel, *Ultramarine*. Sykes Davies was immediately impressed with Lowry's prose style, and later on, at T.R. Henn's request, took responsibility for steering him through his final examinations (probably just one paper), though he himself had only graduated the year before. They met mostly in pubs, and here Sykes Davies observed the hardened young drinker in action and listened to his very tall stories of hard times at sea (largely rebutted in the contributions from Russell Lowry and Joseph Ward in Part 2). He also got a glimpse of how unpredictably violent the normally amiable

Lowry could become. He is wrong about Lowry's father being a shipowner.

This is an edited extract from an interview given on location in a Cambridge pub in 1975 for the 1976 National Film Board of Canada documentary feature, *Volcano*.

What was absolutely obvious to the rest of us, the sort of normal people come up through the usual channels, was that Malcolm had had experiences that we hadn't had, you know. Nearly a year – I don't know how long it was – at sea, when he ran away. He used to talk a lot about it. And it certainly broadened his experience. My experience as an English public-school boy . . . well, I had, in fact, lost my virginity but not on the scale that I am sure he had, going around with those pals of his in boats. This was a big advantage that he had right from the start. He was different from the rest of us. He talked a lot about that sea experience. It meant a great deal to him. This, as I remember, was his own account, but please remember I am talking about forty years ago. I am an old man and I don't necessarily remember everything right. I might even improve on it or make it worse either way.

He ran away to sea, so he said. His father was a shipowner and he could have gone to sea in one of his father's ships, but he had very decent feelings; this is one of the essential things about Malcolm. He was a very gentle, affective chap, and to go to sea in one of his father's ships, all arranged by the family, you know – this was too simple a pattern; it didn't interest him at all. So he ran away to sea in someone else's ship and had some pretty interesting experiences. Among them was the problem that he was a middle-class boy, really, with a middle-class accent and manner and ways of behaving, from an English public school. He had to win the confidence of his mates on shipboard. And he did it in the end.

He came to me one day, when I was supposed to be teaching him – you know he taught me more than I taught him, really. But he said, 'You must come. There's a wonderful film on at the Vic,' – that's one of the local fleapits. So I went with him one afternoon (you understand his evenings were otherwise engaged on more serious matters). And the film was about a middle-class boy who had run away to sea and I thought at once, 'This is Malcolm's own story,' and he was seeing it on the screen. Well, this chap in the film managed to secure the confidence of his shipmates. He did more. There was a storm and he did something very heroic. The ship's mast was broken but he cut it loose. Unfortunately, in doing so, he lost his own life. And the concluding moments of the film were where one of his shipmates is carving under one of the ship's boats an epitaph for this chap with his marlinspike or whatever they had: 'He was a great guy.' Well, Malcolm was deeply moved.

Just at this moment, in this completely deserted afternoon cinema smelling of cheap scent – you know the way they do – a solitary undergraduate in front of us chose to laugh. Malcolm was very powerfully built. He rose and seized this chap by the neck, bumped him up and down in his seat, and said, 'It's more than anyone will say for you when you go, you dirty little rat.' And then the spell was broken and he said to me, 'Hugh, let's go.' I was only too glad to do so; I didn't want to be involved in a fight at that stage in my academic career. We went across the market-place just here. You know, I was doing my best to educate the boy, you understand. He began pulling a little blond moustache he had, a rather small one. Whenever he was embarrassed he used to pull it like this, and he started pulling, so I knew that he was repenting, and you know he said, 'I'm not sure I ought to have done that.'

And I said, 'Well, I don't know, Malcolm. Probably not, really. But you must admit, Malcolm, in a language where you can say things like "Alas, unparalleled", just to say that he was a great guy was a bit flat, you know. There was something on that boy's side.' *I'm interested in how he fitted into Cambridge, because the school he came from was very sober and scholarly.*

When you live in a place where everyone has got 'the troubles', as we used to call it, eventually you are interested in who is going to die and who is going to survive, and you get a pretty shrewd idea in a way. Malcolm had just the same kind of prophetic gift.

I met him in one of the main streets of Cambridge one day with John Davenport, who was one of his boon drinking companions. The pubs opened at ten – there was very little time for repentance. But I met these two about two o'clock one afternoon and they weren't drunk and disorderly, but they were certainly drunk. And Malcolm greeted me, and he said, 'You know, Hugh, John and I are doomed. We're doomed. You are not doomed.' He was bloody well right. They are both dead and I am alive. But he had this sense of some people who are going to scrub along not necessarily living orthodox lives, but they are going to get by. Here I spent forty years at a Cambridge college, you see, without real disgrace of any sort. Malcolm, I think, probably couldn't have done that; he was eccentric by birth, by nature. And one of the signs of his eccentricity, a very interesting one indeed, was that he generated stories. Some of them are true, because I remember clearly. But some – I don't know whether they happened to me or one of our pals, if you understand what I mean. Malcolm just had this capacity. You'd meet someone and they'd say, 'Here's what old Malcolm has done now.'

For instance, take the way he passed his examinations – that's what I was responsible for mainly. Well, when he took his second after two years, his first main examination, he had done some work and he had got a few notes. But he took this pile of notes from St Catharine's . . . down to the Senate House where the examinations were held, and he got a great rock in his pocket – typical sort of combination of prudence and recklessness – and he plunked his notes down outside the Senate House with this rock on them to prevent them from being blown away. And he just got through that time. Well, the next year, at his final examination, he had been drinking more and this time he hadn't got any notes. He'd just got a great fat volume, Professor Saintsbury's *History of English Criticism.* And he carried that down from St Catharine's, a distance of four hundred yards at the outside, reading furiously, and he dashed in and started writing before he had even read the questions. One of these stories is true, because I saw it; the other – well, he had this capacity – he was a mythogenic character. It was partly, I think, because of this extra experience he had during the year at sea and partly it was built in. He was a very remarkable man. And there was always the booze, of course. He drank more than the rest of us and he drank in a different way.

How did he drink that was different?

Steadily and persistently, and at that time, when he was living at St Catharine's, he developed a taste for a pretty grim liquor – he always had a taste for grim liquors. This one was called Moussec, I think, and it was a kind of fake champagne. There was a very high liquid content but not very much alcohol. But his kind of drunkenness wasn't quite alcoholism, you know. It was a different thing, and unless you have been in that state yourself you can hardly understand it. It isn't a question of being drunk from time to time – that's normal, that happens to a lot of good citizens and ordinary people. The point with him and his friend John Davenport was how rarely they were totally sober. It couldn't have amounted to more than an hour or two a month. And it was this persistent drinking; not so that he was ever quarrelsome – he was always very gentle, delicate, polite. They didn't get like that. But they got used to being tight, or half-tight or three-quarters tight. Malcolm, for example, could work a typewriter quite well when he was tight, which I couldn't. . . . He could control himself. If you or I drink a bit too much we'll have one or two bright ideas, with a bit of luck, but after the hangover they'll be forgotten. But Malcolm, since he was more or less pickled the whole time, he remembered things. He didn't behave like a drunkard at all; it was a different phenomenon.

Was Aiken a drunk, too? I mean an alcoholic?

No, not an alcoholic, but he also drank a lot. . . . When Malcolm had left Cambridge I ran into him there in Rye and he was living with Conrad Aiken, and I was living with someone else. We used to meet a lot and we drank pretty steadily. I was drinking then; it was my main period of drinking, as a matter of fact about a couple of months on brandy. . . . But we were never drunk. There was one occasion when Malcolm, just in sheer high spirits, had the idea it would be fun to wheel Conrad down the street. It was at Jeake's House. It was the very street that Henry James lived in and wrote many of his great 'compulations', as the local guide-book called them rather prettily. Malcolm had the idea it would be great fun to put Conrad in a wheelbarrow and tip him into the mud at the bottom of the harbour. Luckily he didn't do it. If he had done it I tell you what would have happened: I'd have had to get Conrad out. Malcolm wouldn't have done it. He would have gone away rocking with laughter. But no, Conrad drank a lot of whisky, rather like Malcolm really. It wasn't a question of being drunk so much as not being quite sober for more than a few minutes at a time in an hour. Conrad is dead, bless him, isn't he? I don't want to malign his memory. I am simply describing what happened.

Was there much literary activity at Cambridge at the time, in which Lowry played a part?

In a minor sense there was. But this particular subculture, to use a term we did not know, centred around an undergraduate magazine that was called *Experiment*. That was run by Bill Empson, Jacob Bronowski and myself. We were the main editors . . . and we did, in a sense, form a circle. But among us there was no doubt that Bill Empson was a genius. He was the chap who would last – we have been perfectly right about that. Malcolm was interesting and valuable to us as editors and we were, I imagine, his first publishers. We published stuff of his above all because he wrote in prose. At that time poetry was the fashionable thing. The notion that you could write creative and imaginative prose was just there, because Joyce was in the background. . . . We knew all about that. Mostly our contributors wrote stream-of-consciousness stuff of unutterable boredom – I cannot describe how shattering. . . . Malcolm came along doing the same kind of thing, but his stuff was different. I still remember reading a script of his in his rather odd typewriting . . . 'My first murder was committed in a windmill.' Well, I must say, that riveted my attention, you know. And I said, 'We ought to publish this stuff,' and we did.

What was the standing of St Catharine's College at that time?

Not quite a major college, but always very interesting because it's been, I'm sorry to say, rather poor. And it was running English as a subject under a very able Director of Studies, Tom Henn . . . who was a wonderful man. He didn't get on with Malcolm. It was just one of those temperamental difficulties, and we've got one principle here: try to be a liberal institution. Never try to join together those whom God has put asunder. If they don't get on, OK. Well, Tom, who was a very humane man indeed, realised he wasn't getting on with Malcolm and asked me if I would take him on, and I did. It meant meeting him in pubs, not in my rooms as most of my students do, but this was understood; it was perfectly all right.

Do you think Cambridge spoiled Lowry?

No, no, not at all. I think he lived a life here between St Catharine's . . . and this pub and several others and, well, I think he got a lot out of it. I think he was happy here.

As a writer?

Yes, he was writing. He was tapping away on the typewriter, you know. God knows what happened to most of it. But we published him. No, I think he was really happy here. He was perhaps better because he didn't persist with Tom Henn or Tom Henn didn't persist with him. It set him free, at liberty. I more or less understood Malcolm so far as an all-too-sane man can understand someone like Malcolm. So we got along very well. And then he had lots of other things, like he played a banjo in a very sailor-like fashion, and he liked singing and I used to sing with him now and again. One of the things I found so impressive was that on these wanderings on the Pacific in a ship, he had been to places that I've heard of, with evocative, lovely names like Port Swettenham. He'd been there. I forget whether he'd been to [Java], but you know that Kurt Weill song ['Surabaya Johnny']?[3] I used to sing that with him. He was doing his best to get those famous breaks and slips on the banjo. No, I think he had a good time. Mind you, he was never going to be very happy, poor Malcolm wasn't. As I said, he was doomed. He knew it, and he was.

---

3 This is not clear from the transcript, but 'Surabaya Johnny' was a popular song and widely sung at the time.

'He Was Afraid I Was Going to Offer Him Tea'
John Davenport

John Davenport (1910–63), the critic and journalist, was editing a Cambridge poetry magazine when Lowry came to visit him in his room at Corpus Christi College. They immediately discovered a common interest in alcohol and later spent a great deal of time together drinking, boxing and sharing experiences in London's 'Fitzrovia'. Davenport had a reputation as a talent-spotter (see Kathleen Raine, p. 53) and soon decided that in Lowry he had discovered a genius (see Arthur Calder-Marshall, p. 78). He introduced him to Charlotte Haldane's literary set, and the two friends spent Easter 1932 together in Devon working on *Ultramarine*. They met later in Hollywood and France, and, at the end of Lowry's life, Davenport visited him several times in hospital. Here he observes very shrewdly Lowry's trick of keeping groups of friends separate and putting on different masks for each of them.

This is an edited extract from an unpublished introduction that he wrote for *Ultramarine* in 1962.

... The years 1928 to 1932, when I was up at Cambridge, were exceptionally rich ones. Idly jotting down the names of those who have since distinguished themselves in the arts I am staggered to find myself faced with over forty of the famous. Each had already given some earnest of his ability in his future field, but four of these young men stood out for us as having already accomplished something. William Empson had already written many of his best poems and completed the first draft of *Seven Types of Ambiguity*; T.H. White had published his book of poems and a novel under a pseudonym; Richard Eberhart had his first book in the press, and, after leaving Dartmouth, had been to sea; now appeared Malcolm, who had also been to sea and who was finishing *Ultramarine*. He was just twenty, but had an aura of experience. I had tamely been to France, Italy and the Netherlands; he had been to Hong Kong and Vladivostok and seen Socotra on the horizon. Furthermore he was the intimate of a well-known American writer, and himself a novelist. He came round to my rooms at Corpus soon after the term began. I was an editor of *Cambridge Poetry*, and Malcolm was paying a round of such visits with the solemnity of a Frenchman seeking election to the Academy. It was late afternoon, cold and dark as only Cambridge can be, and I asked him if he would like something to drink. He afterwards told me that he was afraid I was going to offer him tea. A decanter of whisky put him at ease and we launched a friendship that lasted for twenty-eight years. He was too shy to dine in hall, so we ate dinner in my rooms and went on talking and drinking until nearly midnight, when he had to run a mile to his drab lodgings near the station. I visited him there next day, in a confusion of books, papers, bottles, gramophone records. There were a pair of barbells and a ukulele. Pinned on the walls were restaurant bills from many countries, photographs of pictures by Chagall and Rousseau le Douanier, and other objects, all of which I later learned had some totemic significance. A mysterious order underlay the chaos. The books revealed the eclecticism of the literary workman. Like other undergraduates of that time he had the Elizabethans, Joyce and Eliot, but few undergraduates then knew Knut Hamsun and Hermann Bang, B. Traven and Nordahl Grieg. Nor had they read the whole of Ibsen and Strindberg. E.E. Cummings, Hart Crane, Wallace Stevens and Conrad Aiken himself had merely been names to most of us. Henry James had not been rediscovered, but Malcolm had volume after heavily annotated volume of the Master's works. James Hanley was a new name. Three novellas he had an especial affection for were Mann's 'Tonio Kröger', Melville's 'Bartleby', and Bunin's 'The Gentleman from San Francisco'. Many young men of twenty are as well-read, but Malcolm's reading was integrated in an unusual way. Dante and Faulkner were made to seem part of a whole. His mind was very acute, and he had already felt and suffered deeply, but he presented the world with the persona of a drunken sailor in a dirty sweater playing a ukulele. Each was a true representation of himself. He soon had a number of friends, but he did not like them to overlap, preferring to present a different image of himself to each. I was fortunate in being able to share more than one of his worlds, but the nameless misery that drove him made him often inaccessible. It is of course a commonplace that all men are essentially solitary. In Malcolm's case it was an absolute isolation. On its ordinary level it was simply a form of narcissism. The weakness and the strength of his novels lies in the fact that he can only create *himself*. The protagonist of *Ultramarine* is himself. The Consul in *Under the Volcano* is himself, and so is his half-brother Hugh: this has perhaps been insufficiently realised. The women in his work are seen rather than understood: the Consul's wife is two women, one in the body of another, which explains certain psychological discrepancies.

But to return to these basic dates: in the long vacation of 1930

Malcolm went to Norway to meet Nordahl Grieg,[4] working his passage each way. Although he went to sea many times afterwards it was only as a passenger. That particular need had been worked out of him. During his last two years at Cambridge he had rooms in college, on the ground floor of the big court at St Catharine's. He very much disliked being on the ground floor because of the lack of privacy. The door would often be locked for days, although an occasional jazz record could sometimes be heard: Joe Venuti and Eddie Lang, perhaps, playing 'Going Places' or 'Doing Things'. He was a mystery to his tutor, L.J. Potts of Queens', who, to Malcolm's delight, had translated some Strindberg stories. His vacations were often spent with Conrad Aiken, now back at Rye, as Mr Lowry senior felt himself unequal to cope with his problem child, and Conrad found himself *in loco parentis*. Work on *Ultramarine* continued, but the task was complicated by the fact that present experiences had to be incorporated in the text, which caused Proustian wrestlings. This explains the slowness with which all his work was carried out. It was a ceaseless struggle to maintain an equipoise between past and present. During the Easter vacation of 1932 we went down to Hartland, North Devon. Mr Lowry had suggested that I help to coach him for his final examination that summer. There was far too much to be done, and Malcolm spent the weeks putting his novel into final shape, determined not to touch it during his last term. Nor did he, but concentrated on doing three years' work in a month or so. He eventually gained third-class honours in the English tripos – I suppose because the examiners felt they couldn't plough a genius just because he hadn't read the set books.

Malcolm refused to return home and spent over a year in London. *Ultramarine*, which had nearly five years' work in it, was given a final polish and sent to a famous firm of publishers. They were intrigued by it. Then one of the directors had his case stolen from his car – the engine was running, he was away from it for less than a minute – and the only typescript of the book was in the case. Malcolm took it very well, but the disaster nearly overcame him. He had scrapped the earlier scripts in a glorious gesture of freedom. The absolutely final version had been made in the house of our friend Martin Case, a pupil of J.B.S. Haldane's, whose wife, Charlotte, was a marvellous antidote to academic Cambridge, and in whose house at Chesterton one had perfect food and drink and

4 According to Clarissa Aiken, Lowry spent this vacation at Jeake's House in Rye in Sussex, and she does not mention the trip to Norway. It seems he did meet Grieg, but when is unclear.

endless music. Malcolm spent a great deal of time there. By a miracle Case had preserved all the material abandoned by Malcolm, who wrote yet another version of the book, which this time was sent to Jonathan Cape, who agreed to publish it in 1933.

Jazz, Movies and Literature
Gerald Noxon

For some years a writer and broadcaster for the Canadian Broadcasting Corporation, Gerald Noxon (b. 1910) was the publisher of *Experiment*, the Cambridge literary magazine in which Lowry's first serious fiction appeared. They shared an interest in jazz and the cinema as well as literature, and they clearly found each other's company congenial. When they first met, Lowry was in the process of writing *Ultramarine*, and their discussions on the literary techniques of Joyce, Faulkner, Melville, Bunyan and Conrad Aiken give an insight into the writers who were influencing him in his first year at Cambridge. Oddly enough, Lowry did not apparently mention to him the Norwegian, Nordahl Grieg, although he is supposed to have travelled to Oslo to meet Grieg in the summer of 1930. When Lowry moved to Canada in 1940 they resumed their friendship, and their correspondence suggests that Lowry took very seriously Noxon's criticisms of his work. It was at a house he found for him at Niagara-on-the-Lake in 1944 that Lowry completed the final version of *Under the Volcano*, which Noxon later dramatised for CBS Radio in New York City.

This is an extract from Noxon's article 'Malcolm Lowry: 1930', which appeared in *Prairie Schooner* (Winter 1963–4).

It was in the fall of 1929 that I first met Malcolm Lowry. I was then an undergraduate at Trinity College, Cambridge, in my second year at the University, while Malcolm, although a year older than I, had just come up. His arrival had in fact been delayed for some two years which he had spent working his way around the world as a merchant seaman. He had come up to St Catharine's College, which was not one with a contemporary literary reputation.

Our meeting, since we were in different years and at different colleges, would have been most unlikely had it not been for the fact that I was the publisher of a small undergraduate literary magazine called *Experiment*.

Malcolm was at that time, and continued to be, for the most part, a very shy fellow whose acquaintance at Cambridge was composed not primarily of his fellow undergraduates, but of a wide variety of persons, both of 'town' and 'gown', ranging from bookmakers (turf) to bookmakers (literary). However, shy though he was of most of the academic fraternity, Malcolm was above all a writer, and he knew it. This fact soon became known to the editorial board of *Experiment*, which consisted basically of J. Bronowski, Hugh Sykes Davies and William Empson.

A story entitled 'Port Swettenham', submitted to the magazine by Malcolm, was promptly accepted and printed in the February, 1930, issue of *Experiment*. It was, although very rough and uncertain in many ways, quite obviously a work of genuine literary merit and one of original talent. This was the first publication of work by Malcolm Lowry.[5] He was at the time already well on the way with a novel entitled *Ultramarine*, which was eventually to be published by Jonathan Cape several years later.

By the time his story had been published in our magazine, I had of course had reason to meet the author. It was not easy to know what sort of person he was. I knew nothing whatsoever about his background except that he had been to sea and he appeared to be, through what I later learned to be an extreme shyness, a rather surly, uncooperative, and not very communicative individual. Drink in sufficient quantity would for a time tend to loosen his tongue, but that did not always mean that he was any the more able to communicate his thoughts and feelings to others.

It was quite obvious to me, however, that Malcolm was having a difficult time at Cambridge, not so much on account of Cambridge itself, but on account of what seemed to be the serious problems which occupied his mind and dominated his spirit.

At first, after the publication of his story, I met Malcolm only accidentally, in the street, in pubs, or sometimes at parties. Then, on his own account, towards the spring of 1930 he began to come to visit me in my rooms in Trinity. He was passionately fond of jazz and fascinated by the cinema. I had a phonograph, a small but respectable collection of jazz records – old Deccas and Parlophones, as I recall – mostly blues, for which Malcolm and I shared a particular fondness. I also had a long shelf of film books, which were not very common around Cambridge at that time.

During these visits, which always occurred at night, Malcolm usually stayed only a comparatively short time. If he found someone else with me when he arrived he would usually either refuse to come in at all, or sit silently for a few moments and then, mum-

5 Except for those printed in *The Leys Fortnightly*.

bling some sort of an excuse, take his leave.

Our conversations, apart from the subjects of jazz and movies, were nearly always concerned with the technical problems of the writer. Malcolm was at that time trying very hard to discover a way in which to write the kind of book he wanted to write, a mode of writing which would not only fulfil his own purposes but would at the same time conform to a certain extent to established literary values which he acknowledged and respected. He was deeply concerned with questions of 'métier' as well as the problems of self-expression. Two writers seemed to have an overwhelming importance for him at the time. They were Herman Melville and Conrad Aiken. Later I learnt that a third writer, a Norwegian by the name of Nordahl Grieg, was also very important to Malcolm, but he never mentioned Grieg to me during the Cambridge days as far as I can remember. We did, however, discuss at some length a novel which Malcolm had already started writing, entitled *In Ballast to the White Sea*, and it was in connection with this project in particular that Nordahl Grieg had influenced Malcolm, as I later learnt. The manuscript of this novel was destroyed, according to Malcolm, in a fire at Dollarton in British Columbia in 1944.

In *Ultramarine*, too, the novel which Malcolm was trying to complete while he was at Cambridge, there was certainly some debt to Grieg, but on the whole *Ultramarine* was predominantly influenced by the works of Conrad Aiken in general and by the novels *Blue Voyage* and *Great Circle* in particular.

With me Malcolm chose to discuss principally problems of style and language, not content. He seemed to know what he wanted to say, which was most unusual in so young a writer, but he was terribly concerned with how he should say it. The question always was, how should a serious novelist write in that year 1930? Naturally we discussed the kind of solutions put forward by such writers as Joyce, Faulkner, and Hemingway as well as those put forward in the works of Aiken, Melville, Bunyan, and a host of others.

Basically Malcolm was unwilling to repudiate the legacy which he had found awaiting him in the works of nineteenth-century novelists. While discarding the aridity of a purely realistic style, he was unwilling to adopt the kind of personal stenography which made the works of writers like Joyce and Faulkner superficially difficult for the reader. Nor was Malcolm to be reduced by the apparent simplicity of Hemingway, whose writing he found much too flat for his own purposes. For Malcolm it was necessary that his writing should have a perfectly wrought surface meaning, in the sense of the term established by Flaubert. A competent and thoroughly understandable narrative technique, however complex it might be in form, was a necessity, as was a sound dramaturgy of classical origin. And above all Malcolm knew that he had to use the full range of the English language as it had been given to him to know it and use it. And even in 1930 his command of the English language was amazingly authoritative.

But while fulfilling all the conditions mentioned above, Malcolm insisted that his writing must be capable of carrying meaning at many different depths, on the many different levels of intellectual and emotional communication which he discerned so clearly in Melville, for instance.

Truly, Malcolm Lowry had set himself a problem to which there could be no single, simple answer. He had already committed himself to a struggle which he himself realised could never have a definite outcome. There was no help for it. He could not borrow nor adopt a style. He had to create one of his own to fulfil his own needs, and it had to be forged out of the extraordinary complex alloys which were constantly being produced in what must be called the furnace of his mind. For, internally, Malcolm was a man on fire. His external appearance in 1930 did not give much evidence of his internal condition.

He was a short, compact man, very broad in the shoulders and exceptionally strong. His arms were rather long for his height and when standing he let them hang down at his sides in a curiously fixed curvature. I remember thinking that Malcolm was not bow-legged but bow-armed. His eyes, of an extreme blue, were the most striking feature of his face. I learnt that you could always tell more about Malcolm's state of mind by the look in his eyes than by anything he might say, or fail to say.

In spite of our fairly frequent visits together, with the jazz and the movie books and the discussions of literary style and methods, I did not feel that I knew Malcolm very well, nor could I form any exact notion of the personal problems from which he was obviously suffering but to which he did not refer. All I knew was that I liked him and I knew instinctively that he was a friend.

'The Word Genius Can Be Truly Applied'
Kathleen Raine

The poet Kathleen Raine (b. 1908) took the natural sciences tripos at Girton College, Cambridge, in 1929. She was married briefly to Hugh Sykes Davies, Lowry's friend, 'unofficial' tutor and one of the editors of *Experiment*, in which her first poems appeared. In this extract from her autobiography, *The Land Unknown* (Hamish Hamilton, London 1975), she gives a glimpse of the dazzling array of talented personalities who were her contemporaries at Cambridge in the late twenties and early thirties, including Humphrey Jennings, John Davenport and William Empson. Among these, she singles out Lowry as 'the only one . . . of my then contemporaries to whom the word genius can be truly applied'. Her assessment of Lowry's vision of the holocaust to come is rather generous. There is nothing of this in *Ultramarine*, and Lowry only gave the hero of *Under the Volcano* the power to foresee in 1938 a Europe in flames when he wrote the final draft in 1944, by which time the horrors of the Second World War had become common knowledge.

. . .We knew fairly accurately how we ourselves and others stood years before we had been put to the proof. But I wonder how many of us realised then that Malcolm Lowry, the only one (besides Humphrey)[6] of my then contemporaries to whom the word genius can be truly applied, possessed that gift of which Cambridge values took little cognisance? True, John Davenport, then as later remarkable for his discernment (he was also one of the first to acclaim Isak Dinesen[7] and a boon companion of Dylan Thomas), loyally and constantly, if prematurely, proclaimed Malcolm's greatness. He did indeed publish extracts from his first novel, *Ultramarine*, in *Experiment*; but it was only after many years that *Under the Volcano* showed us who Malcolm really was. Shy, tongue-tied, gauche except when he played and sang to his ukulele, little use at examinations, his gifts were of feeling and imagination; aspects of life little valued in our Cambridge. William Empson, among us in the full blaze of his glory, impressed us more, because his gifts were within the range of our understanding. William was able brilliantly to articulate a student's intellectual and emotional experience. As between William's brilliant gift of discursive intellect and Malcolm's inarticulate, profound feeling and intuitive insight, William's, at that time, impressed us more. Or must I say, impressed me more. Impressed me in part because William's brilliance frightened me and made me feel inferior; whereas Malcolm did not frighten; he was too shy, too vulnerable, to overawe; too disarmingly simple when he sang:

6 Humphrey Jennings, the film-maker.
7 Pseudonym of the Danish writer Karen Blixen.

This year, next year
Sometime, never,
Love goes on and on for ever.
What makes the world go ro-ound is love.

Yet the singer of these simple sentiments possessed virtues and qualities of genius that were no part of our Cambridge scheme of things; Bill[8] had no great opinion of him; and, as always, I followed my foolish head instead of the simplicity of that other faculty to whose recognition the head has, in the long run, to bow. . . .

The man whose name I so briefly, so inadvertently, and so undeservedly, bore at that time, Hugh Sykes Davies, was a friend of so many members of our Cambridge literary circle that, in the matter of friendships (at that time a bond we probably both felt to be far more binding than that of marriage), our Cambridge life went on somewhat as before. Humphrey and Cicely Jennings were our friends; and Hugh was very close to Malcolm Lowry who came, like himself, from a Methodist background. Both played golf with the detached expertise of the intellectual and I have a vivid picture, more like a photograph than like a memory, of Hugh and Malcolm swimming together in Quy fen, while I, in a complex despair worthy of *Under the Volcano*, looked miserably on.

I had of course read the passages from *Ultramarine* published in *Experiment* and the book itself when it appeared. I was puzzled by Malcolm's evident feeling that the stokehole of a tramp steamer and the brothels of Eastern seaports were somehow closer to 'life' than Monteverdi and Shakespeare played in College halls and the civilised minds of Cambridge. Not the point, of course – I missed the point. I did not understand that Malcolm had taken upon himself an exploration of the whole scope of his world, a quest for paradise which must take into account the hells, 'under the vol-cano' on whose green and fertile slopes our Arcadia so precari-ously lay. We all thought of ourselves as the growing-point of our time; but whereas most of us were only the eternal avant-garde, Malcolm really was open to the suffering and heart-breaking aspirations of humanity's collective mind and most secret thoughts. For genius is not a personal gift but precisely that gift of access to the universal which Malcolm had and we had not.

And yet, though we did not know it, under Malcolm's volcano is precisely where we were, Hugh Sykes and I. I was his faithless 'Yvonne', though I did not, like her, in compassion return when I left him. Malcolm's book has, I now see, mysteriously defined the

8 William Empson.

mental climate in which my first marriage had its brief existence. We were, unawares, experiencing just those underground influences, the subterraneous gathering of catastrophe that Malcolm Lowry so powerfully evokes. The uncharted freedom of a Bohemian way of life, just because of its freedom from the ordinary social pressures, reflects, vibrates to, what is 'in the air'.

Hugh, like Malcolm, was very much aware of the Spanish Civil War and was presently to be drawn, like others of that generation (Burgess and Maclean were among his friends, as fellow-members of that élite of élite 'the Apostles'), towards Communism. Herbert Read was related to him; and Herbert's gentle and idealistic form of Anarchism was a gleam of light in the sky over Dis, at that time.

But if we were living in the hells we did not know the place by its true name; this, we thought, is the reality of things, this cynical despair is seeing things as they really are. And the hells have their pleasures, if not their joys; not least among these, as Milton knew, the building of Pandemonium, city of those arts and sciences by which the lost adorn their doomed city. To give expression to despair, to uncover, layer upon layer, with the artistry of a Virginia Woolf, bottomless subjectivity; to strike heroic postures of bitterness; to fabricate opinions – these things have their joyless pleasure. We read Petronius and Lautréamont and *Ubu Roi*; and explored our habitation cut off from the light of heaven by the phosphorescence of Surrealism – soon to be '*au service de la révolution*'. Only Malcolm saw the hells for what they were; and in so doing – like Dante by the mere change of a point of view, under Satan's hairy thighs – was to be free of them, in the end, the volcano under him and the lovely light of Paradise dawning for him, at last, over the cleansing sea of Dollarton. But all that lay in the future. Neither Hugh Sykes nor I myself knew ourselves in hell, having quite forgotten paradise.

'The Flash of These Beautiful Blue Eyes'
Charlotte Haldane

Charlotte Haldane (1894–1969), novelist and former journalist, was married to the physiologist J.B.S. Haldane in 1929 when John Davenport first introduced Lowry into her literary set. 'Chatty's addled salon', as the unimpressed J.B.S. called the glittering company of young aesthetes who gathered at his house, included William Empson, Michael Redgrave, Hugh Sykes Davies and

Kathleen Raine. Charlotte was evidently attracted to the charming, blue-eyed young Lowry and based a character upon him in her third novel, *I Bring Not Peace* (1932). The suggestion contained in the novel that she had an affair with Lowry is discounted by their friends (see, for example, Arthur Calder-Marshall, p. 76), but he did later tell his psychiatrist, Dr Raymond, that he had been 'beautifully seduced' by a married woman, which does seem to leave the matter open.

This is an extract from the 1967 BBC TV *New Release* programme, *Rough Passage*. She is interviewed by Tristram Powell.

The eyes were quite extraordinary, but mostly he'd keep his head rather down and sideways and then suddenly look up at you, you know. And you'd get the flash of these beautiful blue eyes. . . . I thought he was such a striking personality, and I was writing novels at the time and I put him into one of my novels. This was set in Paris, although . . . he'd never been there before, and it was designed as a fugue with four voices. And Malcolm was one of the four characters. I asked his permission, of course. I had to do that to use it. And he said, 'Yes, certainly,' and I dedicated it to him. *And in that book you used some of his poems?*
I used two or three of his jingles, and I've got it here as a matter of fact. I think one of them is very attractive, but you have to bear in mind that he used to sing these, and he had a wonderful sense of rhythm and he'd sort of 'swing it', you know. And so, without the music, it isn't quite the same, but here, for instance:

> I was always dreaming when the day was done,
> My childhood broke through chords of music and of sun.

I think that's lovely. And then:

> If you could solve this beauty you would see the man
> Behind all that I try to be and never can,
> And share the simple music that my heart has seen,
> That's what I mean –
> Yes, siree –
> That's what I mean.

He used to have a slight little American accent when he sang that, you know.

3 Bohemian Days, 1932–6

After Cambridge, Lowry joined the Aikens at Rye; now, according to Clarissa Aiken, he wanted to incorporate a dream sequence from Conrad's new novel, *Great Circle*, in *Ultramarine*. Aiken objected, but it was not the last time Lowry would 'borrow' from his mentor's work, and from other writers. By midsummer Clarissa was not sorry to see the evermore slovenly Lowry depart for London. His father continued his allowance on condition that he stayed at a temperance hotel, but he soon moved into a dingy bedsitter in Devonshire Street on the edge of Fitzrovia, an area popular with such pub-crawling Bohemians as Paul Potts and Dylan Thomas. Now he had a much wider audience and the Lowry myth really took off.

In pubs such as the Fitzroy Tavern and The Plough he became a familiar, somewhat Chaplinesque, figure with his baggy trousers, rolling gait and ukulele at the ready, playing 'hot' music and steadily drinking himself into unconsciousness. It was a memorable performance – the doomed, impoverished genius.

The poverty, of course, was an act (he was getting £7 a week from his father). But he could present a sober enough image when he wanted to, as he did to the poet Anna Wickham. As her son James Hepburn recalls, he clearly enjoyed the easy-going atmosphere and the exuberant company at her house on Parliament Hill. It seemed almost as if he had found a new family for himself.

He had also found a new 'guardian' in his old Cambridge companion Hugh Sykes Davies, who became responsible for reassuring Mr Lowry that his son was being well-behaved enough for his allowance to continue. This kind of arrangement was probably deeply humiliating to Lowry, and John Davenport remembers that he would avoid collecting his money from a city office for weeks on end.

But the myth of the doomed poet, so assiduously cultivated, now threatened to become a self-fulfilling prophecy. He accidentally broke the neck of the Hepburns' pet rabbit, and in October

1932 the final manuscript of *Ultramarine* was stolen from the car of Ian Parsons, a Chatto and Windus editor. Disaster was only averted when a friend was found to have kept a carbon copy of an earlier draft, but the whole book had to be rewritten. It was finally published by Jonathan Cape in June 1933. The reviews were tepid; his family were unimpressed.

Lowry left home for good at the beginning of 1933, after a brawl with his brother Russell. The voyage into exile had begun. The first three months of 1933 were spent in Paris where another old Cambridge friend, the painter Julian Trevelyan, assumed the mantle of 'guardian'. In March he went with the Aikens to Spain where he fell in love with a young American writer, Jan Gabrial. They were married in secret the following January. Love seems to have sobered Lowry, but only temporarily. There were turbulent scenes, and nights when Lowry took off alone around the Paris bistros. When Jan returned to America to break the news of her marriage to her mother, he was left in Paris to turn his new experiences into fiction.[1]

Later that year, in New York, the couple settled down to an apparently happy and productive existence, writing and trying to get published. Jan, politically to the left, was engaged in producing 'proletarian' literature. For a time, the previously unpolitical Lowry began to turn out a more economical and realistic prose, and the highly poetic influence of Aiken was weakened. He was now working on *In Ballast to the White Sea*, which grew to a monumental fifteen chapters. But his 'borrowing' habit threatened to get out of hand, and, according to Jan, one publisher's reader to whom it was sent found himself reading a chapter from his own novel.

By the beginning of 1936, finding the marriage claustrophobic, Lowry moved out, giving the excuse that he suspected he had contracted syphilis from a homosexual after a drinking spree. (His friend, Eric Estorick, confirms that he did spend time with acquaintances who were homosexual.) Jan and he lost touch, and he seems to have spent much of his time in bars or wandering up to Harlem, attracted, no doubt, by the 'hot' jazz and the exotic 'Negro' culture.

His drinking was causing concern to his friends, and in June Estorick suggested he enter Bellevue Hospital as a voluntary psychiatric patient. He was there for ten days before Jan heard of his whereabouts and quickly removed him. But the searing experi-

1 'In Le Havre', *Life and Letters*. 'Hotel Room in Chartres', *Story*. Also in *Malcolm Lowry: Psalms and Songs*.

ence had served its purpose, and he immediately began work on what was to become one of his most brilliantly wrought works, the posthumously published *Lunar Caustic.*

This experience reunited the Lowrys, and in September they left for Hollywood where John Davenport had found a job script-writing. However, Lowry's American visa was due to expire and they needed a cheap place to live. He had also become interested in D.H. Lawrence's Mexican writings, so the couple decided to head south of the border.

They arrived in Acapulco on 2 November – the Day of the Dead – 1936, the occasion in Mexico for a macabre festival in celebration of death. The impact on Lowry was immense. It was, he wrote later, 'the ideal setting for the struggle of a human being against the powers of darkness and light'. That setting and that struggle became the inspiration for *Under the Volcano*, the masterpiece it was to take him eight years and three drafts to complete.

Visits to 'La Tour Bourgeoise'
James Hepburn

After leaving Cambridge in May 1932 Lowry gravitated to London and the Bohemian life which, in those days, centred upon so-called Fitzrovia, an area extending from Charlotte Street to the borders of Soho and Bloomsbury, and pubs such as the Fitzroy Tavern, the Marquis of Granby and The Plough which were frequented by a whole generation of would-be writers, artists and poets. Louis MacNeice, Dylan Thomas, Arthur Calder-Marshall and Liam O'Flaherty were among those with whom Lowry rubbed shoulders. James Hepburn (b. 1907), a young music-hall dancer who had just launched himself into show business with his younger brother, met Lowry when he came to visit his mother, the poet Anna Wickham, who kept a literary salon at her home on Parliament Hill in Hampstead. James and his brother John struck up a close friendship with Malcolm and together they did the rounds of the Hampstead pubs, visited the London music halls and occasionally went to rugger matches. The house on Parliament Hill came to be dubbed 'La Tour Bourgeoise' by a family friend, and Anna Wickham's salon has emerged as something of a literary landmark. Here Dylan and Caitlin Thomas spent the second night of their honeymoon, and here Malcolm Lowry accidentally strangled the family rabbit.

This is an edited version of an interview which James Hepburn gave me on 30 July 1984.

I can't really be awfully precise as to the exact date that I first met Malcolm, but I think it was in the course of the summer of 1932. ... He must have met my mother, Anna Wickham, probably somewhere in London. As a result of that meeting he came up to the house from then on. He used to make a habit of it and he came frequently when he was in England. It was following these visits that he and a brother of mine, who was of the same age as both of us, became friends and we used to roam around together. We went to pubs and rugger matches and I think sometimes to the cinema, and that was how we became associated and how we became friends. . . . He was particularly interested in 'hot music' and he played the ukulele in a way which I think is unique . . . rather in the same way as the guitar was played at that time in such combinations as the Hot Club of France. . . . And the thing in particular I remember about Malcolm was the great capacity he had for enjoyment and for the recognition of what he regarded as excellence, which gave him great pleasure. I remember the smile that would develop on his face when he came across something which he regarded as good. . . . He would play any of the 'hot music' of the time. One of his other friends, Ralph Case, the elder brother of Martin Case, was an extraordinarily accomplished pianist and at that time played 'hot' piano in a way which was very beguiling to us all, and he and Malcolm used to play duets together. And I think that was one of the features of the time. Then my brother and I used to make a contribution by doing a bit of tap-dancing during the 'breaks', as it were. This was the nature of our association, and it's obvious that it wasn't a particularly literary one. The literary discussions took place between Anna and Malcolm and they would talk about writers and writing often far into the night.

What features of his personality stand out for you, or stood out for you at the time?

Well, I think Malcolm had a well-developed sense of himself, and he also, I think, had a well-developed understanding of how he wanted to present himself. In other words, in a sense, you might say that when it came to literary associates, that he had, as it were, an eye to the main chance. And, of course, he also used to run the gambit about the horrors of sailing before the mast in a way that could become tiresome. And I remember, when it did become tiresome, we used to tell him so, and we used to say something to the effect of 'Get orf it, Malcolm. If you hadn't wanted to go to sea there was no goddamn reason why you should have gone.' And he would respond very amiably to such advice, and he would indeed 'come orf it'. But, from time to time, he would return to it.

Did he have much money to live on at that time?

I don't think he was ever really poor. I think that the funds he had in hand would actually vary . . . as to the period in the month. But one never felt he was in any sense on his uppers and . . . actually money was always available to him . . . he had an allowance from his father, but he had to go in person to an office in London, the office of either a business associate of his father's or a representative of his father's business. And he resented having to do this and he dreaded the occasions when he had to go. He regarded it really as a humiliation. Of course, whether that was reasonable in the circumstances, I don't know. I think I could have brought myself to collect a monthly stipend, which never came *my* way.

It's been said by some people who knew him that Malcolm became somewhat paranoid at the time that you knew him. Did you ever notice anything of that sort?

Well, I didn't . . . but he did have a very strong sense of a malevolent destiny which would rise and kick him in the pants from time to time. I remember that and I remember . . . there were times when he was in a depression when he would look almost surly, his head would go down and his eyes would droop; and he would feel, in response to some happening, that destiny was at it again.

I remember one occasion in particular. Malcolm had come to visit us and was talking to Anna in front of the fire in what we then called the Morning Room. My brother George, who was, I think, at school at the time, had a rabbit and we had this in a hutch. Malcolm had seen it and was very pleased with it because it was a young animal and rather attractive. And he was talking to Anna and actually sitting over the fire with the rabbit on his knee . . . he was stroking it and fondling it and suddenly the creature went limp. And Malcolm had, in fact, broken its neck. He was quite horrified, but he didn't see it as anything that he was responsible for; he attributed it to this malevolent destiny which constantly dogged him. . . . I think he stayed that night . . . and next day, after this happening, he met Arthur Calder-Marshall and he had in fact taken the creature away and had it with him in his case. . . .

Then I remember the occasion in 1932 when the typescript of *Ultramarine*, which he had sent to Chatto and Windus, went astray, and I can remember the absolute agony he went through.

Naturally enough; it was the most frightful thing to have happened. And I remember all the drama and the events by which Martin Case was able to reconstitute the typescript from pages which he had had. Of course, that was an agonising time for Malcolm. But it's not surprising in a way; it was characteristic of Malcolm that he had only one copy of the typescript. And that, I remember, was another example of the intervention of his malignant destiny which had, as it were, whisked the manuscript out of the publisher's car.

Did Malcolm talk to you about his family?

Well . . . what I remember of it was that Malcolm had a feeling that he was a disappointment to his father, which he regretted. But in a way he regarded that as one of the facts of life and that he wasn't going to be able to do very much about it. I think he was determined to follow the course which he had mapped out for himself, and the fact that in doing so he was a disappointment to his father was, he thought, unfortunate.

In what way do you think he felt a disappointment?

Well, I think he felt his father would have had certain aspirations for him which were not connected with literature, but . . . had probably come to the conclusion that he *was* going to pursue a career in literature – but that he would have had very powerful ideas as to which course that should take, which were not Malcolm's. I think . . . the arrangements which were made by his father would indicate that he had become reconciled to the fact that he was going to pursue a literary career; but then, it seemed to me, the nature of the arrangement which his father came to with Conrad Aiken was, in a sense, deeply humiliating. You could put it that Conrad Aiken was employed as Malcolm's keeper . . . and I have a gut feeling that Aiken's attitude and that relationship, which was extremely damaging to Malcolm, was more or less forced on Malcolm by his father.

Damaging in what way?

Well, I think in a sense it diminished Malcolm's independence.

Did he talk about his mother?

I don't remember him talking very much about his mother. I think he had a great affection for his mother, and I've never really been able to decide whether his mother was more sympathetic to his aspirations than his father. . . . I'm not sure if my feelings on this are particularly reliable and I wouldn't want much to be hung on them, but I really felt that Malcolm thought his mother was incapable of great displays of affection and I think that he may have felt the relationship . . . rather cold. . . . I think that as a child he may have actually looked to his mother for reassurance and didn't always find that the reassurance came.

Did he mention his brothers?

Not very much. I think he admired them very much and I think he felt that in them was what his family looked for him to be, but that he couldn't fulfil it, because he was made of different material, probably. . . . As a matter of fact I think that when he was with us he was rather happy to be able to forget about his family, and in a sense I think he felt that he would like to be a member of ours.

How did he relate to women?

Well, I don't think that he found relations with women very easy. I don't think that he had a very simple approach to women, and I think that it might be said that he approached women through his writing. I don't know how reliable an impression that is. I mean, if he could present himself as a character in literature he would find it easier than if he presented himself on the basis of a boy to a girl. . . . I don't think he found it, to put the thing in bald terms, very easy to pick young women up. . . . Douglas Day seems to present the fact that there was some kind of affair between Malcolm and Charlotte Haldane. Well, I think that Charlotte Haldane was evidently a bit of a baby-snatcher and that possibly she made a pass at Malcolm, but I never remember that there was any response from Malcolm . . . but I couldn't possibly have known if there had been. . . . I remember them together in so far as we were on several occasions at their house in London with J.B.S. coming in and looking with a rather jaundiced eye at these random young men who were around.

When you read Under the Volcano *and those sections of it dealing with Hugh's days in London, do you recognise Malcolm there?*

Oh yes, indeed. I recognise Malcolm and some of the incidents he writes about. But it's a long time since I read *Under the Volcano*. I find that some of the more obsessive parts become rather tiresome, rather in the way we used to find his obsessive accounts of his experiences before the mast tiresome, and I feel inclined to say, over those passages, 'Oh, come orf it!', which you may find rather a heresy.

The Family Abandoned
Russell Lowry

By the time Lowry left Cambridge he had become almost entirely alienated from his family. He was so noisy and quarrelsome that his father became worried that he would wreak violence on his mother or the servants. In the end it was his brother Russell whom he attacked, and the resulting fight led to them never speaking to one another again.

This is a further extract from the interview he gave me on 2 September 1983.

When he came home on vacation from Cambridge were you still living at home?
Yes, I was at home. I was then at the family office in Liverpool.
Things finally moved towards a final break with the family at Inglewood, didn't they?
I had my quarrel with Malcolm in, I suppose, the early part of 1933. . . . An effort had been made to make Malcolm at home at Inglewood. He was given an upstairs room equipped as a sort of library for him with a desk. It was completely at the top of the house, so he could write his papers there. He could do what he liked, and it just didn't work. And there came a time when he was getting more and more quarrelsome and this was a trouble, particularly for Father, because he was away at the office all day and Stuart and Wilfrid were not at home; they were married and gone. I was also in the office all day, so Malcolm, if he was at home during his vacation from Cambridge, was left at home with Mother and with Mary and Sarah.[2] If he got violent this became very worrying. And he did become very quarrelsome indeed.
Tell me about your own final quarrel with Malcolm.
Well, it had become his habit to go wandering around in the evening, collecting noises and impressions of the dockside and this, that and the other place. This included his famous utterance that the Birkenhead tram did not go 'Ting-a-ling', it said 'Elang-elang'. He had no transport of his own, so he would come home on the last bus at about ten o'clock . . . he just managed to get the pubs closed, get the bus and come home, arriving, I suppose, at half past ten or so. And I would be going to bed and he would come in and we would have a chat. His bedroom was next to mine at the opposite end of the corridor from the parental chamber, and this was jolly as a rule. But he was gradually getting more and more quarrelsome. And there came one evening when he came in in a thoroughly obstreperous mood, and I wasn't in that sort of mood. I wanted either to go to bed or write to my fiancée, or something of the kind. Anyway, I didn't want to be talking to him. And so I told

2 Maids.

him to get out because he was a drunken young bugger and a bloody nuisance. And he wasn't pleased with that, so he hit me and I hit him, and we then proceeded to struggle all around the place. I chucked him out of my room and he eventually fetched up in the bathroom and fell into the bath, and it was all very undignified and very unbrotherly. The house was in an absolute state of turmoil. Neither Mother nor Father nor Mary nor Sarah batted an eyelid, and everything remained totally quiet, and nothing was ever said about it. But Malcolm and I practically never spoke to each other again, which was a pity because it would have patched itself up in time. But there wasn't any time, and that was the end of Malcolm's relationship with the family, as far as I'm concerned, and Malcolm's relationship with me and mine with him.

Do you remember the last time that you saw him?

No, no I don't.

He just moved out of your life.

That's right, yes.

Did you have much news of him after he left? How often did you hear about him?

Well, he maintained a correspondence with Stuart . . . so I heard about him from Stuart every now and again, and of course Father was perpetually worried to death. In fact he was literally worried to death eventually by Malcolm, very largely because he was always running out of money. No one knew where he was. . . . He did those things he ought not to have done and left undone those things he ought to have done. I personally had no contact with him. I did write to him actually to put an end to our previous quarrel, but he didn't reply. Of his 'brother Russell' he still never spoke. But I heard *of* him rather too frequently from Stuart, because these letters were the most obscure things full of think-balloons all over the side and written upside-down and written in the corner – Malcolm obviously writing for his own amusement and not for our benefit. . . . And Stuart would say, 'Oh, no. There's another letter from that bloody Malcolm fellow. I don't know what it's all about. Can you read it?' And we'd try to decipher the think-bubbles, but there was never anything one could do about it. He was just bellyaching about life in general and Father in particular, I think. I don't remember any of the contents of the letters, except that they were long and complicated.

Do you remember the publication of Ultramarine *in 1933?*

I don't particularly remember it. It didn't explode on an expectant world exactly. In fact, as far as I know, it sank like a stone. I bought a copy, which I've still got, but I don't think many other people did.

So the family weren't particularly impressed that he'd published a book?
Not particularly. Why shouldn't he have? No, no, no. We were
getting on with our own affairs. I in particular had just got married.
No, we weren't publicity-conscious at all. We didn't either seek
publicity or want or enjoy it when it came.

'The Doomed Sailor of Genius'
John Davenport

John Davenport continues his account of his early friendship with
Lowry by recalling Lowry's squalid lifestyle in a Bloomsbury
bedsit, his friendship with Anna Wickham, and his reluctance to
collect his weekly allowance. Davenport, obviously a more robust
character than Lowry, did not think, as James Hepburn did, that
having to report to collect his cheque from a City office was particularly humiliating for him. The observations he makes about
Lowry the actor seem particularly acute. His reassessment of
Ultramarine, thirty years after its publication, concurs, oddly
enough, with brother Russell's opinion at the time – that its poor
reception was not exactly undeserved.

Malcolm's London year was quite extraordinarily squalid. He
moved from one room to another in the Bloomsbury area – rooms
that had no heat; rooms that had no light; one room that could only
be entered by squeezing through a broken panel in the permanently locked door. He became a familiar figure in the pubs and
bars of the neighbourhood – the doomed sailor of genius.

It was then that the Lowry legend really began. He was finally
borne away to her Hampstead home by the Australian poet Anna
Wickham, whose sons were friends of his. She was a very tall
woman with a deep voice, living in a large house through which a
gale swept perpetually, tossing leaves and manuscripts in and out
of the windows. Malcolm began to get some sort of order into his
life. I discovered that his penury was imaginary. His father allowed
him £7 a week (more than it sounds today) on condition that he
appeared personally and collected it at the London office of his
firm. These terms were really neither harsh nor humiliating, as
the poor man simply wanted to be assured that his son was alive
week by week. He was disappointed. Malcolm refused to go – he
was too dirty, had no shoes, didn't want to shave. He was forcibly
cleaned up one day and I accompanied him to the City. He walked
into the office quite briskly, exchanged a few words with the chief

accountant, and was handed an envelope which must have contained at least £70. Of course he enjoyed pretending to be destitute. It was another of his masks. He also enjoyed spending the money in forty-eight hours on the sad detritus of humanity that haunted London's Quartier Latin.

When *Ultramarine* appeared it made little impact on the critics. It is not a very good novel, but it contains some fine things; and for a first novel it has a remarkably assured style. I had become so used to thinking it a work of genius that I thought the critics more than usually insensitive; but rereading it recently, deliberately trying not to use hindsight, I realised that they were not altogether to blame. Its principal interest lies in the clues it gives to his later work.

A Guardian in Hampstead
Hugh Sykes Davies

During his Fitzrovia days in London Lowry made contact with his old Cambridge tutor, Hugh Sykes Davies, and persuaded him to act as his guardian, to vouch for him to his father in Liverpool and so enable him to draw his monthly remittance.

This is an edited extract from the interview Sykes Davies gave for the National Film Board of Canada's 1976 documentary feature, *Volcano*.

When did Malcolm come to live with you?
That was after he had gone down. When I was a research student here[3] I was living in some disorder in a flat in Hampstead and I met Malcolm in a pub, one of those pubs that literary society tends to convene around. You must convene around one pub or another, and it is nice to be able to meet your pals. And I ran into Malcolm there one night and he said, 'I'm in trouble, Hugh,' and I said, 'Yes, old boy, I know.' You see, I had been his tutor and that kind of thing, officially. And he said, 'My father won't pay my allowance because he said I drink too much.'

And I said, 'Well, you do really, don't you, Malcolm?'

He said, 'Look, my father says if I could find some responsible person to act as my guardian, then he would pay the cheque to them.'

Well, I saw what was coming, but I was fond of Malcolm – anyone would be – a most lovable chap. . . . So I became his

3 Cambridge.

guardian, you see. I used to receive his cheques from Dad and hand them over to Malcolm intact. And he was living with me. It was rather a nice little flat in Hampstead. There was one other person present . . . connected rather with me than with him. She had a tendency to drink rather a lot, too – one of Epstein's old models. . . .

But there was one morning, I remember, I went to Malcolm's room about ten o'clock. (Life didn't start early, you understand, for this household.) I went in and found him in the middle of dressing and he was pouring amber-coloured liquid from his shoes into a large bottle. Well, I had never seen this done before, and I had heard of lots of strange drinks, like red biddy, you know – bubbling gas through a rubber tube through water and then drinking the product – but I had never seen this done before. And I was a bit astonished and Malcolm realised this. He was a man of great perception. He began pulling this moustache of his the way he did as he screwed himself up to make an explanation. And the explanation was this. 'Well, Hugh, you know, not to put too fine a point on it either, I notice that in this hot weather my feet smell. So I bought a large bottle of eau de Cologne from Woolworth's. I put it in my shoes and leave it there overnight, and in the morning I pour it back into the bottle.' But this was certainly one of his problems. If in fact you were an analyst you would say 'an obsession' or something of the sort. But living the life of a chap who was hardly sober for much of the time, he didn't have that many baths and that kind of thing, and yet he was extremely fastidious. He was, as it were, a man with a dual nature. Fastidious indeed on the one side, but handicapped on the practical side in carrying out a programme of fastidiousness. This went very deep with him, you know. I think very deep indeed.

When was the last time you saw him?

I should say about 1935, when I disappeared into a sanatorium for a year in Switzerland, and this was a break from most of my old friends really.

Were you ever in touch with him again in any way?

No, I heard news of him from common friends. I heard charming stories, for example, about his marriage, his first marriage. We thought she was a bootlegger's daughter or something of the sort, you know. But Malcolm's French was rudimentary, as I know, because I was responsible for teaching him, and he had been told that there was a certain stage in the ceremony at which he must indicate agreement. So the commissar, or whoever he was, said [the words] and someone nudged Malcolm and he used the only expression he knew in French: '*Ça va, ça va.*' I can't vouch for that you know. I wasn't there, but it was absolutely typical of the man. He would generate lots of stories. . . .

Were you surprised when you heard that Lowry had died?

Not at all. He told me he was doomed and I believed him.

Did you hear about it immediately?

Within a week or two. And I went through certain private observances that I usually go through, little private rituals on the death of my friends. I did it for him as I would for anyone who had been a friend.

The Randy Puritan Who Liked His Booze
John Sommerfield

Not long after he moved to London in 1932, Lowry sought out the young writer John Sommerfield (b. 1908), who had written a novel about his sea experiences, *They Die Young* (Heinemann, London 1930). Over the following two years they spent a great deal of time drinking around London pubs. Sommerfield later incorporated Lowry into a novel called *The Imprinted* (London Magazine Editions, London 1977), in which he appears as the doomed novelist, Angus.

This is an edited version of an interview given to me on 8 August 1984.

I was working as a kind of carpenter in a place that made scenery in a workshop off the Old Kent Road. I liked it; it was nice there. . . . I was working away at the bench on some job and some figure, scruffy-looking – slightly sloshed, I could see – came in and asked for John Sommerfield. I said, 'I'm him,' and he said, 'Oh, I want to talk to you,' and he looked around. The bloke who ran the place was around somewhere, and he said, 'Does the bosun mind?' So I said, 'Oh, no.' And it turned out that it was Malcolm. He had read this novel of mine, which I think very lowly of, but it had quite a patch about the seafaring life, which he liked apparently, and he wanted to talk to me about it. So I talked about it and then it was getting on for knocking-off time, so I said, 'Let's bugger off across the road to the pub.' And that was the beginning of a beautiful friendship.

What kind of a character was he to meet?

Well, the thing about him I felt was enormous personal warmth, you know, and sometimes you meet somebody that you im-

:l you get on with and like – some sort of chemistry or
don't know. I just liked him at once and we went to
started drinking and had a lot of fun. . . . The thing
lm was that, despite all the sadness and tragedies and
difficulties of his life, he was an immensely humorous person,
marvellous company – a laughing chap, you know – a great laughing fellow.

How much was he drinking when you first met him?
Quite a lot, but we drank beer mostly, you see, which is not very
harmful. It was only later on when he drank a lot of other things.
But I'm afraid, you know, we were bad influences on each other,
because luckily at that time I was working at this job, so I had some
beer money, too, see? I've known plenty of other people who drank
a lot more than he did . . . later on I think his difficulty was when
he got on the hard stuff. But *then* he didn't get on the hard stuff,
hardly ever.

Which were your favourite pubs when you went on booze-ups?
Well, many. It was more or less in general, you know. We used to
go to several pubs; there were pubs all round there. At that time I
was living near Swiss Cottage and we used to go to the Swiss
Cottage pub a lot when he was at my place, because I remember
spending the whole day with him there when he was going to catch
a train back to somewhere and he kept missing it.

The Fitzroy, of course, was a favourite one, wasn't it?
Yes – I'm not sure really if *we* did any Fitzroy work or not. Probably did, but not a lot, I think. Also we used to sit in these little
Soho cafés like Bertorelli's, which were great for people who were
hard up, because you could have a cup of quite drinkable black
coffee and sit there for hours; they didn't mind.

*In those days Malcolm was living in a place in Devonshire Street, off
Portland Place, I believe. What was it like?*
Well, it was full of cigarette ends and rubbish and had a slightly
broken window and all that. You know, it was just a sort of bedsitter. I slept on the floor there many times. . . . He had a lot of books
there. And that's the only place of his I saw. He did stay a few
times at the Wickhams', the Hepburns' place on Parliament Hill,
because he knew Anna Wickham, you know, the old poetry lady,
who I used to know. . . . Actually she had a terrible row with Malcolm. I don't know what it was about, and I wished I'd seen it,
because people said the invective was something out of this world.
Well, I mean, Malcolm was fairly fluent – but she, you know, she
could really tear people off a strip. I think she terrified him. I was
rather frightened of her. I was always very nice to her.

What were Malcolm's politics in those days?
Well, as far as I know he didn't have any. I was a naïve left-wing political bore at the time and I used to carry on to him about it, and he rather thought I was great for having these ideas, but he didn't – you know – he didn't appear to connect with them at all.
Do you think he was religious?
No, I don't think so.
What about sex and women? Did he talk much about them?
No, not a bit. It always struck me as strange because I once called him a randy puritan, which I think was right, because he obviously did like girls. He was interested in them. He never seemed to have much to do with them; I think he was scared of them in some way, and also he was the sort of chap that would not have casual sexual relationships. . . . He didn't go in for that – not as far as I knew, anyway.
He was supposedly very frightened of contracting syphilis, too, wasn't he?
Well, that was because I think his Dad was a bit of a nut on the subject, and, when he was a fireman on this ship, they got him into a brothel somewhere. He didn't want to go but they shoved him into going and he didn't like it because, I think, he felt sorry for the whore, too. And then, of course, the chap in the next bunk to him had got a terrible dose of clap, you know. He didn't get it, but I think that put the wind up him a bit. But in those days it was much more serious; there were no antibiotics and things. If you got the clap, it was bad.
When he talked to you about that voyage on the Pyrrhus, *do you remember what he said?*
No, I don't. He let me have a copy of the book[4] . . . I admire that book immensely and it always amazes me that people talk so much about his later work; this book, I think, has got a great deal for it, and as the first novel of a young chap I think it's remarkable. It's got a lot of Malcolm in it in the sense that, although he was having a horrible time, it's funny. A lot of it is funny.
That incident of the sailors dragging him into the brothel he must have told you, because it doesn't come out explicitly in the book, does it?
. . . He wouldn't say he was dragged to it. He wouldn't admit to that, because the thing with Malcolm was that, although the conditions on the tramp ships of that time were horrible (I know, because I've worked on them myself), he didn't mind it. I mean, the work was hard, the food was horrible, you usually had bedbugs everywhere: he didn't mind any of that. But what he could not

4 *Ultramarine.*

stand, what made him really unhappy, was that they took the piss out of him for his middle-class attitudes. And, of course, he started off by doing a very foolish thing, without realising it. He got the job through his father . . . and he came down to the dock in the family car and got on to the ship. Of course, that finished him from the start, because, you know, working seamen are just as much snobs as upper-middle-class people, only in a different way. No, he had a very bad time on that boat. The actual physical hardships he didn't mind a bit; he was probably better at taking them than most of the other blokes.

How did he talk about his family? What impression did you get of them from him?

Well, not a lot. I got a feeling he didn't really want to talk about them very much. I got only vague inferences and things. I do realise that there was something between him and his father which he hated, and I did realise – although he never said so specifically – that they were more or less paying him off all the time in money – you know, like rich people who've got kids they don't want to bother about and so they just buy them lots of presents, you know. . . . But he wasn't a bloke who talked about himself a lot, you know.

Was he at all paranoid?

. . . Oh, well, he had delusions of persecution, but they weren't all delusions; he was a man everything went wrong for . . . you know, letters he should have received never got to him; he cut himself when he was shaving all the time – things didn't go his way at all. . . . But one of the things about him, he could laugh at himself. And strange things did happen to him. I remember one very boozy day . . . we went into some draggy little drinking club in the afternoon, and they had a fruit machine – not one of these electronic ones, but one of these things you pull handles to – and for some reason I put some money in there and I got the bloody jackpot for the first and last time in my life. And I think we went on to drinking scotch then, because scotch was comparatively so much dearer than beer. . . . I think that really set the ruin in. And we might have had a meal at Bertorelli's or might not, but I remember walking up Fitzroy Street rather slowly and Malcolm had a bottle of Chianti (I can't think where he got if from; it was actually undrinkable – even I wouldn't drink it after a swig or two)[5] and suddenly Malcolm said, 'My God, look!' I looked round and just going round the

5 Sommerfield did not actually tell the story as recounted above. He said he had told it before and suggested that I take it from previously published versions. So, from here to the end, I have based the account on the transcript of *A Portrait of Malcolm Lowry*, BBC Radio 1967.

corner of Charlotte Street were two large elephants. And I looked at him and he looked at me and I thought, 'Well, if we're both seeing things, it's all right.' Then we ran like blazes round the corner, but there was no sign of an elephant. But what we did discover was a heap of steaming elephant dung in the middle of the road.

John Davenport's 'Tame Genius'
Arthur Calder-Marshall

Arthur Calder-Marshall (b. 1908), novelist, short-story writer, biographer, memoirist and critic, was at Oxford when Lowry was at Cambridge, but learned of his reputation as a 'literary genius' from John Davenport, who himself had a reputation as a talent-spotter. They met for the first time in London in 1932 after they had both graduated, and Calder-Marshall found Lowry charming and very clever, with a tremendous sense of humour. He has given a great deal of time to writing and speaking about him, and in 1963 wrote and narrated the BBC radio programme, *A Portrait of Malcolm Lowry*.

The following is an extract from an interview he gave me for the 1984 BBC radio programme, *The Lighthouse Invites the Storm*.

What is your most vivid memory of Lowry?
Well, there are so many, but I think perhaps the very first sight I had of him, which was at 5.30 one afternoon in Duncannon Street. I was going up to a Lawrence and Wishart[6] party at Gatti's Restaurant which was up twenty-four stairs, with a brass rail running in the middle of the stairs. And, as I was walking up, there, at the head of the stairs, appeared two swaying figures – John Davenport and Malcolm Lowry – both of them so pissed that they were only standing up because they were holding on to the rail. John had this expression of hatred on his face as he saw me, because he'd been keeping me from Malcolm – Malcolm was his tame genius. And Malcolm put out his hand and said, 'Arthur, it's wonderful to meet you at last.' Probably that.
Can you describe Malcolm Lowry to us?
He was a broad man. He had very nice blue eyes and a queer sort of smile; one saw his upper teeth gleaming when he smiled and they, in fact, always reminded me of an animal's teeth – a fox's teeth, perhaps. He was always very conscious of the fact that the

6 A left-wing publisher.

word 'Lowry' is in fact a dialect word for fox, and I am sure that right from the very beginning the fact that he was a Lowry influenced him. He moved with a lumbering gait; in fact I think he got so used to playing the role of the old seaman who had just landed ashore that even if he had this shambling gait naturally, he did increase it. He was terribly clumsy; he had very small hands and he was really incapable of doing any of the sort of skilful things that one would expect. He couldn't even comprise a full octave on the piano. He had a reputation for enormous strength and he obviously had colossal vitality and the ability to suffer the ravages of drink. He wasn't the wonderful swimmer that he was supposed to be in terms of speed. I remember he challenged me to swim a length with him and I beat him by three or four yards, and I don't claim to be a fast swimmer. I never saw him box, but I have no doubt that he was a better boxer than, shall we say, John Davenport, who pretended to be a great boxer. He had a sort of Charlie Chaplin image of Malcolm with the taropatch, which is what he insisted on calling his ukulele. I don't know why, because I cannot find in any dictionary the word 'taropatch'. There was that, plus his little old suitcase, plus his rolling gait, plus his trousers tied up with a tie and an old jacket. He never went in for the sort of matelot's singlet; it tended to be, you know, a shirt with a collar, or without a collar.

What struck you most about him as a character?

The first thing was his enormous charm and his great sense of fun. He loved to laugh, he loved talking about films, and he loved talking about books, especially the funny passages. He had a tremendous sense of humour. He was, in fact, very, very clever. He never gave the appearance of being very, very clever. He was capable of using people, though they didn't realise this at the time. Of course one of the things, as a long-distance drinker, he had to do was, in fact, to get relays of people to drink with him. . . . He was a wonderful fellow drinker. I remember John Davenport, who, apart from Lowry, was one of the heaviest drinkers I've ever met, saying to me, 'I am not in Malcolm's class, I cannot take it, I can't last as long as he does.' He was lovely to meet in a pub and talk to for two, three, four hours, but to live with him . . . to me that would have been hell. I cannot understand how Margerie[7] succeeded in doing it. . . .

Do you think that Lowry developed much over the years you knew him?

No, I would say not. Behind the assumed personalities, Malcolm

7 Lowry's second wife.

remained a little boy who didn't know anything about women; he didn't meet any girls . . . his other brothers were too old to introduce him to girls, and I think he was terrified of girls. I don't think he knew anything about them. His opportunity for meeting girls was very small because his father, although he had this large house outside Liverpool, didn't like parties, didn't like dancing and didn't like jazz. Consequently, I don't think Malcolm had a normal childhood or normal adolescence during the holidays. And of course at The Leys School he didn't meet girls anyway. I think he was very frightened of girls.

He had an obsessive fear of venereal disease, hadn't he?

Malcolm talks about having been shown over a venereal hospital, or venereal museum, at the age of five by Stuart, which is absolute nonsense because Stuart was at the War at the time. . . . Actually syphilis was a family menace in those days. I remember my father in fact was so frightened of syphilis that he told me he never sat on the lavatory seat, even though he was in his own home. Syphilis was, for that generation – not for me, but clearly for Malc – an absolute phobia, which reinforced his secret feeling that he was impotent anyway, I think.

Do you think that Malcolm was inclined towards homosexuality?

Well, he was a very pretty boy. If you look at the photographs of him at The Leys, when he was playing amateur theatricals, he clearly was a pretty boy. I didn't think he was pretty in Cuernavaca in 1937, but Paul Fitte, who committed suicide at Cambridge, was supposed to have propositioned Malc and committed suicide out of pique at being refused. In actual fact he committed suicide because he was being blackmailed for scandalous debts in London.

It has been argued that the Fitte incident was, however, an important event in Lowry's life because he felt in some way responsible and was filled with remorse about it for many years afterwards. What do you make of that?

I think that later on in Canada, as life got more and more boring with Margerie, Malcolm invented episodes in his childhood and youth to make things more interesting for her. The slight infection of his cornea, which lasted for about three weeks, he turned into being blind for two or three years, and Margerie accepted it absolutely as gospel. Equally I don't believe that the case of Paul Fitte had very much importance in Malcolm's life until he got older and was running out of material and had to go on inventing more and more interesting stuff. I read the newspaper account of the inquest, and I don't think there was that much in it. I think it was exaggerated, mind you, by Charlotte Haldane . . . who wrote a novel about Malcolm. She introduced Paul Fitte into it and made him a sort of alternative love interest. That was merely because Malcolm would not go for Charlotte, and I can quite understand why, because Charlotte was in fact so on-coming that she was completely off-putting.

Do you think that the drinking was just part of the Bohemian persona, or was it necessary for his writing?

. . . Malcolm, who was fourteen years younger than his eldest brother and five years younger than the youngest of them, I think drank far more than any of them, at an earlier age, in order to keep up. It was one way of proving that he was grown up, and the youngest in a family is always running to keep up with the older ones.

Did he have a distinctive pattern of drinking that you could discern?

Just continuous – but continuous. I think he got hooked on alcohol at the age of fifteen. He was OK when he became Boys' Junior Golf Champion, and then I think he realised he had got to choose between being fit enough to hit a golf ball or devoting himself to drinking. And the drinking, in fact, did foster all the fantasies which he had to compensate him for being quite different from the rest of the family. The two main fantasies were that he was a jazz musician and that he was going to be a great writer in the tradition of Jack London, who he was lapping up at the time. Well, Jack London had started by getting blind drunk at the age of five, and was an adolescent drunk even earlier than Malcolm. So in saying that he was going to sea, he was deliberately following Jack London's pattern. Of course, Jack London had bloody well to earn his own living; he was fighting to exist. And this is really the tragedy of Malcolm's life, that he was a rich man's son trying to copy the career of an extremely poor juvenile delinquent.

What about his sense of humour? He could cast a very ironic eye upon himself at times, couldn't he?

He certainly regarded himself as a completely comic character. He uses the phrase 'Cheerfulness keeps breaking in', which by the way he didn't invent – he took it from Dr Johnson. Cheerfulness kept breaking in, as he saw himself as a ludicrous character. At the same time as seeing himself as a ludicrous character, when he was taking himself *seriously*, he saw that ludicrous character as being a fraud.

He of course took to romanticising and fictionalising his early life. Were you aware of that?

Oh yes, yes, but it started long before I met him. As I see it, he was conducting the fiction right from the time that he shipped aboard the *Pyrrhus*. He organised the trip aboard the *Pyrrhus* with the press coming along and the family and Momma coming down in the family Daimler to see him off, which of course completely mucked him up with the whole of the ship's crew. But he organised this as a publicity stunt to launch himself as a jazz musician and a young writer who was going abroad in order to get copy. This is in a seventeen-year-old schoolboy who was already beginning to dramatise himself completely. And the trip had to be wangled because his father clearly didn't want him to go. He thought it was a waste of time because he hadn't even qualified for Cambridge. But Malcolm planned it so that Stuart, his eldest brother, would plead with his father saying, 'I think it would be a jolly good idea for Malcolm. It'll give him some experience, and he really *has* got some literary talent.' So he uses Stuart to get his father to use his influence to get him on that trip as a deckhand. He didn't have to fight to get on a ship in the way that Jack London did.

When he came back from that trip, before he went to Cambridge, he made his first contact with Conrad Aiken. What part do you see Aiken as having played in Lowry's life?

Well, after coming back he tried to write a novel about the trip, and he found, in fact, that he couldn't write. He could have written an absolutely brilliant book about himself as a comic figure who wants to be a great writer, but finds he's no good and gets biffed around by the crew of the *Pyrrhus*, as in fact he did. But he wanted to write something that was as portentous as Jack London's *The Sea Wolf* – one of his worst novels – and he found that he just couldn't do it. He then succeeded in inducing his father to pay him seven quid a week at a time when most bank clerks were bringing up a family of three or four on five quid a week. There he was, alone, trying to write this novel, and he couldn't. But he read Conrad Aiken's *Blue Voyage*, which is also about the sea, and he thinks, 'This chap can really do it,' and so he wrote a wonderful smarmy letter of admiration to Conrad Aiken asking to meet him. Now Conrad Aiken was *not* a writer of genius. He happened to have been at Harvard at the same time as T.S. Eliot, Lewis Mumford and Edmund Wilson, and considered himself one of the greats, though nobody else did. So when a schoolboy writes and says, 'You are one of the greats. May I come and meet you?' and then later says, 'My father would pay five or six pounds – I recommend six – for you to take me into your house and tutor me,' Conrad Aiken was terribly pleased. There began a relationship of mutual admiration which was to last a lifetime.

When did you first hear about Malcolm?

When Malc went up to Cambridge, he was rather older than most undergraduates, and of course quite unique in that he hadn't come straight from school; he'd been, by this time, almost all the way round the world as a seaman. He'd been out to America. Conrad Aiken, the great American poet, had hailed him as a young writer of genius. And he was going up to Cambridge really to write the novel which he'd already started with Conrad. I was at Oxford actually a year before. I never met Malcolm at Cambridge, but the year before I'd gone over with the Oxford poets' hockey team and had met all Malc's contemporaries – people like Bill Empson, Basil Wright, T.H. White, Hugh Sykes Davies and so on – all of whom we regarded as brilliant people. 'Brilliant' was the word, but not 'genius'. Malcolm, however, went up as a young man of 'genius' as he'd been hailed by Conrad Aiken.

Now I don't think anybody would have taken that seriously if he hadn't met John Davenport. John Davenport was in a way very like Malcolm. He was fond of booze, he was extremely talented and terribly versatile – so versatile that he was never able to do anything in the arts because he knew that somebody else had done it better. He picked on Malcolm as a fellow drinker, and Malcolm *had* got quite a lot of money. Well, John announced that here was a young man of genius, and he took over the job of being Malcolm's tutor, being paid by Mr Lowry once again. I remember receiving a letter from John Davenport written from North Devon saying, 'Come down and stay with us. We're working on the novel. The bar opens at ten o'clock in the mornings and it doesn't close to residents. Lowry *père* pays.'

Well, I didn't go. I had left university, and like most would-be writers I was having to earn my living at something other than writing. I was trying to establish myself enough to write . . . being a writer was keeping your head above water. You didn't have the money or the time to be a genius, but Malcolm did. He got it established with John and with Conrad that he was a genius. Old Mr Lowry, who, I think, can only be blamed as being a terribly, unintelligently, over-indulgent father, went on paying Malcolm enough money to write his masterpiece. Of course, that was only enough money for him to get tight, and *Ultramarine* took six years, as far as I can remember, from the time he went to sea in 1927 until the book was published in 1933. It was, in fact, the most terrible pastiche of Nordahl Grieg's novel, *The Ship Sails On*, for plot, and of Conrad Aiken's *Blue Voyage* for style. It was interesting, but it was never good as a novel. He couldn't write a novel.

Why did he then produce little after Ultramarine, *do you think?*

Well, you see, *Ultramarine* was based on personal experience, an embroidery of personal experience. He had now got to get some *more* personal experience. He went to see Nordahl Grieg in Norway and, as a result of that, he wanted to make another novel out of the experience, which he called *In Ballast to the White Sea*. This he was talking to me about in 1934 as his next book. It never got written. That was the thousand-page thing that got burnt in Dollarton in Canada twenty-five years later. But there wasn't anything in that trip to Norway to write about.

You don't see it as the great lost masterpiece it's sometimes claimed to be?

Oh, rubbish! No, *In Ballast to the White Sea* was probably more useful as tinder rather than anything else.

But it kept him writing.

No, it kept him *talking* about writing. He went to Paris talking about writing *In Ballast to the White Sea*; he went to Spain talking about writing *In Ballast to the White Sea*, but nothing much was being written. Then, when he got married to Jan Gabrial, Conrad Aiken hoped that marriage would cure him of drink and give him something to write about.

How did Malcolm meet Jan?

She gave my wife and me the 'true' account of the courtship, as opposed to the completely inaccurate one that Conrad Aiken gives in his book *Ushant*. Malcolm took Jan into the gardens of the Generalife on the Alhambra in Granada in Spain. Jan had in fact knocked around quite a lot, so when he fell on top of her she was perfectly prepared to surrender to a fate that was certainly not worse than death. But to her astonishment he told her the story of *Ultramarine* from beginning to end, and said how astonishing it was that she should be called Jan and the heroine of *Ultramarine* should be called Janet. That was the extent of their erotic relationship in Granada.

It wasn't until a year later, when he was in the bar at the Alhambra Theatre, Leicester Square, that he met Jan again. And the fact that he met Jan at the *Alhambra*, Leicester Square, after having last met her in the *Alhambra*, Spain, made him realise that they were made for one another. He then proposed marriage. And Jan, who had been sold the idea that Malcolm was a young genius, really did believe that she was going to be Malcolm's Frieda Lawrence. He was going to write some wonderful book in which she would appear. But he wrote nothing except two short stories, both of them occasioned by her running away from him. She found she just couldn't stand it. He drank just as heavily, he was no good sexually, and she finally went to New York and Malcolm followed. Then the next stage of getting new material came when he went into the most terrible alcoholic fugue in New York, and landed in Bellevue Hospital alcoholic ward. That did give him a really searing experience. That was the basis of *Lunar Caustic*. Unfortunately he was only there for a short time and he couldn't elaborate.

He was incapable of inventing anything. He couldn't take a character and/or a situation and elaborate it into a story. He could only take what happened to him or what he had seen, and embroider it. And it tended to become more and more what he'd seen, because he *did* less and less. He just drank and watched. *Lunar Caustic* got to the length of a novella, but nobody would publish it. He then went to Hollywood, hoping to get a job through John Davenport.

What did you think of Lunar Caustic?

I think *Lunar Caustic* is, in fact, a very fine piece of writing, very fine – got a lot to say for it. Of course it's a very small piece of writing, but what there is of it I think is extremely good. But he didn't finish that for years and years. After Hollywood he went down to Cuernavaca in Mexico, still intending to work on *Lunar Caustic* (though it hadn't got that name at the time) and also *In Ballast to the White Sea*. Then a bus journey that he took with Jan, on which they saw an Indian chap dying by the roadside, gave him the idea for *Under the Volcano*, and he started work on that.

The Lost Manuscript
Ian Parsons

Lowry started writing his first novel, *Ultramarine*, in 1927, shortly after he had returned from his voyage on *Pyrrhus*. It took him five years to complete. In September 1932 he sent it to the London publishers Chatto and Windus. In October one of their editors, Ian Parsons (1906–80), had the manuscript stolen from his car. He had not kept a copy. Such disasters were not uncommon in Lowry's accident-prone life. However, as Parsons writes in the following extract from a letter which appeared in *The Times Literary Supplement* on 13 April 1967, 'People who are accident-prone nearly always believe in miracles,' and, in this case, there was an almost happy ending to the story.

. . . What happened was this. On the afternoon of 2 October 1932 I was due to go on holiday from Chatto's, in which I was then the very junior partner. I set off for Scotland in an old open 3-litre Bentley, of which in my salad days I was the proud possessor, and while proceeding north up St Martin's Lane (a thing you could happily still do at that time) I stopped off at the office to make a telephone call. The switchboard was immediately inside the front door, and my call took no more than a couple of minutes to make; but when I came out my suitcase had disappeared from the Bentley's back seat on which, in default of a boot, I had left it. In it was the MS of *Ultramarine*.

I was duly dismayed at its loss, though rather less so, I must confess, than at the loss of a fair slice of my personal belongings. It was, after all, only a typescript of which the author was liable to have a carbon. So I reported the loss to my senior partners, we alerted the police, and arranged for a suitable reward to be advertised in a number of appropriate places. When, after a reasonable interval, nothing whatever had been heard of my suitcase or its contents, I had perforce to break the news to Malcolm. And of course, being Malcolm, he had *no* carbon. But being already accident-prone I suspect that he was as much invigorated as alarmed by the news. Could he possibly rewrite the book? Yes, he thought, given time he could. So we arranged to pay him a weekly stipend for however long it took him to do so.

All this happened at the end of October 1932. Towards the end of December I suddenly received an urgent message from Malcolm asking me to meet him at a local pub. There, after nearly half an hour of mysterious silence, during which numerous pints of bitter were downed without Malcolm divulging the reason for this meeting, he suddenly came out with the following story. He had gone home to try to reconstruct *Ultramarine*, but had found it quite impossible to work there. He had then visited, in turn, half a dozen places in which he had written parts of the book in the hope that local inspiration would stimulate memory. All to no purpose. Finally he had gone to stay with the friend in whose house – somewhere near Birmingham, I think – he had finished the book. Upon explaining the reason for his visit, the friend went straight to a drawer and pulled out a bundle of heavily corrected half-sheets of typescript. It was the torn-up draft of *Ultramarine*, rescued from the waste-paper basket into which Malcolm had thrown it after typing out a fair copy.

People who are accident-prone nearly always believe in miracles. It is the other side of the same medal. So for Malcolm this unexpected resurrection of his book was a miracle that he hugged to his heart so closely that it temporarily bereft him of speech.

Typically, when at length he was able to unburden himself, he begged me not to let Chatto's feel obliged to publish *Ultramarine* because of what had happened; only if we really believed in its merits and its chances of success. In point of fact we had already, on 21 December, made an offer to Lowry's agent, John Farquharson, on the strength of the report that Oliver Warner (who was then Chatto's reader) had written back in September when the original manuscript first came in. In this he said, 'This is an unsatisfactory work because it is potentially so good and so original.' Then after praising its originality but criticising its lack of form, he went on: 'The man has a real flair for reporting, in which he is brilliant, and he has an ear for conversation which is remarkable. My conclusions are these: (1) I agree with I.M.P. that we should do him, for his potentiality rather than his achievement. (2) I don't think we shall make a penny, and I think he'll get very mixed reviews. . . . He will never, I think, do four-square circulating-library books, but his talent is one to be encouraged.'

I quote this, with Mr Warner's kind permission, not in order to claim credit for our joint perceptiveness, but to explain why the book was eventually published by Jonathan Cape. Malcolm genuinely wanted to relieve us of any sense of obligation to publish *Ultramarine* unless we were *wholly* enthusiastic about it, and we respected his generosity in the only way we could, by withdrawing. It also explains why I'm tolerably certain that the published version didn't differ materially from the original manuscript, despite Malcolm's reference to 'the only real version' and his subsequent plan to rewrite the book. But he was writing fourteen years after the event. Moreover I have just recently confirmed with Frank Taylor, who published *Under the Volcano* in America, that the story as Malcolm subsequently told it to him was substantially as I have given it above. Why on earth I should have been taking away on holiday a manuscript I had already read remains a mystery; an excess of zeal, no doubt, for which I was suitably rewarded.

Call It Misadventure
Clarissa Lorenz

Clarissa Lorenz (dates unknown) was married to the American poet and novelist Conrad Aiken, and met Lowry in 1929 after he had crossed the Atlantic to visit the man whose writing he so admired. She recalls how Lowry spent most of his university vacations with them at Rye in Sussex, and remembers especially the trip which they all took to Spain in 1933. There he drank heavily, exciting the contempt of the local Spaniards, and later met the young American writer, Jan Gabrial, whom he was to marry. It is clear from Clarissa's account that Lowry found her a receptive audience for his woeful tales of a tortured childhood – tales which his brother Russell has gone to such great pains to refute. Nevertheless, she throws interesting light on Lowry's relationship with Aiken.

This is an edited version of her article, 'Call It Misadventure', which appeared in *Atlantic Monthly* (June 1970).

... We first met Malcolm in 1929. Nothing in his cherubic countenance suggested the crucified genius. A snapshot I took of him in Cambridge, Massachusetts, shows a handsome, rugged youth of twenty with wavy brown hair, a radiant smile, and the intense blue eyes of a visionary. He had crossed the Atlantic impelled to meet the author of *Blue Voyage*, having assumed that my husband's novel had been dedicated to him. (We had the same initials, C.M.L., but he didn't use his first name, Clarence.) Presumptuous, wasn't it, and yet he felt something mystic about the coincidence, destiny pointing to Aiken. Under Conrad's supervision, he tinkered with *Ultramarine* for the next four years. An excerpt, 'Seductio ad Absurdum', appeared in O'Brien's *The Best British Short Stories of 1931*, and caused the volume to be banned from British public libraries.

In the early thirties we went to live in Rye, Sussex, where we had Jeake's House, a seventeenth-century edifice named after a family of astrologers and necromancers. This haunt intrigued Malcolm, and it became his second home. As a Cambridge University student, he spent all his vacations with us. His father, a Liverpool cotton broker, staunch Wesleyan, and fox-hunting Conservative, had engaged my husband as tutor and therapist to grapple with his son, a dipsomaniac. I kept my fingers crossed. One genius in the house was enough. For all my maternal feelings toward Malcolm, ten years my junior, I associated him with catastrophe. On his own admission, just to meet him was a disaster. Conrad for a long time suffered fracture headaches – souvenirs of a bibulous wrestling match with his protégé over the lid of the w.c. tank.

They were both night owls, spending convivial hours at Ping-Pong and literary powwows. Their 'pub-crawls' stirred gossip in Rye and upset my domestic timetable. I would sit by the front window, chafing, while the dinner dried up in the oven. One foggy night a couple of muddied, blood-streaked apparitions staggered in, looking sheepish. They had fallen into the river – fortunately at low tide. 'How much longer will Conrad put up with this madman?' My diary gave him short shrift. 'Not to be housebroken. . . . Definitely no mixer. . . . A caged lion. . . .'

Malcolm tried hard not to be a nuisance. A creature of extremes, he either starved himself or gorged – on everything but fish (choking on the bones happened to be one of his many phobias). I kept fearing he would absent-mindedly set fire to his mattress or break a leg falling downstairs. He moved like a somnambulist, his blue blazer spotted and rumpled, a necktie holding up his trousers. Keeping him laundered and presentable called for finesse. His socks created minor crises. One day he decided to buy a pair of argyles.[8] 'About time, too,' Conrad grunted. 'But don't go near the gasometer or there might be another Neuenkirchen disaster!' Malcolm's deep belly laugh resounded through the house. . . .

Our demure young housemaid adored him. 'He's a real gentleman.' Jenny sensed his sweetness, humility, and loneliness. He had endured four years of near-blindness as a boy, forbidden to read, write, or play games because of a chronic ulcerated cornea in both eyes. The youngest of four sons, he called himself the runt of the family, although he won the schoolboy golf championship of England while attending The Leys in Cambridge (where 'Mr Chips' was a master). He was a fine swimmer, a great hiker, and he even broke a record for lifting barbells.

With women he was shy and taciturn. On one of his solitary tramps along Romney Marsh skirting the Channel, he mailed me an apology in rhyme, for what offence I don't recall. The note vanished, doubtless into Jenny's apron pocket. She saved most of his discarded scribblings. However disorganised he may have been in other respects, Malcolm was a disciplined writer, productive for long, sober periods, endlessly revising and turning out draft after draft – totally committed to art. . . .

In the course of working out his oedipal problems by proxy, he wanted to use Conrad's dream, recounted in *Great Circle*, of eating the father's skeleton. That, he was told, would be carrying things too far. The Aiken touches deleted, *Ultramarine* went off to Chatto and Windus, only to be stolen from the publisher's car, where he left his case momentarily. While the firm advertised in vain for the manuscript, friends of Malcolm's salvaged fragments of the only other copy, and he supplied the missing pages. Jona-

---

8 Socks with a coloured diamond pattern.

than Cape (who had turned down *Great Circle*) accepted *Ultra-marine* with a £40 advance.

In April 1933 Malcolm accompanied us to Spain for a much-needed holiday. A university graduate of twenty-four, with a third-class tripos in English, he looked neater but much heavier, a beer drinker and 'perpetual source of anxiety to a bewildered father', as he confessed. Lowry senior still trusted Conrad to wean his prodigal son from the bottle, an onerous job for any father surrogate. . . .

Conrad dozed fitfully in the train to Granada (a seven-hour endurance test). Malcolm had carried off his hotel key for the second time. He read *Ulysses*, perspiring in his short sleeves. Whenever the locomotive laboured uphill at a snail's pace, he leaned out the window and gesticulated at the engineer to hurry up. The closer we came to the Sierra Nevadas, the farther away they seemed, elusive as paradise, their snowy peaks lost in the clouds. Beyond this apparent mirage was the Alhambra, our destination. A request for two rooms had brought a garbled wire from the Carmona pension: 'Reserving both rooms.' Conrad said wryly, 'They must have known you were coming.' Malcolm chuckled. I hoped his sense of humour would survive Ed Burra's darts and barbs. The young surrealist painter, who would be joining us later, spared no one in his caricatures.

We were parched by the long, hot journey, and longed for a cold beer. The Carmonas' son-in-law, Tende, a scrawny, lynx-eyed youth, met us at the station and invited himself along with us to the Hollywood Café, where a Negro jazz band performed. 'Travelling a thousand miles for this?' Malcolm said plaintively. A paunchy Spaniard at the next table hooted, 'What a fat belly!' Conrad's retort 'Look at your own' jolted him. Tende sniggered and kept goggling at Malcolm's drinking capacity. I foresaw trouble. . . .

Malcolm had a keen eye for symbols. He was fascinated by my account of an ironmonger in Granada wrapping up some nails in a photogravure page depicting the Crucifixion. One moonlit night, while admiring Granada from the embankment, Conrad tossed English pennies over the parapet. They hit the monastery roof 300 feet below with a faint ping. When Malcolm imitated him, his coins dropped soundlessly into a void. 'No echoes, no answers – the story of my life,' he said with detachment, as we strolled into a wineshop nearby, a rendezvous for artists. There Conrad made a discovery. Among the paintings that patrons had left in lieu of cash were two self-portraits by Sargent and a watercolour of his niece, the Cynthia of *Blue Voyage*. 'By Jove, this is uncanny!' Malcolm blinked with amazement. 'Coming across your heroine in the Alhambra!'

. . . Conventional tourism was anathema to him. He preferred his own inner landscape and orbit, sampling the cantinas. Sober or not, he observed life with an artist's eye, selecting meaningful material, whereas I snapped pictures indiscriminately and filled my diary with a hodgepodge of impressions.

The pension saw less and less of him as the days flew by. Tende would lurk in the background at mealtimes, pointing him out to newcomers with a sly, 'Psst, *el borracho!*' A barfly? That nice, quiet young man? The ladies looked at him askance, and he pretended to be oblivious of them. Ed Burra's arrival complicated life still more. The frail, pixilated artist appeared in a dusty green suit and dragging his luggage, which included a laundry bag. . . .

Before long my fears were justified. One day at lunch Ed did a caricature of Malcolm as a blimp in a sombrero. Tende pounced on it with glee, passing it around the patio and drawing giggles and guffaws. 'That punk,' I sputtered, aching to wring his puny neck. Malcolm got to his feet, snatched the sketch, added a pipe to the mouth, tore it up and flung the pieces in Tende's face, then berated the artist. 'That was an unkind thing to do,' he said with characteristic restraint. 'The trouble with you is that people are too good to you.' Ed shrugged and twinkled, 'Oh, you don't know half the things they say about me!'

Ed could kill his detractors with a pencil. Malcolm had no such outlet. He had been initiated into sadism at a tender age, he told me, in a rare burst of confidence. 'My nanny used to whip me daily with brambles until I bled. I thought it was the customary thing so I never complained. My parents gave her the sack only after the family gardener told them he saw her hold me upside-down over my bath.' Sadism he felt throughout Spain – a terrified urchin held by the heels over a precipice, a donkey hobbling on fettered forelegs, a little girl blithely twisting a dragonfly on a spike.

Ed's mischief had emboldened Tende into stepping up his baiting. He told Conrad that Malcolm was known all over Granada as *el borracho* and the Civil Guard were watching him. 'Once I see him in the Hollywood Café, he asked for *aguardiente* [brandy] and two women.' The day I caught sight of him he was lurching through the streets jeered and laughed at, children and adults turning around to poke fun at him. Scattering them would only have doubled his humiliation. He stopped at a music shop, listening to a flamenco record, a fixed smile on his face, then continued on his zigzag course. ('. . . man no longer belongs to or understands the world he has created. Man had become a raven staring at a ruined heronry. Well, let him deduce his own raven-hood from it.')

... [Malcolm] wasn't allowed to live in London or go to sea again, and he dreaded being cut off from the parental purse. Con-rad began to talk of releasing him, much though we needed those monthly 20-guinea cheques. The whole dilemma cast a pall on us.

In the next several weeks his drinking tapered off and he bore Tende's torments like a Spartan. But even an English gentleman has his breaking point. One afternoon in May, during a period of regression, he started climbing Alhambra Hill when he heard the derisive '*El toro, el toro*', Tende with some friends cavorting behind and aping his wobbly gait. Malcolm seized his *bête noire* by the scruff of the neck, rammed him uphill a hundred yards or so, flung him down, picked him up again for a repeat performance, then left him in the dust. 'Where did you deposit him – at the Puerta da la Justicia?' Conrad inquired sardonically, as his protégé related the triumph with pardonable pride. 'Three cheers,' I rejoiced. 'That's my boy!'

From then on he had no more trouble with Tende. But fate had other entanglements in store for him – an exotic American girl who came to the pension with her French escort. Malcolm, instantly smitten, stole her away, and for the rest of her brief stay they were inseparable, doing the town and roaming the foothills, falling into a brook one morning, he looking like a mesmerised owl, to quote Conrad. I was glad to see him relate to another human being besides his mentor, but I had misgivings about this glamour girl in the large picture hat who found him fascinating and so handsome.

Their romance touched off arguments about virginity and Spanish morality, causing a flutter. The ladies mellowed toward our paying guest, waxing lyrical over his transformation. He had come out of his shell, reborn, shedding radiance in all directions, loving everybody.... Now he bathed daily, shined his shoes, borrowed my nail-file, and absent-mindedly wore his shirts wrong side out. Conrad's violent reaction mystified me. 'All this prim-ping and preening is positively revolting!' There were acrimo-nious exchanges after Jan left with her Frenchman.

Late one night they staged a terrific row in the patio. I returned from a stroll to hear Malcolm bellowing, 'And what about inces-tuous Susie?' a reference to *Great Circle*. In an alcoholic stupor he then threatened to kill Conrad, not for the first time either. Ed turned a ghastly green. I asked, 'What's all the rumpus about?' An ominous silence broken only by the whoo-i of owls, Conrad mute as a graven image.

Twenty years later he supplied the answer in his autobiography, *Ushant*, Hambo speaking. ('Well, it was . . . understood between us . . . You had eaten your father's skeleton – why then shouldn't I eat yours? Not symbolically only, either, my dear old fellow . . . You as much as admitted that now it was my turn – my turn to kill you. First by taking Nita. Yes. For of course we both knew that both of us were powerfully drawn to that open wound . . . Not so? Yes – in the shadow of the Hundred Fountains, at the Alhambra, you proposed to share her, as foul a sort of voyeur's incest as any second rate god could imagine. . . .')

The rift shortened our holiday by a week, Conrad now determined to drop his protégé. Adios, adios – Spanish farewells are like Beethoven finales. The Carmonas loaded us with lunch baskets, wine, and two enormous bouquets. A melancholy quartet entrained for Algeciras. . . .

Next morning we boarded the *Straithaird*, encumbered with baskets, shawls, donkey trappings, Spanish posters, and Egyptian runners. Frayed nerves and edgy tempers prevailed. Conrad, almost knocked down by playful moppets, was tempted to pitch the noisy brats overboard. Malcolm shared a cabin on that hectic voyage with 'three Somerset Maugham colonels who were dying of the hiccups'. This evil genie pursued him. A disenchanting letter from Jan in Lisbon kept him fastened to the desk, penning an interminable ship's log, when he wasn't in the bar. What Conrad called the first fine careless rupture marked the beginning of an ill-starred marriage. . . .

An Encounter on the Left Bank
James Stern

The short-story writer James Stern (b. 1904) was a lifelong friend and correspondent of Lowry's from the moment they met in a Paris bistro in the winter of 1933. That first encounter on the Left Bank was characteristically Lowryesque, as was their second meeting some fourteen years later in New York (see p. 146). Stern discovered that his new acquaintance was not only a formidable drinker, but also a prodigious walker, yarn-spinner and clown. He also attests to his extraordinary capacity to remember things which happened even when he was apparently unconscious through drink.

This extract is from an interview he gave me for the 1984 BBC radio programme, *The Lighthouse Invites the Storm*.

How do you remember Malcolm Lowry? What did he look like?
He looked very powerful. He had a huge chest. He was short in the leg and immensely strong. And he was always scruffily dressed. . . . I was in Paris when I first saw him. I was on my way to a party at the studio of Julian Trevelyan. It was pelting with rain, and in those days, if you went to a party, you were expected to take at least a bottle of wine with you. I was in the Rue Daguerre, where Julian lived . . . and I stepped into a bistro to get some wine. There was one other man in there besides the man behind the bar, and this man was lying flat on his back on the floor with a guitar on his huge chest. He had a blue tweed coat on and I think he was snoring. What attracted my attention was that his feet were dry although it had been raining for hours. And I thought to myself, he must have been lying there for most of the afternoon. Anyway, I ordered a glass of wine for myself. Then I heard a sort of a groan behind me and this figure rose to his feet, came over towards me and said in very English English, 'Excuse me. Could you perhaps be British?'

And I said, 'Oh, is my French as bad as all that?'

'Oh, not at all, not at all. It's just those bags, those grey flannel bags.' And he reached out his hand and grabbed mine. It was a very small but immensely strong hand. Then he told me his name and this was a bit of a shock because I'd just read his first book.[9] And I had just published *my* first book.[10]

So I asked: 'Malcolm? *Ultramarine* Lowry?' And he stared at me and asked, 'What's *your* name?' and I told him. Then he said, 'What! *The Heartless* Stern *Land?*' And that was how we met.
Was he drunk?
Not then. He must have been there for hours, sleeping it off. But he was very gay when he realised that we knew each other through our first books. I can't remember whether he was invited to the party, but anyhow we arrived at the party together. I had a bottle in each hand and I saw many people I knew there, all of them dancing. Forgetting about the bottles, I clapped my hands over my head. Needless to say, the bottles smashed. Instantly there was an uproarious howl of laughter and a clatter of breaking glass. Then I bumped into a dancing couple and put out my hand to save myself from falling. Unfortunately my hand grasped what the French call

9 *Ultramarine.*
10 *The Heartless Land.*

a *tuyau*, one of those pipes attached to a stove. Of course it was 'red-hot'. I let out a scream and the next thing I knew I was being carried up a ladder into a room above by my new-found friend, who laid me on a bed and put something soothing on my hand. Gradually the pain lifted and we joined the party. But not for long. After a couple of drinks, we set off for what Malcolm called 'a little walk'. That walk lasted twenty-eight hours.

By this time what impression had you got of him as a character?

Well, the most obvious thing, of course, was that he liked the bottle and never had any idea where he was. I knew Paris pretty well, otherwise I don't know where he would have gone to. And we walked a very long way and we were walking a very long time. We stopped about every twenty minutes or half an hour to have another one, and it went on like that all night.

Finally, I remember we came to Les Halles, the market, towards dawn. And by this time he was swaying a bit. He marched into a bar – one more – and asked the woman behind the counter, who looked almost as strong as he did – huge biceps she had – for a glass of Calvados. So she poured him out a tiny little glass of Calvados. His French was almost non-existent, so he said, 'That is a thimble.' And he asked me what on earth the French for 'thimble' was. I couldn't remember, so he stuck the glass upside-down on his little finger and said, 'Thimble, Madame! Thimble!' whereupon he got a slightly larger glass. So then he asked for a 'proper glass', in other words a tumbler. And so he had his tumbler of Calvados. Then he began to sing – groan and sing till the sun came out; that was about nine or ten o'clock in the morning. We got to the Luxembourg Gardens and in the Luxembourg there's a statue of George Sand, more or less recumbent. I sat down on a bench and he walked over to the statue. He had finally bought a *bottle* of Calvados from the woman in the bistro, and now he began having a swig. Then he offered it to George Sand, whereupon I burst out laughing. It was really a very funny sight. And then he sat down beside her and began to recite some kind of poetry – in English, of course. After that we staggered off to my apartment.

Then an awful thing happened. I lived on the sixth floor in a street that was then called René Pauline . . . Malcolm was going up the stairs very, very slowly, and just as we got to my floor and I opened the door he collapsed and seemed to be utterly unconscious.

Of course, after twenty-eight hours of walking with Malc I had quite forgotten that my sister, who was about eighteen and had never been abroad in her life, was coming to Paris that very morning. I was absolutely horrified, but I thought it's no good telling Malc because he's unconscious. Well, finally, my little sister arrived. She rang the bell and I opened the door.

She saw this figure lying on the floor and she had a frightful shock. Needless to say she had never seen a man drunk, and she said, 'Oh, poor man! Is he hurt? Can't you put him to bed?'

And I said, 'No, he's too heavy.'

'But what's happened to him?'

I said, 'Well, we've been out celebrating his birthday.'

'Oh, you mean he's drunk?'

And I said, 'Oh, no, no, no. He may be a little bit drunk but he's not disorderly.' And out we went, me and my sister, leaving Malc there. I don't know what happened then, and whether he was still there when I got back I can't remember. The only thing I do remember is that he never said anything about it until fourteen years later, when we met in New York. Then he asked me quite suddenly and almost aggressively why I had told my sister that he had been drunk that morning, which certainly surprised me. You see, I don't think he ever lost consciousness, however drunk he was.

The First Wife's Story
Jan Gabrial

Jan Gabrial (b. 1911) was the only child of a Jewish concert-master and conductor from Amsterdam and an American teacher of German extraction from New York. Her father died when she was thirteen. She went to the American Academy of Dramatic Art and was on the stage for two years before a car accident led her to turn to writing. It was in Granada in Spain, in May 1933, that she first met Lowry. She was touring through Europe and North Africa; he was spending a holiday with Conrad Aiken and his wife Clarissa. Their courtship and marriage were periods of blissful companionship punctuated by quarrels, mutual recrimination and near catastrophes. This pattern, which was to become a feature of their fractured romance over the next six years together, was to be captured in short stories such as 'Hotel Room in Chartres'[11] and in *Under the Volcano*. After their break, Jan wrote a story called 'Not with a Bang',[12] which told of their dramatic parting and dealt

11 Published in *Malcolm Lowry: Psalms and Songs*.
12 Published in *Story*, September – October 1946.

openly with the theme which came to dominate their marriage – the compulsive love which was, at the same time, mutually destructive. Jan comes over as an outspoken and revealing witness to her life with Lowry. From her account we can now fill in details for the year 1935 which previous biographies leave all but blank, and we can now place Lowry's stay at Bellevue Hospital Psychiatric Ward as taking place in 1936 and not 1935, as previously thought.

This is an edited extract from an interview she gave in 1975 to the Canadian film producer, Robert Duncan.

When you married Malcolm in Paris in 1934 it was all quite sudden, wasn't it?
No, not at all, no. We had fallen in love in Spain the previous year. We wrote many letters back and forth. Let's see, I think it was probably May when I met Malc. I'm pretty sure it was . . . somewhere towards the middle or end of May 1933. At the time I met Malc I was twenty-one, shortly to be twenty-two (my birthday is 11 June), and Malc was three years older.[13] I had been looking at the Edward O'Brien book.[14] There had been a short story of Malc's in it. It may have been 'On Board the West Hardaway'.[15] I'm not sure. Anyway I had thought it magnificent, so when I met Malc travelling with Aiken I was quite into the work of both of them, and already these were the two men that I admired tremendously for their talent. . . . I met them at the Villa Carmona near the Alhambra in Granada. Aiken was there with his wife and with Malc.
How did that meeting happen?
I met Jerry, who was Aiken's wife at the time, at the pension and she asked me if I would like to go into town. She asked me to go with her to see the flamenco dancers. Then through her I met Malc. Aiken I knew very little of. I think I talked to him.
When you met Jerry, did you realise that she was Aiken's wife?
Ah, yes. Oh, sure, sure. She was Mrs Conrad Aiken.
And you had gone to the pension with every intention of meeting Aiken?
Oh, no, no, no, no. I was travelling through Spain. There's a town in the south of Spain that is famous for its gorge, and I had spent a couple of days there. And previously I'd come up from North Africa. Actually my trips had wandered around through Europe

13 There's a miscalculation here. Malcolm was born on 28 July 1909, so if Jan was twenty-two in June 1933 she would have been born in 1911, making Malcolm two years older than her.
14 *The Best British Short Stories of 1931.*
15 In fact it was a story called 'Seductio ad Absurdum'.

down into Tunis, Algeria and Morocco. . . . After I had wandered around in Morocco for a time I came up through Gibraltar into Spain.

Anyway, while I was at this gorge in southern Spain I met a very kind and very nice man who was from Syria. His name was Calef. We had a completely platonic friendship; he did get a little bit enchanted with me, but I told him I was going on to Granada and he decided that we would write, to keep in touch. . . . Anyway, after I was about a day or so at the Villa Carmona, Calef called me and told me he was going to come up and join me – this was just before or while I was first meeting Malc. . . . Well, Calef arrived and I was really very mean to him. By this time I was so enchanted with Malc, and you know this was someone to whom I could really relate because of the fact that I knew his worth. He had interests that I could involve myself with. We could talk, we could discuss. It wasn't something that was kind of abstract and rather flattering to my ego. So I was really very unkind, because when Calef arrived I barely saw him. I spent my time with Malc. Calef and I did not have an affair and, when I left, he took me to the train and said goodbye. He then went on to wherever he was going and I never saw him again, never heard from him again.

I went on from there, probably to Seville, and Malc wrote me a letter from wherever he and the Aikens had gone, saying, 'The thought that you might have given somebody else what you would not give to me is more than I can bear,' or something like that. We were writing back and forth, very passionate love letters, and this went on for the whole time that I was wandering through Europe. Finally we agreed to meet. Malc was back in England by the time I had reached France. I spent some time hiking through the château country; then, when I got back to Paris, I decided to go to London and I would join him there. I had found a pension or boarding house there that I had heard was very good and made arrangements to go there and stay. I made a date with Malc – that he would meet me at the American Express, if I recall. That was where we were going to reunite. And we did. I think we went to two or three pubs that he was very fond of. I remember one called the Marquis of Granby, and The Plough, and there was another, probably The Fitzroy. We went to a few of these and agreed to meet that night for dinner. It was a cold, rainy London night, and Malc was two hours late, and by the time he arrived I was already wet, hungry and very disenchanted. And I didn't realise, because I didn't know him well enough then, that he was fairly well bombed by the time he turned up. So this was the way our relationship went in London – good periods, difficult periods, good periods, difficult periods. . . .

I remember one . . . little episode. Malc asked me if I wanted to fly with him to North Wales. Tom Forman, who was a friend of Malc's, was going and they were going to stop at this marvellous place, which was like an Italian village, but it was in Wales on the water. Tom was a pilot, and I remember we took off on this rainy night in this little bit of a tiny, tiny plane that just barely held the three of us. I'd never been in a plane and I must have been out of my tree, but anything that was a new experience I thought was a fun thing. We landed somewhere in a cow pasture and I couldn't understand a single word that anybody was saying; it was some- where where people had heavy English accents. We eventually managed to get to another airport and then there were more stops, and finally we landed in Birmingham. Birmingham and Bismarck, North Dakota, I think, will go down in my memory as the two most God-awful places that I've ever been in my life. We had steak and kidney pie, which was cold and which I threw up as soon as I got to my room, and it was an utterly disastrous town and gloomy. But the next day we went on . . . to this little hotel in the mountains in North Wales. And it was cold as the hinges of hell. It was bitter and I had utterly inappropriate clothes; I had things like frilly blouses, which were in no way suitable. And suddenly one day Malc's father was about to turn up, and I was furious because the hotel had no heat, and Malc insisted that I stay in the hotel room the whole time so that his father would not know that he had a girl with him. So I said, 'Well, I can be Tom's girl.'

He said, 'No, no. He's downstairs!'

So he was very much afraid of his father. And so I did stay in the room, fuming. That episode was really less charming than the times that we had spent wandering around in London.

Did you meet any of his family at all?

Never. Never met anybody. I came back to England alone. I was going off alone. I left them in Wales and came back to London and took quarters, and they came back about ten days later. By then we had warmed to each other again, and weighing all the pros and cons and everything, we decided we would get married.

Had the affair been consummated?

Not really. Malc had held me, but we were both fully dressed. We were in the lobby of the sitting-room of the hotel in Wales and he had been terribly embarrassed because he had ejaculated and felt very self-conscious about it. I do remember that last night I was in London before I took off to France. (I wanted to be married in

France because I loved Paris. I thought it would be a marvellous experience to be married there. I was wrong.) But that last night . . . there must have been some consummation because I remember we stayed at Hugh Sykes Davies's place for a couple of nights while Hugh was away, and I do remember Malc cooking sausages. And I remember our – you know – sleeping together, but sexually it was not much of a much. I think we were both nervous and both kind of groping. There must have been a tentative kind of consummation, but I doubt very much that there was. . . . You know, none of the birds flying into the sunset or the skyrockets going off that you see in 1930s' movies when they're trying to indicate what's happening.

Was he a virgin at the time, do you think?

I think so. I have a feeling that he was. He told me, I think, that there may have been one – someone, I don't know, a maid, a barmaid, somebody in his father's house or something.[16] But you know, with Malc you never could tell, you never could be certain. He did not know what to do. He was very inexperienced. I had had very little experience, but not a whole heck of a lot, and I didn't know a whole great deal more than he did. Actually, the first time that I ever really had a full consummation with anyone came with Malc when we were in Paris, after we were married. And it was a very revealing thing for both of us. You know, we both felt, 'My God! We can!' You know I had thought that I must be frigid and he had thought that he was impotent, with problems. So then it got very funny. I mean, then he would – you know – sing the 'Star-Spangled Banner' to try to prolong things or whatever, keep from coming too quickly. And sex became a kind of fun thing for us. But it took a long time, which I think it does very often. I've never been the sort of woman who found that you sleep with somebody right away – you know, everything goes, like that. Maybe with somebody who's very skilful . . . I don't know.

Did you both go to Paris together?

No, I went to Paris ahead, to get everything taken care of, and Malc was sort of lining up things in England. He was not going to notify his father and I was not notifying my mother. I guess it was really necessary. He thought if his father knew about it, then he might cut off his allowance. I felt that if I told my mother at that stage, that all she would do would be to worry. She wouldn't know what I was marrying and who he was, and I thought I had better wait until I went home, tell her about it then, and kind of bring her

16 In view of Lowry's known fear of women, this could be another Lowry myth – a story told to impress Jan.

up-to-date as to what the whole thing was. Don't forget this was back in the early 1930s. It wasn't like today where you say, you know, 'Come and meet my roomie.'

So I went to Paris ahead of time to try to get the papers together and Malc came, I think, around New Year's Eve[17] – he was always arriving on some kind of a day that had some kind of a meaning. The symbolism of things was very important to him. . . . We were married on 6 January. I had finally got things together, but in the middle of all this my purse had been stolen together with my pass-port and all the papers I had accumulated. And at that time getting married in Paris was not easy. In fact one of the things they wanted was a certificate from every place we had lived for the past six months. That wasn't very simple to take care of. I think Julian Trevelyan solved a lot of it by slipping somebody ten francs, if I remember. But anyway, I had found a lovely apartment . . . and rented it, and it was delightful . . . utterly lovely.
Where was it?
It was at 7, rue Antoine Chantant. So, that was taken care of. It had a bedroom – a small bedroom – and a bathroom . . . it had a lovely living-room with an extra bed there, with a skylight and a fireplace and beautiful old French furnishing – things that were inlaid and so forth. . . .

Well, everything was marvellous until the morning of the wedding. The morning of the wedding we were not speaking to each other. I don't remember exactly what the quarrel was about, but I do remember it was very difficult. Then we went and got married. Julian stood up with us, Julian and Brock and Louise. Louise had been Julian's girlfriend; she had been living with Julian. She was a girl from Brooklyn who looked like Juliette Greco, the actress, a very beautiful and exotic-looking gal. And Brock was an English artist whom she fell in love with while she was living with Julian, and so she moved in with Brock. . . . So those were our witnesses. And then I had invited friends of mine plus whatever friends Malcolm had that I hadn't met. I think we had maybe ten or twelve over that afternoon or evening. Dinner was a little pot-luck thing at the house. I didn't know how to cook; Malc didn't know how to cook. I think we bought things and brought them in. Then we set about to try to get *Ultramarine* translated into French for the *Nouvelle de Français*.
Is it true that at the ceremony, when asked if he would in fact take you for a bride, he said, 'Ça va'?

17 James Stern remembers meeting Lowry in Paris in the winter of 1933, so it is possible that he arrived there earlier than Jan recalled.

Malc didn't know two words of French and '*ça va*' were not two that he knew. No, it wasn't. Actually it was one of those mass weddings that the French perform in which the whole room is full of couples that are getting married. It's like a courtroom and we were married by the mayor. You know, each couple went up and did their thing and this whole torrent of French was poured out. We laughed later, and we said that actually I had married Julian because Julian was the one who said '*oui*' when we were asked. No, Malc didn't say '*ça va*'. It's one of those apocryphal stories that somebody thought would make a good story. He was numb. I don't think he said anything. Anyway, we got the marriage licence book, which I still have, which had a place in it for fourteen children, and, as I say, we had a party and then things got very lovely. We were both enchanted with the idea that we were husband and wife. The words seemed marvellous. We were utterly delighted with our roles. Then we got started to meet some of the French writers and some of the people in publishing in France.

After the wedding, how long did you stay on in Paris?

We stayed in Paris . . . until . . . I think it was early April. We took a lot of trips. We went to Chartres, and 'Hotel Room in Chartres' was written about one of our little scenes – the quarrels and . . . the make-up. But the reason we separated at that point was to try to work things out – he with his father and me with my mother, so that when I could come back to Europe we could be open about everything. (You know, it was ridiculous; even then I was writing letters to his father for him because he couldn't write to his father.) Well, I came to the States in July – again, I guess, around the birthday. After I'd been in the States about two months I got a letter from him saying that he was coming over. The plan had been that I was going back and we were going to find a little town in the South of France, and we were going to settle down and write. That would be our sort of starting-point. Instead of which, for some reason or other, I think his father insisted that he move here, over to the States.

His father knew you were married at this time?

Oh, yes. . . . He had agreed to make an allowance of $150 a month. But the attitude was negative; he was kind of nebulous . . . while I was in the States Malc sent me a couple of stories that he had written, and I had taken them around the publishers. I took them to several magazines and finally placed one – I think it was 'Hotel Room in Chartres' – with Whit Burnett[18] and I interviewed an

18 Editor of *Story* magazine, in which Lowry's 'On Board the West Hardaway' was published in October 1933.

agent because . . . we wanted to get *Ultramarine* published in the States. So I acted as a sort of advance guard . . . I had some busy things to do there as far as he was concerned. Then I made a few trips. I went down to Washington DC, which I had not been to, and then he came over and wanted to go to the New England area because of the *Moby Dick* aura, and we went up there. We spent the summer in Provincetown . . . Provincetown was great. We had a place right on the sea, with two rooms, a kitchen, bath and a little beach which was completely private and where we could go out at night. We would walk into the sea with no suits and swim, and, although we were never intimate, we knew and used to go to beach parties with Ed Wilson . . . Provincetown was a fairly sober time. We didn't have the violent quarrels and things there. It was pretty good.

And then you went back to New York?

From Provincetown we went to New York and spent some time with my mother. My mother absolutely adored Malcolm. She didn't know at that time that he had a drinking problem. I had not told her. And she just adored him. And he was very fond of her.

Your mother was living in New York at this time?

. . . Our house was in Bayside, Long Island. But Malc and I went to New York also because it was getting to the fall and that was the time when things began to ferment literarily. And obviously we wanted to get back in touch with editors. . . . We probably got back to New York, I would say, some time in September. We stayed with my mother . . . and then I went into New York because I knew the city better than Malc did. And I found an apartment on Perry Street – 99 Perry Street – which I thought was charming. Malc liked it, everybody else hated it. My mother hated it. I thought it was delightful. For one thing, it was the first actual place we had other than Paris. The rooms in Provincetown, while they were on the sea and everything, were very simple. This had built-in bookshelves and a sort of federal look about it, and I believe it had a fireplace, and I enjoyed it.

Then we got very active. I think through Whit Burnett and Martha Foley, we got very active in the current literary movement in New York. And there was a man whose name I can't remember now – he was a jewel of a thing – he was probably about seventy and he adored giving cocktail parties for writers. Anybody in the literary movement – editors, whatever. He was on Lenin Street in the Village, if I'm correct . . . and we were on his list and used to go there very often. We met Bennett Cerf and a number of then prominent people and many who were not prominent, and never became so. And, by and large, it was not a heavy drinking period, as I remember. Then I developed a breast abscess and went into St Vincent and was there for about ten days, and I think Malc went on to it at that time. I remember being very hurt because he didn't come to see me. . . . He came to see me once, and he didn't come to pick me up when I was ready to leave. I got home and the place had been broken into, which was a sort of accompaniment of many of our experiences. But we stayed on in Perry Street, and I'm trying to remember what he was working on. He was working on a book that had to do with Paris.

Do you think he was working on In Ballast to the White Sea?

No, he didn't begin that until we were living on 47th Street. We went back and spent Christmas with my mother on Long Island. And we gave up the Perry Street apartment, but I don't remember why. I think there was some violent drinking scene and I went back to Long Island and then Malc followed me. . . . It was a bad scene there around that Christmas. It was the first that my mother knew that he was drinking, and I remember he started saying something against me in front of her and at that point she turned against him. She said, 'I can say anything I want, but *you* can't say anything against my daughter.'

We stayed with my mother for a few months and then – I think it was maybe the early part of 1935 – we went into the Hotel Somerset. I don't know exactly [why] . . . I think we were planning to go to Mexico, and we decided that instead of taking an apartment we would go into a hotel and live there on a week-to-week, month-to-month basis. Then we would get [tickets] and take off to Mexico. . . . Also I think it might have had something to do with Malc's visa having to be renewed periodically – I can't be sure. . . .

Anyway, we did stay there and actually, during that year, we both did quite a lot of work. Malc worked on *In Ballast* – I think we had about maybe fifteen to twenty chapters of it. I did the typing. He used my father's old typewriter and I had a portable Corona. He banged it down on the other and then, when it had to be submitted, I would type it up on the better machine. And that was the time he acquired Harold Matson as an agent. I think there were a few times when they were a little disenchanted with each other. I remember one time Harold sent the book, or part of the book that he had, to a number of publishers and it had come back, and we suddenly discovered that the chapters were all mixed up in it; they weren't in sequence. Then the other thing was we found that one of the chapters, or something in there, had been lifted almost verbatim from Burton Rascoe. We found that out because it was sent to Burton Rascoe to read and he was very upset by the whole situation.

Then it began to get a bit frayed again. Always, as it seemed, when we got in closely with people, we would have the scenes and the arguments. I'm not trying to say that we lived in blissful harmony; there were scenes and there were drunken periods and tears and whatever. But this was something that I felt able to cope with and able to live with at that stage, because these periods were not that prolonged. They lasted maybe a few days and then we would be back and working normally. Frankly, it's been so long since I learned how to quarrel with anybody that my memory of the mechanics of it is somewhat hazy. . . . Malc was like a child when he was angry; he would fling out and want to hurt. But mainly our relationship was very good.

Then I think the thing started when he started going to Harlem with this group that included Tony. . . . After we'd had about a year at the Somerset, I guess Malcolm was beginning to feel smothered – that the four walls, the whole scene was closing in on him. So he decided he wanted a separate room. And that was when we went up to 86th Street and found this place where we could get two rooms. But they were not adjoining. His room was down the hall on the same floor as mine. I thought that was perfectly rational. I mean, I could see his point, and, being an only child, I was used to privacy, too. And we really hadn't had privacy. Then the other thing was that each of us slept kind of differently. Malc was given to insomnia; I wasn't. I hit the sheets and I'm out. So it was kind of hard on us sharing the bed; neither one of us was used to it. So I think the whole idea was to get a little bit of physical and emotional separation without losing touch. But that only lasted a week and then Malc moved out. And that was when I got the letter that, you know, he was – we thought maybe something had happened with Tony.

What was that, now? I don't understand that.

I didn't either, at the time. I was absolutely frantic because there had been no real notice of it. Apparently he had gone out drinking with Tony and other people. And Tony was a homo. I think he was French . . . I can't remember too much about him. . . . I used to keep very, very close diaries, but it turned out not to be a good idea because Malc got into them and read them, and so I stopped writing the diaries.

Did he go out with Tony?

He said he wasn't sure what happened and Tony had syphilis and he didn't know what the situation was. He wanted time to test and find out if he had it. And so he did go through the whole thing. As I look at it now, I see that that may just have been an excuse. Maybe once he got started with the drinking he just wanted to get back into a heavy drinking session. Who knows? Anyway, I went down to visit him and I was horrified because he was living in some dreadful little room. I don't even remember where it was, but it was in the Village. And he seemed terribly slummy; it was that business almost of being on another ship that's going somewhere else. I think he said it would take two months, or maybe three, before he could be sure that he didn't have syphilis. Anyway, we said we could not get back together until he was sure.

And did you ask him how he thought he had contracted it?

He said he thought he might have had an affair with Tony; he didn't know. We were always very frank about anything bodily with each other, so it never occurred to me that he could have any homosexual tendencies, which is perhaps rather strange. But he was utterly not. He was not a turntable at all. It wasn't as though you had the feeling that he'd just as soon it was a man as a woman. No way. Sex was something that he agonised over, in a way. I don't think he ever felt really sure of himself sexually, even when he had good periods, because – you know – of the physical thing. Then perhaps there's the fact that, by the time that I met him, he hadn't really had the kind of youth that men should have had by that time. You know, the time in which they get to know their manhood. I really don't think he ever did find it. He could have, I think, through analysis. But at that stage, no matter how good the relationship was for periods at a time, it wasn't enough to make up for all that had gone before. . . . Who knows? Maybe that complete devotion that he had to writing, that immersion in writing, was a sublimation for the fun and games that men of twenty-four generally indulge in.

So how did he finally end up in Bellevue? What happened there?

Well, apparently he just kept drinking so long that Eric Estorick had him committed to Bellevue. And Estorick called me and . . . I went over to Bellevue to see Malc. . . . He looked so shrivelled somehow. And he was wearing some sort of a mouse-nothing-coloured – a dust-coloured robe of some type. And he looked, well, as though he were really in hell. And I felt that I had got to get him out of there, that they would just destroy him there. . . . It was the worst possible place for him and I think I felt quite bitter that that was where he had been taken and where he had been put. It seemed to me there had to have been some obviously better solution. Then, by the end, I guess we started planning again about

Mexico. We planned to go as soon as he was sure that the syphilis thing was behind him. But we started out, I think in September, to come to the coast[19] to go to Mexico and to get his passport and visa renewed. And by that time we knew that John and Clement Davenport were going to be on the coast, and we were going to stay with them. . . .

So how long was he in Bellevue?

. . . I would say maybe ten days. It wasn't a prolonged situation. He wasn't there for months or anything like that.

And then you signed him out?

If I had to – I guess that was probably what had to be done, yes.

And then did he come back to live with you?

No. He went back, I think, to his room until he had clarified this syphilis thing. I had taken an apartment in the meantime, a little one-room-type place up in Central Park West, and I was living there, and we met periodically. I was doing some writing and we met a lot at night, too long walks at night. . . . It was difficult, the whole marriage, because we never settled down and said, 'Ah, there was never that.' It was always, 'Well, we've survived that.' But then we were uplifted again because we decided we would take a trip across the country on Greyhound, which at that time cost about $35 or something. . . . With a few exceptions, like the time I kicked him in the ankle in Chicago, it was a really interesting trip, a fun trip. We wandered around the places we wanted to go, and whenever we wanted to get off the bus and stay somewhere, we did. We loved New Mexico and we loved Arizona. And we came into California in the most dramatic way possible. We crossed into it at about five o'clock in the morning, when the sun was just coming up, and I still wish I could find out which way we came, or which route, because it was like going into the mountains of the moon. There were great shaggy cliffs touched by the sun, and there didn't seem to be any signs of life, and it looked absolutely barren and, oh, terribly kind of primitive. It could have been any place that was not of this world. And we came into Los Angeles, and we . . . stayed with Clement and John for a month, and then we came to Mexico.

19 Southern California.

Adventure and Suffering in New York
Eric Estorick

Eric Estorick (b. 1912), Director of the Grosvenor Gallery, first met Lowry in New York. In 1936, when Lowry's health seemed to be deteriorating, he introduced him to a psychiatrist who arranged for him to be admitted as a voluntary patient to the city's Bellevue Hospital. This was something which displeased Jan, who immediately had her husband removed. However, it was an experience on which he based the novella *Lunar Caustic*, published after his death. He began it following his release, calling it originally *The Last Address*. It was rewritten twice, once under the title *Swinging the Maelstrom*, and finally pieced together under Lowry's preferred title, *Lunar Caustic*, by his widow, Margerie Bonner, and the poet Earle Birney. Estorick's reminiscence includes the story of a dangerous expedition the two men made into New York's Harlem. Lowry later described New York as 'a city where it can be remarkably hard . . . to get on the right side of one's despair'.

This is an edited extract from an interview given to me on 14 May 1984.

I was a secretary-assistant to Waldo Frank, a kind of doyen of the liberal left who was then in his sixties, and it was really through Waldo Frank that I first met Malcolm. . . . We met in Frank's studios on West 83rd Street in 1934 or '35 . . . and I do remember observing at that time that Lowry was far less interested in the momentary politics and the realistic aura of the time than I was, and that he lived very much in an amused world of his own. . . . I happen to be an only child, and, when I brought Malcolm home to meet my parents, somehow between my mother and Malcolm there seemed to be an instant flow that I think had more to do with the drama of the kitchen, because Malcolm was not Jewish and we are and were. He had a mad love for chopped chicken liver, and my mother made mountains of it, and the more she made the more externally exuberant he became, and the joy of the moment expressed itself, so that both my mother and father enjoyed it so much when he came into the house. Malcolm also brought a kind of romantic image. When he spoke he spoke dramatically with great articulation – not intellectually, except when he wanted to be intellectual to discuss concepts. I think the reason he had such a good time was that he relaxed with my parents. We all relaxed. We were only youngsters at the time; I was twenty-two.

In addition to chopped liver, he had a great love for pork chops, and someone had said that the only place he could get really good pork chops in New York City was in Harlem, and he insisted that we go to Harlem. And that's where we got into a terrible mess, because the night we went to Harlem he was fairly loaded. . . . I don't think we had any dinner up in Harlem, but Malcolm and I must have been given the eye by a couple of pimps who asked if we were interested in girls. I know that the approach was made to Malcolm who was – what shall I say – more at alcoholic ease than I, who was sober and tense. We followed these two chaps into a Harlem tenement and went up about three floors. And as we began to climb I sensed that what was going to happen was that we were to go up to the roof and they were really going to go for our wallets. There were windows in the hallway and, as we passed from one floor to another, I grabbed at my wallet which was in my back pocket and threw it out of the window. I know that the guy who was by my side quickly drew a knife and slashed at my trouser where I had taken the wallet, hoping to grab the wallet, but the wallet had gone out of the window. Malcolm was perhaps half a storey ahead of me and the moment I threw the wallet out of the window the two fellows reversed themselves and ran like mad down to find it.

And I called to Malcolm and said, 'Let's get the hell out of here.' By this time he was sufficiently drunk to be indifferent to danger and he wanted to keep on walking, and I said, 'Malcolm, we just better get out of here.' And we went out of the front of this Harlem tenement with the alley by the side. I went to see if I could trace where my wallet had come through the window, but I didn't find it. All I could see were cigarette stubs being thrown out of the windows by leering blacks who were wondering what the hell white boys were doing in the building. They knew darned well what we were doing in the building, but it was simply a very hostile and frightening place. . . .

But Malcolm, I know, was going through a rough period with Jan at this time. She wanted to write, or was writing. She was a strong-willed, beautiful girl, seemingly quite disciplined, and Malcolm was certainly not disciplined. I think the great rival for Jan's affections was the bottle, really. Then they separated, and I think she left New York and he stayed on for a while.

. . . I introduced him to a number of friends of mine, including the husband of a fellow student of the graduate school at NYU, and he was on the medical staff at Bellevue Hospital. . . . I believe it was he who advised Malcolm to go in for some treatment, and he did. Now the time span eludes me, but I know at one point I had a violent phone call from Malcolm, being very angry that I introduced him to this doctor who advised him to go to Bellevue, because what wasn't known to Malcolm, certainly, and not to me – and I don't know if it was known to the doctor – was that there was a periodic check-up in the background of the patients. And, if one wasn't a citizen, there was the danger of being forced to leave the country. Nothing terrified Malcolm so much as the thought that he might have to go back to England. And he was very, very angry about this, and I think he left the hospital immediately and shortly after that went out west.

New York was a very open place in those days, an unbelievable place. . . . It's a period that I'm still romantic about, and Malcolm was a part of it. He was there as a visitor, but his tentacles were so sensitive, and his response was so warm. He was a dear person, yet strangely aloof and removed. I think this may have had something to do with sex, though I can only speculate on this. His marriage had gone sour – I know that in some of his drunken sprees he had been subjected to attempted sexual assaults by some English friends who had come over from England at the same time . . . they were not part of his literary world, and so their perspectives and their needs and their interests weren't anywhere near the same as his. But I think that that left a kind of a cloud. . . . I was told, long after he died, that there had been an event at Cambridge of which I know nothing, which had a marked effect upon him. I don't know. I still prefer the memories of Malcolm that I've been telling you about in this abstracted way.

What struck you about his character?

He was to me unique and humorous and with a fantastic wit. . . . As I say, I met him at Waldo Frank's, and Waldo must have said some nice things about me and given him the impression that I could show him about New York, so he was at his ease with me and I was happy to meet him and I found him always stimulating. I was troubled at the times when alcohol took him from active communication into mumbling and separateness, and that did happen from time to time. It certainly happened in the Harlem situation. But he recovered; he would recover quickly. . . .

. . . Even to this day there are many aspects of his life which remain a mystery to me: his coming over from England, some sort of a dread or something. I know that his references to his family were always cuttingly oblique: on the one hand they're lovely, but they don't want me and I don't want to be there. . . . I know that he often alluded to home without that being a horizon that drew him.

He was a complex boy, but of course you felt that he was a young writer who was fantastically articulate. He was mad about the American poet Conrad Aiken. Yes, he would quote Aiken and would talk about Aiken, and I believe he had visited Aiken. Aiken meant a great deal to him. . . .

What do you remember of Jan?

She was a slight girl, had a very attractive face. I think there was a Polish connection somewhere. I've forgotten exactly, but she wanted to write and was writing. It was a time when there was a rage for what is euphemistically known as 'proletarian literature', and I think she was writing a book about miners and mining, which was a subject which must certainly have bored the pants off Malcolm, who was not interested in social reality, as I've tried to point out before. . . . I realise that Malcolm was perhaps the first young *artist* that I had met. I may be using the word 'artist' in a special retrospective way, but he was already beginning to be my idea of what I subsequently got to know and feel artists were and are. . . .

There was social rage which I think Jan was much closer to than Malcolm. Malcolm simply removed from it. I'm sure there were other rages of the independent creative world. He was the artist and was trying to be the artist rather than the propagandiser, the carrier of a banner. Now I may be talking absolute nonsense, but this is what I feel, and this is the way I remember the flags, as it were.

If you read Lunar Caustic, *he seems to see New York as a bit of a mad-house. Did you sense he feared the city? How do you feel he reacted to New York?*

First of all, I think he was a man of great physical strength. By that I mean he had recuperative powers, because if you saw him a day or two after an alcoholic bout he was in great shape, and his articulation and his general enthusiasm were there. It was only in that period before Bellevue, where the drunkenness seemed to go on uninterrupted for many days, that articulation ceased. And that kind of human situation has always frightened me in life. He was strong, he had great recuperative powers, was enormously enthusiastic, and I think he was sensing and recording everything in that way that the artist records and assimilates, digests and ultimately egests for his work. Though he died early he at least left a little body of work, and especially the last novel. It's terribly tragic, and his ending, of which there are so many differing tales, is equally tragic and mysterious.

4 Mexico and Hollywood, 1936–9

A clear creative pattern had now emerged in Lowry's work. He sought experience and then embodied that experience in his heroes, who stand, on his own admission, as autobiographical representations of 'the abominable author himself'. In Mexico he sought and found the material for a masterpiece.

After their arrival, the Lowrys seem to have settled into a relatively comfortable regime. They rented a villa in Cuernavaca, a resort town high in the Sierra Madre just south of Mexico City, with spectacular views of the volcanic mountain Popocatepetl. Malcolm, now a fully-fledged remittance man, received $150 a month from home, and they shared expenses with a lodger. The trio went sightseeing together, savoured the strange mixture of Indian and Spanish cultures, and discovered the fiery local liquors, tequila and mescal. There were occasional drinking sprees when Lowry would perform his now familiar disappearing act, something which Jan seems to have come to live with. It was too much for the lodger, however, who soon departed.

But the beautiful landscape of Mexico and its strangely intimidating culture had come to haunt Lowry. He saw it as an infernal paradise, a Garden of Eden into which a vengeful God had introduced the ever-present threat of death and damnation. If the magic mountain of Popocatepetl represented the possibility of eternal life and beauty, the sewer-like *barranca* which ran through the town could only stand for the gaping jaws of hell. He put all other work aside to start on *Under the Volcano*.[1] He must have worked at it steadily because, according to Conrad Aiken who arrived in May 1937 to obtain a divorce from Clarissa, and bringing with him his wife-to-be, Mary Hoover, he had by then a complete draft to show to his old mentor.

Aiken's arrival obviously disturbed this settled lifestyle. The left-wing Jan and the reactionary Aiken clearly disliked one

1 In his correspondence, Lowry refers to the book simply as *The Volcano*.

another. Lowry again began drinking heavily and on Jan's birthday, 11 June, was too hungover to join her on a celebratory trip to Mexico City. Jan left alone, taking the opportunity to visit a few other places which interested her, and did not return until just before the Aikens left in early July. In his autobiography, *Ushant*, the poet suggests that Jan went off on an adulterous adventure, a story she hotly denies. But the visit had given Lowry some more material for *The Volcano*, in particular a political argument which Aiken claims he reproduced verbatim.

Free of visitors, things returned to normal, and the couple seem to have stopped drinking and to have tried cultivating the healthy life. In September, however, a visit from Arthur Calder-Marshall and his wife, Ara, brought this idyll to an abrupt end. An evening at a local nightclub launched Lowry on a monumental bender, and in exasperation Jan took off again. Calder-Marshall observed the curious effect this desertion had on Lowry: he was devastated, but here was another dramatic event to incorporate into his book.

When Jan returned, the villa had been burgled and Lowry, still drinking heavily, left shortly afterwards for Mexico City. She settled their affairs in Cuernavaca, rejoined her husband, and finally, in December, returned to America alone. This time it was her turn to put the experience into a story, 'Not with a Bang', published nine years later in *Story* magazine.

Lowry now took what Calder-Marshall believes was a quite deliberate plunge into hell. He left for Oaxaca, 'the city of dreadful night', as he called it. There his drinking landed him in jail – the victim, he claimed, of fascist policemen who accused him of spying. In a series of dramatic, almost hallucinatory, letters to John Davenport, his paranoid fear of authority bordered on hysteria. There had even been, he wrote, an attempt to castrate him. In Oaxaca he also met and was befriended by a mysterious Zapotecan bank messenger, Juan Fernando Márquez, an ardent supporter of Lázaro Cárdenas, Mexico's socialist President, whose attempts at reform had provoked a sinister fascist paramilitary organisation, the Sinarquistas, to acts of murder and intimidation. The threatening town and its dingy cantinas, the mescal-inspired hallucinations and Juan Fernando were eventually incorporated into *The Volcano*, and it is the Sinarquistas who finally murder its hero, the Faust-like British Consul, Geoffrey Firmin. Also brought in were the faithless wife, partly modelled on Jan, and those recollections of a tormented childhood and sufferings at sea dredged up from the semi-mythical past. All this was set against the landscape of Lowry's infernal paradise, under the snow-capped volcano with the hellish *barranca* yawning beneath, waiting to swallow the body of the guilt-ridden Consul. The single day in 1938 on which the action of the book takes place and into which so much of Lowry's experience was poured was, significantly enough, 2 November, the Day of the Dead.

As it turned out, Lowry himself was not in Mexico on that particular day. He left in July and returned to Los Angeles, appearing unannounced before a startled Jan and clearly the worse for wear. She seems to have hoped to salvage the marriage and tried to get Lowry senior's help to send Malcolm to an expensive clinic for treatment. But Mr Lowry placed his son in the charge of an attorney called Parks who sent him to a place not much better, it seems, than the snakepit-like Bellevue, from which Jan had rescued him in 1936.

Their attempted reconciliation lasted almost a year. Then Jan discovered that Malcolm had been taken on by Margerie Bonner, an ex-silent-film actress four years his senior, who was to become the second Mrs Lowry. She began proceedings for divorce, and in July 1939 Parks, on instructions from Lowry's father, spirited him away to Vancouver. Canada was to become his home for the next fourteen years.

A Visit from the Calder-Marshalls, Cuernavaca, 1937
Arthur Calder-Marshall

Following the departure in July 1937, after a two-month stay, of Conrad Aiken, his wife-to-be, Mary Hoover, and the artist Ed Burra, the Lowrys went on the wagon. That was how Arthur Calder-Marshall and his wife, Ara, found them when they visited their villa in September. This was the first time he had seen Lowry for three years and the first time he had met Jan, who appeared discontented and bored. A casual invitation for a drink launched Lowry on the alcoholic spree which led to Jan's departure and his own descent through the cantinas to the jailhouse in Oaxaca. It was, in Calder-Marshall's opinion, a conscious decision on Lowry's part to plunge into hell in the hope of coming up with a masterpiece.

The following is an extract from an interview he gave me for the 1984 BBC radio programme, *The Lighthouse Invites the Storm.*

You met them then in Mexico in September 1937, and by that time he had already written something, hadn't he?

He'd written a long short story which is now one of the chapters in *Under the Volcano*, but it was entirely different because at that time the Consul was the father of Yvonne rather than her husband.

What condition was Malcolm in when you found him?

Well, actually, when we landed in Cuernavaca, he and Jan were on the wagon. They hadn't had a drink since Conrad Aiken and his wife had been down four months before. While the Aikens had been staying with Malcolm, there was a terrible booze-up. Jan just popped off to see a chap or a couple of chaps in Taxco – according to Aiken, anyway. She couldn't stand being in this terrible little villa with Malcolm, you know. It was getting on her nerves, because he was impotent and he wasn't really working properly. He was producing just these dreary bits of manuscript. Aiken, as I say, got him on the booze and then there was this period of three months' sobriety. I could feel that they were going absolutely mad with one another. They were bored to tears and it was then we made the mistake of saying, 'Well, come out and have a drink' – that started another alcoholic fugue.

What were your impressions of Jan?

Jan was a small woman. I thought she was a Jewess from the Bronx, but I don't know. She was very American – the sort of ambitious young literary woman, of whom thousands abounded at that time, who would love to have married a writer who'd become a great success, like Sinclair Lewis or John O'Hara; it wouldn't matter how drunk they were as long as they produced a really best-selling book. That was what she was waiting for Malcolm to produce, and he wasn't producing it. She was attractive but all I remember is that she had a slight scar on her nose through having had a motor car accident. She was one of thousands of young women.

So you met them at their villa?

Well, we drove down from the Cuernavaca Inn, which was a very civilised, modern inn with a swimming pool and so on, and we got into the Calle Humboldt, which was off the Plaza, and immediately got into what looked like a road in Flanders during the War in which the shell holes hadn't been fully filled in. It had been raining, and the coffee trees and banana palms were dripping. We drove into this little villa, which was terribly tumbledown in the sense that it hadn't been painted for years, and the paint was peeling off the door, and it looked as though there was nobody there. I knocked on the door and I was just going to say, 'They're not here, let's go away,' when the door opened and there was this girl in blue denims, barefoot, blinking because of the light.

She said, 'What do you want?' and I said, 'We're the Calder-Marshalls.' Immediately she shouted, 'Malc! Malc! It's the Calder-Marshalls!' and there was a sudden feeling that *something* had *happened, somebody* had come from *somewhere.* And though, as I said, we'd never met, she'd heard of us. We went out on to what was called the verandah. It was a tiny verandah, just big enough for four people to sit on it. The railings had been eaten away by white ants, and we managed to find four chairs the canvas of which had not completely gone.

Malcolm came down. He'd been having a siesta by himself and he was rather bleary-eyed. He insisted on giving me the old Spanish *abrazos*, and he was terribly welcoming. We talked about old times and he told me what he was doing. But there was a terribly awkward feeling at the same time, as if there was a strain between him and Jan. She kept on putting in little things, sort of ticking him off for not being successful in the way that she thought I was successful, and so on. Malcolm had this paradise thing about how lovely it was to have the sober life and the swimming in the pool. The pool was about twelve feet by eight and was covered with dead butterflies and various insects.

Then Ara whispered to me, 'Do you think they'd be very shocked if we asked them for a drink?' Well, we went. That was at six o'clock in the evening. At twelve o'clock, Jan said she wanted to go home. Would I drive her home? We were in a nightclub, the only nightclub – a dreary little place, overcrowded if ten people were in it.

I said, 'Let's *all* go,' but Ara said, 'No, I'm enjoying it here.'

'*I'm* enjoying it, too,' said Malc, 'but I will come back with you to see everything's all right.' He came back and saw that Jan got into bed alone, and that was all right. Then he came back into the car and said, '*Now* the drinking can begin!' That was, as I say, quarter past twelve. We left Malc at 3 a.m. He was still drinking.

Were you aware at that time that he was going to turn this short story into a book? Did he talk to you about a projected novel?

Our plan was just to stay one night in Cuernavaca, go down to Acapulco, then work our way back slowly through Mexico and back to Hollywood. But at eight o'clock the same morning Malcolm presented himself at the Inn. He hadn't been to bed – I don't think. I'd still got the most ghastly hangover, and he brought his story and wanted me to read it. He was going to sit there until I had read it, so I said, 'Well, we can't go to Acapulco today.' I read it after having had a swim, and it was *terrible*. I knew that I couldn't say anything even to improve it, because his mind worked in a totally different way to mine. . . . All I could do was to say, 'I'll give you the name of my New York agent, Ann Watkins. Send it up to her and see what she says.' And that's what he did. He intended to turn it into a novel, but I thought I don't see how *this* can ever become a novel.

Wasn't it about this time that Jan left him?

Jan left him two days later.[2] I suddenly realised that with Jan's leaving him *we* had to look after him. We took him to a doctor and the doctor said, 'This man is suffering from an excess of alcohol. . . . I'll give him strychnine and brandy in a bottle. He can take that four times a day. No alcohol apart from that.' Malcolm was terribly excited by the strychnine and brandy, and that, of course, became a part of the novel. There it is in *Under the Volcano*. He was terribly upset by Jan's desertion, although she had in fact deserted him three times before. 'But to be deserted by my wife!' That also became part of the book.

Then he went back to change his trousers at the villa, after four days in the same clothes. He rang me almost at once and said, 'Could you please get the police at once? We've been robbed!' I took the police down and we searched the place. All Jan's clothes had gone because she'd taken them. I said, 'Well, what else has gone?' The police began looking for clues, even picking up my cigarette butts, thinking that they had been left by the robbers, and so on. Malcolm was really more concerned by the fact that he couldn't get a clean pair of trousers on because they wouldn't fit. He couldn't understand why they'd shrunk. Suddenly he said, holding these trousers, 'Extraordinary thing!' All the police crowded round, looking at the table he was looking at, and he said, 'Before the burglary there was only one copy of *Story* magazine, now there are two!' That was the burglary. I paid the police off and sent them home, and Malcolm got another bit for *Under the Volcano*. There *was* no burglary.[3]

Do you think that he was devastated by Jan's leaving him?

I think he was, but I think that, in fact, he had formed the plot of *Under the Volcano*. I think *Lunar Caustic* was . . . his first attempt to write what became *Under the Volcano*, by exploiting his only original thing, which was the capacity to drink more alcohol than anybody and go into an alcoholic hell. I'm quite sure that when Jan

2 For Jan's account of their parting see pp. 121–3.

3 According to Jan's account there was a burglary later, which she discovered on her return. See p. 121.

left and he went to Oaxaca and landed in prison – not as being a spy but merely because he was an old drunk – for him it was a terrible fascist plot. This plunge into hell, he realised, was what was necessary. He was obsessed with Faust and he had sold his soul to the demon drink in order to get a masterpiece. This I regard as being his taking a quite deliberate plunge into oblivion and being terrified, hoping that when he came out the other side he would have a masterpiece – which, of course, he hadn't.

What sort of political animal was he?

He wasn't. I remember . . . all the boring bits about Hugh, the Communist,[4] came from me. I was frightfully, boringly Communist when we went to Cuernavaca, and I kept on about the Party and God knows what else. Malcolm was listening to it all in order to reproduce what was necessary. But Malcolm's own politics was a sort of play-acting, especially when he succeeded in escaping from the brandy-and-strychnine-and-nothing-else regime and was back on the bottle in the Plaza in Cuernavaca. I remember a terrible evening in which he was drinking tequila one after the other – the most appalling drink – and talking about the Spanish Civil War to a drunken bus driver who'd come up from Acapulco. And they decided that they were going to go away at ten o'clock the next morning and drive down to Veracruz and ship across to Spain and fight for the Spanish Government. I thought, God, I can't stand this any more and, when I couldn't persuade Ara to go home, I said, 'I'm sorry, I'm going to sleep on that bench.' I went to sleep and next time I woke up it was six o'clock in the morning. . . .

Marriage beneath the Volcano
Jan Gabrial

Jan Lowry (as she was in 1937) continues to tell of her marriage after she and Malcolm arrived in Mexico. Here she recounts what happened between them in Cuernavaca, some of which is described from a visitor's point of view by Arthur Calder-Marshall on pp. 110–13. Jan particularly objects to the account of their life at this time which appears in *Ushant*, the autobiography of Conrad Aiken, who stayed with them for three months in 1937 and whom she clearly disliked. In this section of her reminiscences she throws interesting new light on the version of those

4 In *Under the Volcano*.

times in Lowry's novel, *Dark as the Grave Wherein my Friend is Laid*, and in Douglas Day's *Malcolm Lowry: A Biography*.

This is a further extract from an interview she gave in 1975 to the Canadian film producer, Robert Duncan.

Did you in fact go to Acapulco, and did you in fact arrive on the Day of the Dead?

We did. We arrived there on the Day of the Dead, and the first thing we saw, looking out from the balcony of our hotel into the street, was a child's funeral going by, with the little white casket and the musicians playing very merrily and very festively. Then, that evening, we went down to the cemetery and everybody was picnicking, and there were the sugar skulls and the strumming musicians. So it was a wonderful introduction to Mexico. Then we came back to the Plaza. The whole town was primitive and sort of unborn at that time. And I remember we spent about three or four hours at some little booth, talking about Mexico to the man who ran it – a black man who had been all over the world in tramp steamers. We were pretty enchanted. We drank beer and we drank things out of coconut shells.

Did Malcolm express any sort of awe about Mexico at that time?

No, it was just another place we were visiting. He enjoyed the colour and you felt that all your senses were involved with it. You know, the smells were strong, the tastes were strong, the feeling of the dust in your face or under your feet was strong. . . .

Can you remember where the money was coming from? Was that Malcolm?

Malcolm had at least $150 a month, and that was ample. We paid $44 a month, or something, for the house we rented in Cuernavaca. It had a pool and gorgeous gardens and we had a maid. We paid her, I think, $17 or 18 which we then raised to 22 because she did the laundry. The gardener was around $12, and then we had a little boy called Humberto, who ran errands and who had the face of an angel. We found out later that he slept all over town and smoked pot; but I think he ran us into $4 or 5 a month or something. We managed very well. Food was inexpensive. The maid cooked out of a charcoal brazier. I'd give her whatever was required and she used to do the marketing in the morning. . . . It was a very simple, pleasant life. . . .

By the way, there's a misapprehension I want to clear up. I keep reading that Malc came out here[5] to work on a script with John

5 To California.

Davenport. This is not true. He did not do any screenwriting. There was talk that he might, later on. But one of the reasons we went on to Mexico at that particular time was because his visa was about to expire and we had to go somewhere to get it renewed. We had wanted to go to Mexico. I had wanted to go down there and he was, I think, as fond of travelling as I, so we went down to Mexico. We had a six months' permit, and then, after six months, we had either to come up to the border to renew the permit and stay on, or else find someone who would vouch for us. The owners of the house,[6] Mr and Mrs Baldwin, had an attorney in Mexico City who then volunteered to do this. . . . Subsequently he was very sorry because, after I left, I think there were a few problems to work out.

Was Malcolm drinking heavily when you first arrived in Mexico?

It came and went in spurts. . . . At the time we left Los Angeles, during the trip down to Acapulco, no, he wasn't. He wasn't in Mexico City, where we next stayed. . . . I think it didn't really start until we got into Cuernavaca and we'd settled into the house. We had a man called Alan from California who was staying with us, sharing expenses. It was a three-bedroom house, and it cut down expenses considerably to have three of us in it. He paid one-third and we paid two-thirds. . . . He was also interested in writing and we used to take trips together into the countryside, to Cuautla and Iguala and Tepotzlan. . . . We spent three weeks of the month in the house in Cuernavaca and then we would travel for a week.

Who was Alan?

I can't remember his last name – it was something like Fernandez – but he was from California. He was of third- or fourth-generation Spanish ancestry. He would go on the trips that we would – you know – make it to the countryside. On one of those trips, I remember, Malcolm got terribly drunk. I think we fell in with a Mexican film-maker who had some friends and a couple of actresses with him. We all got wandering around and went pub-crawling together, and that, I think, was the first time Malc fell off the wagon. It lasted for about three weeks. He took to wandering around. We would get back to the house in Cuernavaca and he would vanish immediately and go into the pubs in town. And, after about two or three sessions like that, Alan said, 'Well, I can't take any more of this, you know. All I am is a nursemaid. I'm running after Malc all over trying to get him to at least come back to bed. So is somebody going to stab him or run him down in the street with a horse?'

6 In Cuernavaca.

I remember we had a talk, Alan and I, about this business of his being a nursemaid, and I said, 'I think one of the things that's a problem is that, whenever we go anywhere, we head for a bar. Of course, that's all Malc needs, and I think it's going to be better all round if you leave. Just leave us to work out our particular situation together.' ...

Anyway, after he left ... Malc, who had been making notes all through this, ran into a serious programme of writing, and things worked out. There was an earlier drunken period. We moved into the house ... probably around 19 November ... so it was in December that we had one of the first really heavy drunken periods that I remember. It was the Saint's Day in Guadalupe, which I think is 10 December, if I'm not mistaken. There was a big religious festival at the church in Guadalupe on the evening of the tenth, and people went from all of the outlying villages and, of course, from Mexico City. So we went into Mexico City and our hotel was very near to the Zócalo, which is the big plaza, and they had buses which ran out to Guadalupe. And I remember we went out to this enormous cathedral with a very festive atmosphere and I remember the lights and the candles and the incense and that kind of thing. It was absolutely packed. When we got there I don't remember whether we had bottles or what the situation was. But Malcolm and Alan were both very drunk and I was certainly feeling no pain. There was an enormous press, just a press of bodies going into the cathedral, with the religious statues and the incense and the bells and the music and a very fiesta air in the streets outside, and we all got separated. And, somewhere or other, probably around four o'clock in the morning, I found myself trying to make my way back. How I did it I don't know, because I don't remember knowing much Spanish or even having very much money. But I got back to the hotel from Guadalupe, and then the next day Malcolm and Alan turned up.

That was the first of the binges that I remember – the one in Guadalupe. . . . But . . . these heavy drunken periods were interspersed with quieter times. It would seem to me that things were going very, very well. We were working. I was writing, Malc was writing, and there would be a sense of fulfilment and a sense of richness. Then, all of a sudden, the wheels would get clogged, and things would break down and Malc would vanish. And usually it would last for two or three weeks. He wasn't *gone* for two or three weeks . . . he would come home for a few hours and then he was off again.

Was he working on The Volcano *at this time?*

No, at that time I think he was working on short stories. We were working on notes. He'd started the idea of *The Volcano*, but he hadn't actually got too much of the formula; it was kind of beginning to try to take shape in his mind. He was using bits and pieces of places and people, like . . . the painted house at the end of the street which was inhabited by a man called Forget. Now you talked to me about the Consul. Actually it wasn't the Consul who lived next door to us; it was some member of the Consul's staff who was there with his family. He was a lame man, if I remember correctly. And they looked down upon us. Their house was quite grand.

Which Consul's staff was this?

American, I think. Their house was larger, much more impressive, sort of a little Mexican hacienda, and set in huge grounds with lots of flowers and lots of trees. It had a great sense of privacy which seemed quaint and pretty and very unprepossessing. Today it would probably be considered rather grand.

So what started the binges, do you think?

I would say that basically the main periods of drunkenness with Malc occurred when people that he knew came down, people like Conrad Aiken, for example. When Conrad, Mary and Ed Burra turned up, then the whole thing completely disintegrated. Conrad, I know, said that on my birthday I left to go and visit two silver-mine engineers, or something like that, which, of course, is a lot of poppycock. What actually happened was that I wanted to do something kind of festive on my birthday, which was ɪɪ June. And I had, I think, talked to Malc and we had some kind of an idea that maybe we'd go into Mexico City, instead of which Malcolm had gotten quite drunk the night before. . . .

Anyway, I took off. I wanted to see Guanajuato, the old silver town, and Morelia and Lake Patzcuaro where they have the marvellous butterfly boats. And so I decided that I would take the bus into town and catch a train and make the trip. Don't forget that I had spent a couple of years before I met Malc wandering around Europe and North Africa, travelling everywhere by myself. I was a very confident traveller and very used to wandering off; it was a normal way for me to live. So I went down to the bus and Malc turned up with a little package of store earrings for me and which he gave me. Conrad later magnified these into silver earrings that were passed through the bus window and regarded contemptuously by me, which is again poppycock. I was miserable, but I wasn't contemptuous.

What in fact happened when he handed over the earrings? The story has always been that you rejected them.

No, I took them – and I took them with me. There was no reason to reject them. They were very cute – they were little straw-hat earrings with dangles on them. As a matter of fact I have copies of postcards and notes that I wrote off at that time. I wrote to him constantly during the trip and he wrote me. . . . On my trip I met a couple of people who were silver-mining engineers and whose address I took, but to the best of my recollection I never saw them after that. When I left Mexico[7] and Malc was staying behind (and the reason for that I'll come on to a little later), I wrote to this man – José or whatever – and said, 'Malc is coming to Oaxaca. Will you look after him?' . . . Also the man who lived next door, who was in some position with the Consulate. . . . I asked him to look after Malc in Oaxaca. And what happened I'm never quite clear. The stories that I got are kind of mixed, but Malcolm wound up spending four or five days in jail in Oaxaca. That I heard all about when I was back in the States.

Now people give very odd and distorted pictures of what our life was actually like in Cuernavaca. The other day I was looking through a book that had a quote from Conrad Aiken in which he talked about Malcolm falling into this dreadful, stinking sewer that ran past our house. Well actually there *was* this little stream that ran through the grounds which I did discover later was a disposal system, but which was not stinking at all. It looked perfectly clear water; we never saw anything in it that would have given you pause. Malc did not fall in it at any time. It was just one of the many distorted pictures. There's another thing over which I must take issue with Conrad. When I lived in Mexico I wore the Mexican sombrero, blue pants, denims. I lived in denims and I lived in *huaraches*, which are flat shoes. I would have been out of my mind had I worn high heels anywhere in Mexico. Of course I used to wear high heels when we went to Mexico City and I dressed, but where Conrad got the heels on the verandah from, I will never know, because they were *huaraches*. But, as I say, he seems to have a fascination with high heels and shit, so probably he saw what he wanted to see and he remembered and believed what he wanted to remember and believe.

You didn't get on with Aiken at all?

Disappointingly, no. I was not aware that he disliked me so when we met in Spain, because we really had very little contact then, and I ran around with Malc. I didn't eat at their table[8] – I had my own

---

7 The following December.
8 At the Villa Carmona.

table and he and Malc and Jerry ate together. I doubt whether I said hello and goodbye to him, you know. I mean, I said, 'I love your poems,' or something bright like that, but then I found out later from Malc that he really disliked me intensely, and he wove this story that I had arrived with a Frenchman and left with a Frenchman.

Later, when he came to visit us[9] I was delighted because I thought, you know, that maybe there would be a chance for us to get to know each other and be friendlier. And there was nothing there that was ever antagonistic except one scene in which I said something about women having the right to be sexually satisfied or needing the release of sexual satisfaction. That is the only time, if I recall, that he was ever actually rude or aggressive to me, because we went with him when he was getting his divorce; we went with him when he was getting married. . . .

He was not, as I remember him, a particularly funny man. Maybe he really was. I remember just bits and pieces of him . . . I remember . . . that he was quite bitter because of the fact that nothing he had written had ever earned him more than $800. . . . He was also quite a reactionary man, and we were very liberal at that point. . . . Conrad's ideas were in quite the other direction, it seemed.

Later on I was surprised to discover the extent of his dislike of me, and I often tried to work it out. The only thing I could think of, which is not a very generous thought on my part but which might have some truth in it, is that up until the time that I came on the scene he was more or less Malcolm's ex officio guardian. And he was receiving an income from Malc's father, which Malc told me was extremely helpful to him at that time because he needed the money very badly. And, you know, I may have been the one that cut off the [money supply]. Who knows?

What did Malc think of Aiken?

Malc's conversation about Aiken went along two different channels. . . . Obviously he admired him tremendously, was very close to him, and yet he would speak very disparagingly of him, both of his attitude towards women and his general spitefulness. But at the same time I think that perhaps he looked to Aiken for the relationship that he never had with his own father. Again it was this symbolism thing, just as when he met Nordahl Grieg. It wasn't as though he were meeting another writer, someone he had read and whose work he had liked – it was as though he were meeting some

9 In Cuernavaca.

sort of *doppelgänger*, or some aspect of himself. I think in a way he felt that he was part of Conrad and Conrad was part of him. I found the letter that he had written to Conrad, shortly after we were married, saying that he had married me out of vanity. It was almost as though he were writing to his father asking for absolution.

Did he start to tell you about doing the short story of Under the Volcano?

Not as a short story, no. It was always going to be a novel. . . .[10]

But he called it Under the Volcano?

Oh yes, he called it *Under the Volcano.* Right.

Can you remember when he mentioned it to you? Did he walk in one day and say, 'I think I'm going to call it Under the Volcano'? *Or did he mention [being inspired by the two volcanoes]?*

Well, of course, it was difficult not to be aware of them because we lived right under them. The path of our house framed them. You looked out on these two gorgeous volcanoes, and under the volcano, that's where we always were. I remember thinking that it was a great title. . . . But, if I'm not mistaken, Malc began fairly early, once we had the house and Alan was gone and we were able to get to work. I think really it was about that time when he started on *Under the Volcano.* He was fascinated with Mexico, but he was also very much under the influence of Lawrence at that time, not necessarily literarily (from a stylistic point of view) but as a literary figure, and Lawrence, too, was very involved with Mexico. Before we went down to Mexico originally, on our way by bus to visit the Davenports, we went to Taos[11] and visited the house where Lawrence and Frieda had lived. So I guess really . . . this was when *Under the Volcano* was probably starting, because I don't think he was working on anything else. Now, when we lived in New York he was working on *In Ballast to the White Sea* and *The Last Address*[12] but when we went to Mexico he left all of that behind. Every time Malcolm went anywhere he left everything – clothes, books, manuscripts, whatever, wherever he happened to have been. And so when we got down there it was almost like starting all over, and I think he must have started *Under the Volcano* quite early. . . .

---

10 Conrad Aiken claimed that the first draft of the novel was complete by the time he arrived in Cuernavaca and that he read it there along with *In Ballast to the White Sea*, which Jan claims Lowry left in New York. Arthur Calder-Marshall remembers *Under the Volcano* only as a short story from his visit in September 1937.

11 In New Mexico.

12 The first version of *Lunar Caustic*.

Do you remember when the Calder-Marshalls came?

Yes. The Calder-Marshalls came down, I would say, within about three weeks of our break-up. I think they wrote us that they were coming, but they did not stay with us. Conrad and Mary stayed with us, and Ed Burra – the Calder-Marshalls . . . stayed at a hotel on the outskirts of the town which was quite pretty. And we used to get together with them. I was very fond of them both. Ara was a gorgeous and funny and spritely and feisty gal. . . . He had been, as I remember, active in the Communist Party in England, which I think he was maybe in the process of drifting away from. . . . They were delightful. They could handle their liquor, and so, from their standpoint, it was not their fault that drinking was a bad thing for Malc. But of course it was. So again the thing got untenable. The drinking got heavy and I decided I would go to Veracruz.

There was a town to the south of Veracruz which had been the scene of a film that Paul Strand had made . . . *Redes* . . . which had come out maybe a year or so before. And I wanted to visit the place because the photography in it had been gorgeous. So I went to Veracruz and then I went to this little town, and then I spent a few days in Mexico City.

When I got back the house had been robbed and completely cleaned out, and at that point it looked like utter dissolution. Malc was drinking, the gardener had fled, the cook was arrested and put in jail and was going to sue us . . . all in all the whole thing had just disintegrated into a kind of Walpurgisnacht. Malc, as I remember, went into Mexico City, the Calder-Marshalls had left and I remember that I was left to deal with things. As I recall it, there was one suitcase of mine that had apparently not been opened or from which anything had been taken, so I had a few things in there, and I took that. Everything else was gone from the house. The robbers had even stripped the mats off the floor. There was no point in staying. I settled things up with Mrs Baldwin, who was our landlady, and I went into Mexico City. And Malc and I contacted each other there.

Did you tell Malc at that time that you were leaving him?

No, I wasn't sure that I was. . . . I did not leave Malc with the idea that I was leaving the marriage. I left Malc because I had reached the stage where I felt there was just nothing else to be salvaged. You know, Mexico had become the worst place in the world for him. What I didn't realise then and what I do realise now is that at that altitude, drinking – and especially the kind of things one drank in Mexico, mescal and tequila and so on, which were very raw and usually you threw the tequila into beer and drank it that way – is more likely to affect you than if you were at a sea-level motel.

So actually, when I left, I left because I wanted to get my head together; I didn't know what I was going to do. . . . I didn't have any money of my own; I certainly didn't want to take any from my mother, because she had already helped me out during the years that I was in Europe. . . . She was a teacher, she was not wealthy and she was not young. So I decided to come up here[13] where at least I had the offer of a job. The salary wasn't magnificent – $25 a week or something like that, which at that time was enough to get by on. . . .

As I say, I had not planned to leave Malc – it was just that there was nothing to stay in Mexico for. Malc was at this point going completely to pieces . . . I was very frightened of leaving him in Mexico; I didn't think that he was able to cope. At the same time I felt that if I stayed . . . there was nothing to be gained because we had reached the point where we were talking past each other. The level of communication was gone and I didn't know how to get him out, so when I came up here one of the things that was on my mind was that maybe he could get into some analysis, because Malc was completely fascinated with the idea of analysis. I was a little afraid of it at that period, but he was not. And I felt that if he could get into some place like the Menninger Clinic, if his father would have him go there, that there he could dry out and begin to get his own fears faced up to, because there were fears that I knew nothing about. Apparently there were nightmares that he was subject to that must have been horrendous. Whether these were from drinking I don't know, because Malc in his drunken periods would take anything. He would drink hair tonic. I remember once he drank a bottle of olive oil. It was in a hair tonic bottle and of course he thought it was hair tonic. But he would drink anything he could find, you know. So there was a feeling in my mind that if we had a separation from each other and if he could get somewhere and get straightened out, then we might be able to get our lives on the right basis. . . .

It would have destroyed me had I stayed with him. . . . The relationship at that time was sort of like trying to talk to something behind glass. And also, at the end of 1937, I was twenty-six years old and I guess my idea was that I had to get away from the whole setting. I had to get away from Mexico, which was destroying both of us then, and get back to some place where I could, as the kids

13 To Los Angeles.

say today, get my head together and decide where I was going to go with my life from there. . . .

How did you get from Mexico City to California?

Well, there are papers that have English sections and they have ads. . . . There was an ad about a car that was leaving and coming up to the States and they would take paying passengers. I contacted the person who put in the ad, I think through Wells, Fargo. He turned out, as I remember, to be a fairly young doctor. . . . It was his car and I agreed to pay half of the expenses going up. He was going to be driving straight to Los Angeles, which was fine because that's where I was going. I don't think I met him until the day that I left. Malc saw me off and I think that the man who worked for the Consulate was with us also, because I wanted him to meet Malc so that he would be able to keep an eye out for him. . . . I didn't drive because I didn't know how to drive, and the doctor dropped me off at the hotel I was going to stay at in Hollywood and . . . I never saw or heard from him again. I didn't even know his name.

So was Malcolm in Mexico City saying goodbye to you?

Oh yes, oh yes, oh yes.

It wasn't a case where you'd just said, 'Okay, I've had enough'?

No, no, no, no. He knew I was leaving, and, in fact, it was either the night before or a couple of nights before that the episode with the dog took place.[14] I think it was a couple of nights before because I think otherwise, if he hadn't sobered down a little, he would probably not have been there, you know. . . . Well, I left Mexico probably early in December of 1937. Then, all of a sudden he showed up[15] roaring drunk on the day of his birthday. He didn't announce that he was coming, and he was staying in a downtown hotel.

He knew your address?

Yeah, yeah, he knew my address. Sure – I'd been writing to him constantly.

Was he writing to you at that time, too?

Yes, yes. They were self-justifying letters, and by that I mean they were, 'If you could understand what I'm going through. If you knew, you'd know why I did this.' That kind of thing. Now when he showed up, seven or eight months had gone by since I'd seen him, and he was very drunk and very boisterous. And I just dissolved, because at this time . . . I had had visions that maybe he

14 See Jan Gabrial's story 'Not with a Bang'.
15 In Los Angeles.

would come up and maybe things *would* work out for us. Also I was beginning to feel that there was no way for us to go ahead unless he could somehow or other get face to face with whatever it was that was causing this drinking. So the first thing I did was get a friend to help him. He wanted to go out to the beach. We thought that if he could get out to the beach it would help. So we found a place out, I believe, on the Malibu Coast – not the colony, but a room on the ocean – for him. But the drinking continued. I was in constant contact with his father during these months because I wanted him to do something for Malcolm. By the way, I was not receiving any money for this; I was on my own. I hadn't asked for any; I didn't want any.

I had written to his father at some length about the Menninger Clinic, and in return he suggested that we get in touch with a man in Los Angeles that he had picked out and of whom I was not fond. I thought he was utterly unsympathetic to Malcolm and to me . . . I was not having much to do with him. But he was the one who came up with a drying-out place in the town of La Crescenta near Glendale which, as it turned out, was only slightly better than Bellevue.[16] I remember little about that period, except I do remember picking up Malcolm after he had got out there. And again he was as he always was after a bout of this sort, rather pale and drawn and very pathetic-looking. He took a room in town and went out and made his own associations. We were drifting apart at this stage, but I had not come to any decision about divorcing him; I still felt that maybe there was something to be worked out about our getting back together. I had not seen a lawyer or even thought about it.

Then, after one of our visits. . . . I called him. And I heard this sort of harridan voice on the other end of the line saying, 'Tell her to go to hell! Tell her to go to hell!' That kind of brought it home to me that the whole thing was becoming ridiculous, that obviously Malc was involved. I was going along my own lines and probably the only sensible thing to do was to get a divorce. So the next day I made inquiries and found out about an attorney and started the divorce proceedings.

Then you assumed that the voice. . .

That voice, I'm sure, was Margerie.

So when you got the divorce in California, did you see Malc very much while those proceedings were going on?

I don't even remember, because I don't think we had any commu-

16 In New York, where Malcolm had been in 1936.

nication after that. It's rather silly to say I was rather shocked and hurt, but I suppose in a way I was, because there had been no indication of any interest on his part going on, and perhaps if I had known that there was, the whole thing might have been different. In other words I guess what I am saying is that it would have been a far different relationship if things could have been open and above board all the way through. I have a bad habit of talking too much and trying to be completely open, which is probably not the smartest thing to be. In this particular situation I think if Malc had said, 'Well, you know, I'm seeing someone else, and I'm really involved and I think we'd better try to work out what to do,' that would have been fine. That would have gone beautifully. But the way it came, it seemed to me to be really rather vulgar. So at that point, you know, I just said, 'Well, look at the picture the way it is. Don't start looking at "What if . . ." and "But on the other hand. . ." This is the way it is and this is the picture you're looking at and you might as well – you know – leave it.'

So after that I don't think there was any communication until . . . I remember writing him a couple of times in Canada, and then getting back a strange letter which apparently Margerie had written. I was going up there on a trip and I wrote them saying . . . we should get together to see each other. And I remember I sent him a story that I had had published, too – the first one I'd ever had published. I sent it to him and I got back a rather snobby letter about it which probably he didn't even write, something to the effect that he would probably die and I would live on. I don't know, I don't remember quite what, but it was something to the effect that he thought that I was picking his bones, or picking his brains. *But how did you know where Malcolm was?*

There must have been letters or communication or something because I did know he was in Canada and I did write to him and he must have written to me. . . . Anyway I sent him the story and got a letter back. . . . I didn't know that he was with Margerie. I thought he was up there on his own, and I fully hoped that we could at least keep in contact with each other. I saw no reason why not. Nothing had happened for us to part as enemies. I hadn't just gone, in spite of the stories that I see are perpetuating about my leaving with somebody who lived in Santa Barbara[17] or something. I wish I had the game instead of just the name; it would have been a lot more fun. Actually, it was very sad leaving in Mexico because he was seeing me off, you know, and I guess we were very young, and we

17 See Douglas Day, *Malcolm Lowry: A Biography.*

didn't want to realise that maybe that was the final goodbye. It didn't seem so at the time, except that it was. You know, we'd been so close together.

It must have been very rough for you, a young woman.

Well, there was something in our relationship which I've never had with anyone else before or since. First of all he wasn't a man who got up and went to an office. He never had a job; he would never have taken one, probably. I don't know if the idea ever entered his mind, because he was a writer and that was the complete filling of his whole existence. That was the whole. Everything else really existed on the outside. You can start all the legends you want about who was responsible for this and who was responsible for that, but it was Malcolm who was responsible all the way through. The notebook was never out of his hand, the pen was never out of his hand, and his mind was constantly involved with that. But it was an intense relationship because of the fact that we were together day and night, except when he was drinking. The conversation was eternal. We took walks, we went horseback riding in Mexico; I'm a terrible horseback rider, but Malc was good. He was a good athlete, I understand. He played tennis and golf and he liked to work out. He was a good swimmer. There was a kind of communication that I've never had with anybody else.

He was intensely easy to talk to. We used to get up in the morning and sit down to breakfast, and at two or three in the afternoon we would still be sitting there talking. Everything that he read was retained, and of course we both read widely. We discussed books, we discussed whatever. We went to lots of movies and both enjoyed films. I guess about the only thing he wasn't good at, except with a glass in his hand, was social congress. That seemed to make him uneasy and then he would over-compensate. This happened in New York constantly when we went to the many, many literary cocktail parties there, and so often he would wind up getting drunk and insulting somebody or yelling at somebody there, which was his particular way of reacting to drink. I think if he had had the feeling that perhaps I was sympathetic to his drinking, which I wasn't, he might not have been so belligerent. I guess the thing that bothered me more than anything was that I hated to see him stumbling and falling over his words and reeling, and seeing this marvellously versatile, wonderful gift that he had with words somehow being so bastardised the minute he got into heavy drinking.

So you discovered he was in Vancouver, and he wrote to you or you wrote to him.

Yes, there was an interchange of letters, but the last letter was the one that Margerie obviously wrote, which was the reply to the one in which I said I was coming up and that I would be there and could we meet and say hello or something. Well, I got back this typed letter which said, 'Don't come. I don't want to see you. It's not going to serve anything.' I have the letter, but I don't remember the exact details of it. . . . Anyway, it was a letter of rejection. . . . I figured, well, OK, if that's the way it is to be, that's the way it is to be.

When you finally got the divorce through, was there any settlement made by the Lowry family for you, because they must have felt pretty. . .

I don't think they felt anything. I mean they just felt that Malc was a problem and here was something else that had gone bad. And they didn't offer. I would have been very surprised had they offered, and I didn't ask for anything.

So there was no payment at all to you.

No, there was no payment whatsoever. The only thing that there was – the attorney did get his fees from the Lowry family . . . which I think was probably around $500 or 600. And I remember the last day when I went into his office after the hearing and I think I had a few things to sign, and he said, 'I'm giving you a cheque for $250, which is half of my retainer, because I feel that we didn't handle it too well,' or something like that. You see, when we got into court, I tried to use non-support as a reason for the divorce in order not to cloud Malcolm's relationship with the immigration officials by bringing in the drinking aspect of it, and that is what my lawyer had counselled as well. But they wouldn't allow it; the judge would not accept non-support. And so . . . then I was kind of floundering around, and I think my attorney felt a little badly for me so he gave me a cheque for $250, just voluntarily. I had not asked him for it and I certainly didn't turn it down. But that was not from the Lowry family, and there was no settlement whatsoever. If it had been a settlement of $250 from the Lowry family I wouldn't have taken it because I think it would have been an insult. But I don't believe in alimony; I never have. And I certainly don't believe in it if there are no children and if one is young and able to get work. I feel that that's leeching on to something.

5 Canada with Interludes, 1939–47

Initially things went badly for Lowry in Vancouver, with yet another attorney playing 'guardian'. He expected soon to rejoin Margerie and once attempted to re-enter the USA, but was stopped at the border for being drunk and (in more ways than one, it seems) having no visible means of support. Margerie gave up a well-paid job in Hollywood to join him at the end of August, and when the Second World War broke out in September he seems to have made some sort of attempt to enlist, but was told, he said, to wait. The call never came, though what kind of a soldier or sailor he would have made is a matter of speculation.

There followed a period of semi-squalor during which he wrote to Aiken, begging for money and help to return to America. Unfortunately Aiken was broke, but did write to Mr Lowry offering to take responsibility for Malcolm. The long-suffering father declined; Vancouver was where he had sent him and Vancouver was where he wanted him to stay. He wrote to the prodigal asking for a letter showing some sign of repentance if his support was to continue. Fearful of being cut off, Malcolm duly obliged, even though it meant being stuck in a place he had come to detest.

Wartime regulations, however, made the transfer of funds to Canada difficult and Malcolm and Margerie had to find somewhere cheap to live. In August 1940 they discovered a squatter's shack on the beach at Dollarton, on Burrard Inlet, just north of the city, at $10 a month and moved in. It was an idyllic setting, with deep woods meeting the shore and clear water lapping right up to the porch at high tide. This was 'Eridanus', the northern paradise which Geoffrey Firmin glimpses on his path down to hell in *Under the Volcano*. The doom-laden writing inspired by Mexico gave way to a new lyricism.

They settled down to a healthy existence, swimming and exercising daily, and enjoying the friendship of local fishermen who taught them how to survive in their primitive surroundings. In

November the divorce from Jan came through, and Malcolm and Margerie married on 2 December.

They had begun rewriting *The Volcano* together, and now Yvonne, the Consul's wife, took on more of Margerie's character. The following interview gives an idea of their relationship during those productive years. Margerie also seemed to influence him politically, and he started to move more to the right: 'a conservative Christian Anarchist' was how he later came to identify himself. He wrote to Conrad Aiken complaining of a variety of ailments, in a letter which suggests that he was in danger of becoming as confirmed a hypochondriac as he was an alcoholic. The second draft of Lowry's novel was sent to his agent in New York and was rejected by thirteen publishers, but he quickly embarked on a third. Margerie, meanwhile, had written a mystery novel which was accepted for publication in June 1941.

As Lowry read, more strands were added to the densely woven text of *The Volcano*'s narrative. When he encounterd Cabbalism, the Consul, already an Adam, a Christ and a Faust figure, became a black magician. This allowed Lowry to add a whole new system of signs to the already complex pattern of literary allusions, foreign phrases, references to tarot cards and films which together give the novel so rich a texture. The hallucinatory visions of the alcoholic Consul enabled him to create a strange world of telling symbols and fateful coincidences where time revolved inexorably back upon itself, like an infernal machine invented by the gods to destroy mankind for abusing its magical powers. It became the kind of novel that can be read in many ways: as a religious revelation, as a political warning or as a Cabbalistic myth, for example. It is also a novel which challenges and subverts the realistic conventions which dominated so much fiction of the 1930s and 1940s. In one sense it is the story of two lovers' inability to connect; in another it is a late thirties' vision of the impending European holocaust.

The holocaust, it seemed, was about to consume the Lowrys, too, when in June 1944 their shack burned down. (Later Lowry implied that he might have played the arsonist.) The manuscript of *In Ballast to the White Sea* was lost and *The Volcano* barely saved. Another disaster had seemed to threaten just before this when Lowry read Charles Jackson's recently published best-seller about a drunk, *The Lost Weekend*. However, he appeared to recover from both these set-backs enough to depart for Ontario, where his old Cambridge friend, Gerald Noxon, found them a home. At Niagara-on-the-Lake, on Christmas Eve 1944, *The Vol-*

cano was completed. (That, at least, is the story: things did have a habit of happening to Lowry on significant calendar dates, and he may well have planned it that way.)

Returning to Dollarton in February to rebuild the shack, Lowry heard of his father's death. He could now look forward to receiving money from the estate, though not immediately. In November he returned with Margerie to Mexico, the scene of his calamitous past, and on New Year's Eve a reader's report from Jonathan Cape, asking for cuts in *The Volcano,* reached him in Cuernavaca. He immediately began composing a remarkable fifteen-thousand-word reply defending everything he had written; it was all there for a purpose, he said. But he became depressed and on 10 January attempted suicide while drunk. The couple left for Oaxaca where Lowry learned that his friend Juan Fernando Márquez, the bank messenger, had been shot in a cantina in 1939 at the very time he had begun rewriting *The Volcano.* It was as if he had scripted the death himself; his hero in *The Volcano* had died in exactly the same way.

Things got no better. In March Lowry was warned of possible deportation proceedings because of a debt incurred in 1938, and from then on he was harassed by the authorities. He could, of course, have bribed his persecutors, but chose to dig in his heels. The good news that his book had been accepted simultaneously by both Cape and the American publishers Reynal and Hitchcock brought a moment of joy before the axe fell. On 4 May the couple were deported. But it was all grist to the Lowry mill, and out of the trip came *Dark as the Grave Wherein my Friend is Laid,* published after his death, and the unfinished *La Mordida,* which he worked on between 1945 and 1949.

He seemed to relax only back in Dollarton among his friends and neighbours along the shoreline. Margerie had a second novel accepted, but it was her turn to suffer a Lowryesque disaster: it was published with a chapter missing! By November they were able to afford another trip, this time to Haiti via New Orleans, then finally to New York in time for the publication of *Under the Volcano* in February 1947.

'His Mind Was Just Like a Fireworks Factory'
Margerie Bonner Lowry

Margerie Bonner Lowry (b. 1905), Lowry's second wife, met him on a blind date in Los Angeles in June 1939. It was, it appears, 'love at first sight', and according to Lowry's biographer, Douglas Day, they 'took up with one another immediately and uxoriously for the rest of the time he was in Hollywood'.

Margerie Bonner had been a silent-film actress. She had married at eighteen and divorced at twenty. After the arrival of talkies, she turned from acting to radio scriptwriting and cartoon animation. When she met Lowry she was personal assistant to Penny Singleton, who was the star of the 'Blondie' films. Shortly after their meeting, with Jan petitioning for divorce, Lowry was removed to Vancouver by an attorney acting on the instructions of his father. The following month, August 1939, Margerie gave up her job and joined Malcolm in Canada. They married in December 1940 and their home for the next fourteen years was to be the beach at Dollarton, north of Vancouver, where they lived in a series of wooden shacks built on the water's edge.

There have been suggestions that Margerie is an unreliable witness, that she was inclined to exaggeration and went to great trouble to conceal the difficulties that had developed in her marriage, especially at the end. She was certainly industrious in building up her husband's reputation after his death and, although criticised for editing several of his unfinished novels for posthumous publication, claimed, with some justification, that she had always performed that role for Malcolm when he was alive.

This is an edited version of an interview she gave to Laura M. Deck, an undergraduate student at Denison University, Ohio, in January 1974. It was first published in *The Malcolm Lowry Newsletter* (No. 3, Fall 1978; No. 4, Spring 1979; and No. 5, Fall 1979).

Douglas Day seems to want to say that Malcolm was a one-book man. Do you think that's true?
Well, I think *Under the Volcano* was the most important thing he ever wrote, but I think some of the other things are important, too. A great many great artists have been finally known for just one book mainly.
What other works would you say are the most important to study . . . were the best?
Well, *Lunar Caustic* definitely, and certainly 'The Forest Path to the Spring',[1] which I think is very important because he was trying something that had never been done before, and I think he brought it off. He was trying to write of happiness on the note of high seriousness which is usually reserved for tragedy and I think

---

1 Included in *Hear Us O Lord from Heaven Thy Dwelling Place*.

he brought it off. A great many other people think so too.

How much did Malcolm read? He is always talking about other authors. Was his knowledge as vast as it seems?

He read constantly, and yes, it was every bit as vast as it seems. He was extremely erudite. He read everything, he forgot nothing. And he continued to read. He had certain books by his bedside which he would reread and reread. William James's *Varieties of Religious Experience* . . . and he constantly read the Bible, and he always had some kind of poetry beside him. Usually something of Dostoevsky's. And he'd dip into those and then we would go into the library in Vancouver and come back with a sackful of books. Oh yes, he read constantly and he read enormously widely. . . .

Do you have anything to say about the way in which he created?

. . . He wrote in longhand, and a good deal of the time standing up at his desk . . . he would make a first draft, then he would give it to me and I would type it. And then I would go over it and make my suggestions for cuts and changes and he would go over it and make his suggestions, what he thought, and then we would sit down and talk it over. Sometimes it would be fiery and sometimes not. Sometimes he would say, 'You want me to cut the best thing I've ever written?' Then he would go back and think over what we talked about and the suggestions we had made. Then he would write another draft and we would repeat the process. This would go on and on until we got something that satisfied us both. But he rewrote everything many, many times.

Did he write many things down in journals before he developed them into his works?

He kept notebooks – constantly kept notebooks. Oh, anything could go into them . . . a conversation he had overheard on the bus, or the way the mountains looked that day, or an idea for a poem, or some sign he noticed that intrigued him. Just anything, it was just a hodgepodge. Often he used his notebooks, too – they weren't just trash; he used them. For instance, when we went to Mexico together we both kept notebooks; he taught me to keep them too . . . and when we came back he used the notebooks to write the draft of *Dark as the Grave*.

Was Dark as the Grave *an account of exactly what happened on that trip?*[2]

Pretty much. It's quite close.

Did he identify Sigbjørn Wilderness[3] *as himself?*

2 *Dark as the Grave Wherein my Friend is Laid* was based on a trip which the Lowrys made to Mexico in 1945–6.

3 The central character in the novel.

Up to a point, yes. I think most writers, like most artists, identify themselves to some extent or another with their protagonist, don't you?

Do you think he identified more closely than other writers?

In some cases, yes. But you see everyone thinks that the Consul[4] was totally Malcolm; as a matter of fact a large part of it was Conrad Aiken. And he was extremely different from Malcolm. For one thing he was twenty years older than Malcolm and in some respects the Consul is far more Conrad Aiken than he is Malcolm, in his cynicism, his political views. Hugh,[5] of course, is the other side of the coin. You see, Aiken was like a father to Malcolm. He took over being his guardian from his real father and they were very close. But he was twenty years older than Malcolm and he did have different views and they used to contend with each other about them, but in other ways they were very close.

Where would you say that Hugh was? Was Hugh just the opposite? Did Malcolm identify with him?

Yes, he did – the sea voyage, the music composing and all of that.

How much of Yvonne[6] was you?

Well, that's difficult to say. You see at the first draft in the story it was his first wife, Jan, and she left him. And they had a pretty rough time, I gathered. In the first draft she was a rather unpleasant character. . . . I think that as he worked down to the second and third drafts and began to change this and that he just threw the earlier ones away. . . . So then Yvonne began changing from the unpleasant character to a more sympathetic character, and that part of it was me. And I think that's one reason why she doesn't quite come off, because he makes her such a sympathetic character that she couldn't possibly have betrayed him as she did. And yet that was an essential part of the story.

Some people have said that all three characters were just an extension of one. Do you think they were different aspects of the Consul's character?

You could say that in a sense. You could say that the two men were, but I don't think you could say that Yvonne was an extension of Malcolm. She was very definitely a woman. And though, as I say, she was rather unsatisfactory because she was so sympathetic that she couldn't have betrayed him and yet she did, you get into a little confusion there. But to say all of the characters are an extension I think is a misrepresentation. . . .

4 The central character in *Under the Volcano*.
5 The Consul's half-brother in *Under the Volcano*.
6 The Consul's ex-wife in *Under the Volcano*.

He spent ten years –

Nearly ten years from the time he started the book till the time he finished it.[7]

It seems from the letter that he wrote to Cape[8] explaining the book that he was amazingly conscious of every image, every thing he put in The Volcano.

Oh he was, he knew exactly what he was doing. I said to him one time, 'Malcolm, you know you're so erudite, in these references you can make and the allusions to this and that – there won't be very many people who will read the book who will be able to absorb it all, to understand or to get all of these references,' and he said, 'Well, it doesn't matter because they are all in the subconscious or unconscious mind of the civilisation of the western world. And the impact will be there whether they realise it or not.'

Do you think that he had a heightened awareness or an observation of the world around him, of civilisation in general, that was perhaps greater than others'?

I think he was twenty years ahead of his time most of the time. He knew things, he could predict things, he was very wise. All of his senses were heightened: his hearing; his eyesight was simply amazing considering the trouble he had with his eyes when he was a child. My eyesight, even now my far vision – I could get in the Air Force with it it's so good. . . . And his was so much better than mine that we would be riding along somewhere and he would see a sign and would say, 'See that sign? It says so-and-so,' and I'd say, 'You're guessing,' and we'd get a mile or so further and I would see it and, sure enough, he was right. And his ears, his hearing – if we'd be in the cabin he'd say, 'There's someone coming down through the forest,' and five minutes later I would hear it.

Would you label him a genius?

Yes, I would.

Did you recognise that immediately when you met him?

Fairly soon, fairly soon. He was the most extraordinary person I ever met in my life. He just wasn't like anyone else I had ever known. He was an extremely complicated person on the one hand and a very simple one, almost childlike, on the other. He was generous to a fault; he was loyal; he was extremely kind. He loved animals – he got nearly frantic during the hunting season when people would shoot animals. He said he loved the earth and he

7 Lowry began the novel in Mexico, possibly in December 1936, and completed it on Christmas Eve 1944.

8 See *The Selected Letters of Malcolm Lowry.*

hated the world, all the people pressing in on you and trying to take advantage of you and vying with you and he said that progress didn't always progress straight ahead. Sometimes it progressed in the wrong direction. Look at the mess we're in today – he predicted it. He saw it coming. He's been dead nearly seventeen years and before that he saw it coming. He said we were headed for an awful mess. . . . He was much happier when he was away from people and just alone with me and quiet, and never wanted more than one or two friends at a time. Many people in a room just threw him because he would get their vibrations to such an extent that he would just nearly go crazy.

In other words, he was very sensitive to other people?

Very. He would tell me things about other people and I would say, 'Oh, Malcolm, that's not right,' and sure enough, a few months later I would find out he was absolutely right. He knew.

Was writing a difficult thing for him?

Yes, he really struggled. Until he'd get going. He'd sit down and start to write and I'd hear sort of groans and faint moans and once in a while a sniff or two and during that time I wouldn't dare make a sound. I just kept absolutely dead quiet. And then after a while the groans would cease and the sniffs would go quite frantic and then there would be dead silence. And then I knew that he was so completely concentrated that the house could fall down on his head and he wouldn't know it and I could go ahead and type or do anything I wanted to. He wouldn't know it; by that time he would be so totally concentrated I would say that he was disconnected; if you spoke to him he wouldn't even know it. He had powers of tremendous concentration. Sometimes when we were together even with a couple of other people around some idea would suddenly come into his head and he'd simply sit and look and you would speak to him and there would be no reply. And Gerald Noxon and I have this expression, 'Well, he's disconnected,' and he *was* totally disconnected. This would go on sometimes five minutes, sometimes half an hour, and all of a sudden he would come out of it with some remark and then he was connected up again and he would talk. But during the time he was in a state of concentration he heard nothing that was said to him. It was amazing.

Would you label him a perfectionist?

Oh definitely.

Was he ever really satisfied with anything he wrote?

No. Never would have been. Wasn't even satisfied with *The Volcano*: 'Why did you ever let me publish it?'

Do you think that had things turned out differently and had he lived longer he would have published some other works to go along with Volcano?

Oh, yes, he definitely would have. He was working right up to the day of his death. He worked all of the time; in fact, he never stopped.

Some of the things don't quite have the impact. . . .

They don't have the impact, the magic or the complexity, but you see that was because he didn't finish them. He would have gone on developing and rewriting and deepening and broadening and they would have had. That's the way he got his tremendous effects, and his thickness was rewriting and rewriting and broadening and deepening as he would come to a scene and see more possibilities in it.

So it really was necessary to take ten years to achieve that?

Yes, it really was. There are tremendous changes from the early versions. Even the version that he sent out in 1940 or 1941, which was a tremendous step forward from the earlier version, of course got turned down by everybody in New York, thank God, because it was simply not comparable at all to the finished version; it was a different book. The plot, the storyline, was the same, but the writing. . . . Of course at the time he thought it was a mortal blow, but later he read it over and said, 'They're absolutely right; it just isn't any good, I'll have to work harder on it.'

It sounds like he was a man of extremes. Would he swing from one mood to another?

Yes, he was either very happy or in a state of despair. He didn't have very much tranquillity . . . he'd get writer's blocks from time to time and then he'd get into a real despair and that's when he would drink, when he couldn't write. I think it was because as long as he could work, as long as his writing was going well – of course he never took a drink during all the years, the last three or four years, that he was doing the final draft of *The Volcano*, nor did he want it. We had it in the house in case friends came and he would serve it and he would drink a cup of tea or something. He wouldn't take a drink. He said it would cloud his critical vision of it. So he said that you might get certain inspirations under the influence of alcohol but you'd better sit down the next day stone cold sober, take a good hard look at them and throw them all away.

I was curious, in Under the Volcano, *when he talks about mescaline and supernatural ideas. How did he really view them for himself?*

Or for anybody else. As he said, you may get all sorts of inspiration but you had better sit down and look at them with a hard cold eye the next day.

In October Ferry[9] *when he's talking about 'the element follows you around' . . . was he haunted by things like that? Did things like that really bother him?*

Not only bothered him, they actually happened to him. Coincidences of the strangest kind constantly happened. At first I was almost frightened and then I just got used to them and we'd say, 'Oh well, the demons are on the job.' Well, of course, he had his good demons and his bad demons.

Did that all tie in with the interest in the occult?

Yes, to a certain extent he was interested in the occult, but as for the Cabbala, he was interested in it for a while, and he studied it all right, quite deeply. Because he found a vast source of poetic images that he could use and once he had used all he wanted to of it, he then dropped the Cabbala. . . . He used it, yes, although he was a believer in the occult and he was a deeply religious man – he would go into church and cross himself and pray and kneel down and pray for himself and for me. He was an absolute believer in life after death. Absolute . . . you couldn't shake him. He said, 'If I should die before you I will be with you constantly.' He was deeply religious – deeply. Not in any orthodox way – he didn't belong to any church. He said he thought the Catholic Church was the guardian of mysteries and he approved of the fact that the doors of the Catholic churches were open and one could go in at any time and pray. He prayed constantly. His patron saint was St Jude, the saint of hopeless and desperate causes. And he used to write on the top of a page when he was writing a new draft or something, 'St Jude help me.'

In Under the Volcano *the characters which I personally labelled 'grotesque' – the people with one leg sitting in bars that the Consul would run across: what did they mean to him? Were they symbols for evil?*

Yes. Of course when he first started to write he was living in Mexico with his first wife and he was spending a good deal of time in bars. But he took notes even when he was drinking. He took notes of these odd characters and conversations with them. And he had his notebooks. He'd sit in the bar and take notes, so we're told. He would; I saw the notebooks, there they were. Snatches of conversations and descriptions of the people in bars and things. . . . I don't think they're all the same. For instance, the old woman with the dominoes obviously was a good spirit. She tried to help the Consul. Some of the other ones were evil. They were human nature as you find it, good and evil.

9 *October Ferry to Gabriola.*

It has been said that Lowry was an unusually egotistical man in that he viewed the whole world as a part of himself; that he had a subjective view of the world and put himself in every situation. . . .

I suppose it's true to a certain extent – that he was the centre of his universe all right. On the other hand he was so amazingly perceptive of other people, so sensitive to them. The things he would tell me about people and I wouldn't believe him, and he would turn out to be right every time. He was extremely sensitive to other people and their character and their *being*. And he was extremely compassionate.

Was he pretty secure with his idea of himself as a writer? Was that a part of it, his lack of jealousy for other writers?

My sister said to him one time after *Volcano* had made its great success, 'Malcolm, you must be very proud, aren't you?' and he said, 'I am proud before men but I am humble before God.' I think up to a certain point he was perfectly aware of his ability but in the end he was humble, he was never arrogant or proud.

Did he ever get to a point where he was discouraged enough that he threatened to quit?

He never threatened to quit, but he got awfully discouraged and he got writer's blocks sometimes when he couldn't work, and he'd sit and try and struggle and groan and carry on something fierce and suffer. It was horrible – it was torture when he couldn't work.

From the start, he knew he had to write?

Yes, from the time he was a child practically, it was the only thing he ever wanted to do. You know, he wrote when he was at this little prep school, The Leys, in England. He wrote stories and articles and edited the paper.[10] He was writing from an early, early age and he knew it was all he ever wanted to do or could do.

What would you label as unique about the way he writes? Or that you think makes him stand out among writers today?

I think there are several things. Of course he had tremendous style, which many writers today don't have. He really has a style that's unique. You can't mistake it. I think he has a breadth of vision that's extraordinary, and of course this is especially true of *Under the Volcano*; it was written on so many different levels. It can be read as simply a novel on the surface, or it can be read as a political tract – the Catholics think it's the greatest religious book since *Pilgrim's Progress*. They are all for it, they say it's a great religious experience. The occultists and cabbalists of course say that . . . and so on. It is written on a good many different levels. . . .

10 He did not in fact edit *The Leys Fortnightly*.

Did you have to do much adding or revising, or did you publish [his later writings] the way he had them?

Pretty much. I did very little in the way of editing. I did a little. I always did – he always was inclined to overwrite and I would have to cut. He said he thought he should pay me a salary because I edited it before it got to the editor.

So you were always a part of his writing?

Oh, definitely. I certainly was. He told everybody he couldn't have written anything without me.

Did he discuss plans he had for writings with you, too?

Oh, yes. And we'd discuss them and I would encourage him or not, however I honestly thought. You see, close as I was to him and his work, I was always able to be objective about it, which was why I could help him. I never got too deeply caught up in it so that I couldn't stand back and look at it with a hard critical eye.

Was it hard for him to do that?

Sometimes it was, yes. Awfully. He would get started and then he'd write and he'd get off on a long dissertation about something that really had nothing to do with the point in fact. He'd just get interested in something and his mind would go *racing* off on this thing and I had to cut it out and say, 'Now, Malcolm, you've got to cut that out, it slows down the action and kills the pace; it has nothing to do with the storyline – you're just riding a wild horse off somewhere.' We'd cut and cut and at first he'd kick and scream and carry on something terrible: pace the floor. He never swore, he said that swearing was an indication that you had no vocabularly. He used very little slang and he never swore except on *rare* occasions. In the end he would say after much torment and carrying on, groaning and pacing the floor, 'Well, I guess you're right. I will never publish anything that you don't approve of.'

Was his use of everyday language unique?

Yes, it was. Absolutely amazing. He used this tremendous vocabulary that he had just in speaking and talking in everyday language, but he never talked down to anybody. He always assumed everybody had the same level of intelligence as he did. He never talked down. Some of his friends on the beach, the old fishermen, he would discuss his work with them and of course they couldn't possibly follow it but they'd sit there and look wise and nod their heads and feel so happy. He didn't do it on purpose to flatter them, he just simply never talked down to anybody. It didn't matter who they were.

What was it like to live with him? Was it extraordinary? Was it different?

Very. It certainly was. It was different in every way I can think of.
As I say, he was the most extraordinary person I ever knew. He
was one of the wittiest people and he used to – unless he was in one
of his black moods – he'd have me in gales of laughter half the time
and I'd say, 'Oh, Malc, I should write this down for posterity.' Of
course I never did. But he was *so* witty and it was just like that
[snapping her fingers], it would just flash and flare out of him. He
was a wonderful conversationalist. We would talk the sun down in
the sky and the moon up. I'll say one thing, I never spent a moment
of boredom with him. I had some pretty bad times with him and I
suffered deeply at certain times, but I was never bored. He kept
me above myself all the time. He didn't live on the same level of
consciousness as most of us do. He'd cut across it at an angle
which made everything very intense. He was constantly aware of
everything. He didn't know how to relax. There wasn't much
serenity in him. He was constantly aware of his surroundings and
himself and people, happenings and events.

*If I was to do some reading by other people, would Grieg and Aiken be the
most important for me to read or would there be other authors, like Melville, Poe, T. S. Eliot. . . ?*

. . . He was greatly impressed by the great Russian writers – all of
them from Gogol right on down to Chekhov; the whole lot of them
– Tolstoy and particularly Dostoevsky. He was very impressed by
all of them and he had read them not just once but many times. He
was conversant even with Kafka; he was very much impressed by
Kafka and certain French writers, certain German writers; he was
very well acquainted with all of Goethe, even the *Conversations
with Eckermann* and the *Elective Affinities*. He'd read him all, not
just *Faust*. He uses the *Faust* legend and the damnation and so on
all through *The Volcano*. . . . The Consul is certainly a Faustian
character – among other things.

*I can't imagine a mind like his. He just must have been truly, truly
brilliant.*

He was, he was; absolutely amazing, just amazing. I said sometimes that his mind was just like a fireworks factory somebody
dropped a bomb in. He just kept going, never still. Like a racing
engine.

*You talked about how he said it would appeal to the subconscious of peo-
ple who didn't even understand it. Did he expect a lot of his readers?
Would he expect them to want to delve into the different meanings and
levels of his work?*

Of course, everyone has their ideal reader who will understand his
work and really read it. But as he said, it could be read on so many

different levels. And of course that's true that there are various theses that have been written about *The Volcano*. They will pick one level and mostly harp on that.

Do you think that most people in sizing up Malcolm have done him an injustice?

No, I don't think most people have. I think that in the main he has had excellent criticism. He's had some people who have gone flat out and said he was the greatest writer of the century and the one English writer who is going to still be read a century from now, and you can't have much more extravagant praise than that.

Was he ever under-confident about himself? Do you think he realised what he was? Not that he would be boastful about it. . . .

No, he was incapable of boasting; he couldn't do it ever. In many ways he was very humble and in certain ways very unsure of himself. Not so much of his talent but himself as a person. For instance, he was an extremely handsome man if you've seen pictures of him. And he thought he was hideous. He had no personal vanity. Absolutely none. And I'd tell him how handsome he was and how beautiful he was and he'd just pat me and say, 'Oh, dear, that's because you love me.' He had no personal vanity. He was unsure of himself in his looks and as a person even though he had beautiful courtly manners. The most beautiful speaking voice I ever heard in my life.

Was he unsure of himself in his writing? Did you have to sometimes reassure him?

No, he was sure of himself there. I didn't have to bolster him up there. I had to more, as I say, edit and cut and make him stick to the storyline and stick to the pace and not go wandering off on it along an imaginary journey. And even then he'd be pretty sure of himself and it would take me a while to say, 'Now this will have to be cut, Malcolm, we just can't use it.' Oh, he was in love with words; he would just spin them off.

There are seemingly autobiographical elements in the works. Would you still label them fiction?

There are certain autobiographical effects and efforts in practically every writer's work. He writes what he personally knows about, as a rule, unless he's just writing science fiction or something. . . . I think Malcolm is in the main more autobiographical than most authors, because I think he thought of himself essentially as a poet and the centre of his universe, and there is a certain autobiographical element in practically everything.

Under the Volcano *began as a short story, didn't it?*

Yes, it did. It was published in *Prairie Schooner* in its original form.

It's the eighth chapter where they take the bus trip and find the man dying by the side of the road, that's what it is. And I think in that version Yvonne is his daughter and he was her boyfriend or something. It's so long since I've read it. He wrote that that was the first thing, and it was from that he just expanded *The Volcano* both ways.

Was The Volcano *to be kind of the keystone of the rest of what he planned?*

Well, it was to be the *Inferno*. *Lunar Caustic* is of course the *Purgatorio*, as it turns out, and of course the 'Forest Path' is the *Paradiso*. *The Voyage That Never Ends*, it was to be called.

I think Douglas Day paints many times an ugly picture of Malcolm.

He does. I think that Day underestimated him in many ways. I think that he wasn't aware. . . . I think Malcolm was almost beautiful; he had the most perfect features. Look at that portrait. It was posthumously done just from snapshots. But . . . for one thing, he had a wonderful physique and he kept himself in beautiful condition, he exercised and played tennis, swam and took exercises. . . . He had beautiful skin, it was practically always tan. He had natural pink in his cheeks. He had the most extraordinary blue eyes you've ever seen in your life. They were so blue they just blazed, and his hair was copper-coloured. That is, it was brown and had copper lights on it. His colouring was beautiful. He had a remarkable smile and beautiful bone structures in the cheekbones. I think he was one of the handsomest men I've ever seen in my life, and he was meticulous about shaving every day except when he had his beard and then he trimmed it very carefully; clean shirt every day . . . and all this business about his being so sloppy – I never saw any evidence of it except in his worst stages of being drunk.

How extensive was his drinking? Day talks about him drinking to avoid writing, drinking to try and write. . . .

Well, most of the time when he turned to drinking it was because he couldn't write and he was desperately unhappy because he couldn't write. So to say that he drank to stop himself from writing or so that he wouldn't have to is absolutely wrong. And also his drinking followed no pattern – he could go years without taking a drink. Then all of a sudden he would just drink for weeks and weeks. Nothing you could predict. And on other times he would just drink socially, just normally, a few cocktails before dinner, and eat dinner and go to bed and read. And just a few drinks like that wouldn't set him off. Very frequently on a Saturday night, when he'd worked hard all week, he'd relax a little bit and we'd have a gin and orange juice before dinner, and eat dinner and go to bed and read – we always read in bed; sometimes he read aloud to me – he read nearly all of Shakespeare aloud to me in bed. It was quite an experience because his voice was like a trained actor's, it was so magnificent. And his accent was so beautiful. So, that would be that and it wouldn't set him off. It would be some emotional problem that would set him off.

It was just something he would turn to when emotionally upset?

Yes, he was a schizophrenic and a paranoiac, there isn't any doubt about that. And he was aware of it, he knew it. We discussed it. And eventually he went to a mental hospital in England and they tried to help him, but he was too intelligent – he could talk circles around his psychiatrist.

Was it something that he had a difficult time living with?

Yes. He did have a very difficult time living with it. For instance, I remember one time when we had gone in town for the winter and taken an apartment in town because it just got too rough on the beach that winter – there was a lot of snow and we did that sometimes when there was a very bad winter – and he wasn't drinking at all, he was working on *October Ferry* and working hard and all of a sudden he stood by the window one day looking out, and he said, 'You see that man on the corner down there? He's been following me for the last two weeks, you know. You must've seen him.'

I said, 'Oh, Malcolm, *King Lear* from nine to ten, *Hamlet* ten to eleven, *Troilus* eleven to twelve – there's nobody down there following you.' If I could make him laugh I could make him snap out of it. But he really did have these persecution things: 'they' were after him. Paranoiac.

Which had to do with his being fearful of customs officers?

Terrified, simply terrified. He would simply almost die when he had to. Actually, he didn't like to travel. He did it for my sake because he knew I wanted to travel, so he did it for me and it nearly killed him.

Then it was just part of this complex, this fear of being followed and being watched? Could he set himself apart from it?

Sometimes he could. He had a terrible fear of traffic, too. I had to steer him across the street or he'd have been run down. He said they all seemed to be coming at him from all directions.

Do you think he was, as Day says, in certain ways kind of childlike?

Yes, he was. As I said, he was so extraordinary because he was the most complex human being I've ever known, and in other ways he was childlike. There was a childlike simplicity, not childish, a certain simplicity about him. A sense of honour and loyalty, decency.

6 Under the Volcano and After, 1947–9

The Lowrys arrived in New York on 19 February 1947, publication day for the American edition of *Under the Volcano*. Albert Erskine, his editor from Reynal and Hitchcock, knew that he was meeting a new celebrity; the advance notices were glowing. The *New York Herald Tribune* acclaimed the book as an achievement 'of the Joycean order', adding that 'few novels convey so powerfully the agony of alienation, the infernal suffering of disintegration'. The *Saturday Review of Literature*, also acknowledging Lowry's debt to Joyce, claimed him as an 'apt, not aping, creative pupil'.

He was now subjected to a series of celebratory parties. Prominent literary figures turned up to meet the new-found prodigy, but by now Lowry had come to feel extremely uncomfortable at such gatherings. He did not seem to know how to respond to public adulation. Even with his well-rehearsed repertoire of performances, he did not seem to have an act to fit the occasion, except the old one – perfected in his Cambridge days – of doomed genius. For that he needed to drink, and drink made him unpredictable; he could slump into apparent unconsciousness or become embarrassingly aggressive. At James Stern's party he simply withdrew into silence, only coming alive when, having a nose-bleed in the bathroom, he was able to convince himself that he had tuberculosis, and was discovered acting out the tragic part in front of the mirror. Of course, he was a natural subversive. An occasion as dignified and pretentious as a literary get-together was something he would probably have enjoyed disrupting.

The book was destined to become a best-seller, but again his reaction was the unexpected one. 'Success,' he wrote, 'is like some horrible disaster, worse than your house burning.' Nevertheless, he was deeply wounded by a stinging attack on *The Volcano* by Jacques Barzun in *Harper's Magazine*, charging him with 'imitating the tricks of Joyce, Dos Passos and Sterne' while giving us 'the mind and heart of Sir Philip Gibbs'. Barzun also accused him of borrowing the styles of Henry James and Thomas Wolfe. Ever sensitive to the charge of plagiarism, Lowry wrote a pained letter of protest to Barzun, who replied courteously, clearly surprised that his review had been taken so personally.

After *The Volcano* and *Dark as the Grave*, Lowry seems to have run out of steam. He had largely rid himself of his obsession with Mexico, though there was another novel with a similar setting which he began, then quickly abandoned. Yet another work was sketched out at this time but never completed, and 'October Ferry to Gabriola', a short story set in his Canadian paradise, was laid aside for future reworking into a novel.

In November Cape published the English edition of *The Volcano*. The reviews were mixed and sales were poor, and the first edition was eventually remaindered. In his own country Lowry was to remain a minority cult figure, an influence on other writers, rather than a writer with a general following, until after his death, when interest in him was rekindled.

The Lowrys were now en route for Europe. A French edition of the book was being prepared and it seemed a good idea for him to be in Paris to advise the translator. But there he reverted to his old ways – the disappearing act and the crawls around the sleaziest of bistros, which is where Norman Matson encountered him. The city seemed not to interest him, as Clarisse Francillon, his translator, recalls; it was just another place to get drunk, another stage on which to perform. But even at his most difficult he could charm away wrath and dazzle with occasional flashes of brilliance.

Margerie, however, was to experience him at his very worst. On holiday in Cassis, in the South of France, he attacked her and became so incoherent that she thought urgent psychiatric treatment was required. There was talk of sending him to Jung's clinic in Zurich, and Stuart Lowry flew out to see them. His long-suffering family, however, were not prepared to fund such a trip and Malcolm was finally admitted to the American Hospital in Paris where he recovered sufficiently to leave for a holiday in Italy. There he spent time in a sanatorium and another attack on Margerie was reported. For a time he seemed to recover, but when they returned to Paris to meet Albert Erskine he had another relapse and it was decided instead to return to Dollarton.

In January 1949 they flew back to Canada, with a brief stopover in London where Lowry was reunited with his old friends Davenport, Calder-Marshall and Sommerfield. He told Calder-Marshall that he was next going to write *Under Under the Volcano*, but Calder-Marshall thought Lowry was in such a bad way that it would never get written.

The return to 'Eridanus' seemed to restore his sanity. There, at least, he did not have to meet hosts of strangers, and he appears to have come to terms with his alcoholism sufficiently to start writing again. He began working intermittently on two or three projected novels, but was unable to complete any of them. However, he did manage to produce a series of short stories included later in *Hear Us O Lord from Heaven Thy Dwelling Place*, published in 1961.

He had taken to writing standing up, and developed varicose veins which required treatment. The poet Earle Birney gives an interesting picture of Lowry at work at that time. In July he injured his back in a fall from the pier at his shack, which put him into hospital for a while. Now he dropped fiction-writing to collaborate with Margerie on a remarkable film treatment of F. Scott Fitzgerald's *Tender is the Night*. It was yet another Lowry project that came to nothing.

Celebrations and Blood
James Stern

James Stern, who had first encountered Lowry in Paris in 1933, met him again in New York in 1947 on the occasion of the publication of *Under the Volcano*. He found Lowry painfully shy, especially with women, and stunned by the success of his novel. He later wrote that 'the beastly book seemed to go off like a hundred skyrockets at once'. At a final party which Stern threw for his friend in New York, an event occurred which seems almost to have been an augury of the downward slide to follow.

This extract is from an interview he gave me for the 1984 BBC radio programme, *The Lighthouse Invites the Storm*.

How did you first hear of Under the Volcano?
I knew a very nice man called Albert Erskine, who was married to one of my oldest friends, Katherine Anne Porter, as her second husband. He was Malc's publisher, and I'm sure he gave me a proof copy of *The Volcano*. Malc, of course, was then in Vancouver and I think I sent a wire of congratulations. Very shortly after that he and Margerie went to Haiti, and I got a letter from him in Haiti saying he was arriving in New York and could I find a hole for them both. A few days later they arrived, and the 'hole' I found for

them was in a hotel, now gone. Anyway, that's where we met again, for the first time since 1933.

How had he changed?

He had changed very little. He always used to make fun of me, because I liked to drink wine. I remember the first time I met him – in Paris – he looked at my glass of wine and said, 'Red wine! That's been the end of many a good man.' I was in the bar of the hotel, and he came in and he saw the red wine, and he said, 'I know who you are all right.' He'd remembered the red wine from our first meeting. I saw quite a lot of him then, and introduced him to a good many of my friends. But he was quite hopeless in company. Lots of people came to see him and shake his hand, but I don't think he spoke at all. The only exception was when occasionally I took him to meet somebody in their own home. But most of the people I introduced him to were women, and he was very bad with women. I took him to see Dawn Powell, I remember, and Djuna Barnes. But he hardly spoke.

What was your impression of Margerie?

I saw so much less of her . . . because he was almost always alone when I saw him. I don't remember Margerie coming to the parties we gave . . . but they were very large parties and I wouldn't remember.

Can you tell us about the famous party where he ended up in the bathroom?

That was at my flat. . . . I've read stories about this party, where forty or fifty people were supposed to have come. That's quite impossible because they couldn't have got in. I expect there were fifteen perhaps. Malc just stood by the door while people came in and shook his hand and said a few kind words. And he was speechless. Whether he was drinking more then, or had drunk more then, I don't know. After about an hour, as people began to move away, he disappeared. But he couldn't disappear very far without leaving the flat. He had nowhere to go but the bathroom. So I went to the bathroom and there I found him. He had a habit of staring at himself in the mirror, and there he was staring at himself in the mirror, blood pouring out of his nose. He was wiping this blood off his face and throwing it all over the bathroom. He was convinced that he had TB, and he looked rather pleased about it, snorting with laughter. He was a hideous sight and so was the bathroom. He was taken straight to a doctor.

Second Encounter
Norman Matson

Norman Matson (dates unknown) was the brother of Harold Matson, Lowry's literary agent in New York. They first met at the end of 1934, when, according to Lowry's first wife, Jan (see Part 3), she and Malcolm had moved to New York from Provincetown, Massachusetts, to involve themselves in the current literary scene. Matson is wrong about Lowry being from Canada; he first went there in 1939. He is wrong about Oxford; Lowry went to Cambridge. And he is probably wrong about their second encounter being twenty years after their first. The last time Lowry was in Paris was from December 1947 until January 1949, although not continuously. This seems to be the period during which Matson met him.

The following piece was originally written for *Malcolm Lowry: Psalms and Songs*, edited by Margerie Lowrie, New American Library (New York 1975).

I saw him first at a distance. He always had a quality of standing alone, of seeming to be far away, not because he himself felt aloof but because he *was* solitary, and was horrified by the world. When I came into the recently converted speakeasy he was at my right, and though we had not before seen each other he at once raised a hand and smiled. Lowry was born (the bookflap tells me) in 1909, so then around 1934 he was rather young, much younger than I, but he did not seem of any particular age. We had a mutual friend who had arranged this encounter without himself taking part. Now, having met, we moved to the bar and were served whiskey by a fat, unamiable crook, a veteran of the illegal days.

Both of us, Lowry and I, had been to sea for long voyages. Not much before this he had been in the Orient, and he was then involved in a novel whose name and subject escapes me.[1] He was different from anyone I had ever met. He was a stranger, from Canada.[2]

He said with a friendly, self-commenting smile, 'You know I'm a Norwegian, too.'

But he was only half,[3] unlike me. He said after a third drink that I should try to remember his other half was Irish.

1 *Ultramarine.*
2 In 1934 Lowry had never been to Canada.
3 No, but his grandfather, Captain Boden, may have been.

In his pictures he is a handsome man. What I remember from this first meeting was a muscular, medium-sized (my size) man, grey as of face and hair, though his hair couldn't have been. We talked about something or other but not politics or 'ideologies' – he didn't give a damn. He was a writer with a capital W, un-published,[4] but confident and wholly – a writer. I might have asked him why he was, being that kind of metaphysical bore – why was it important to be a writer? I didn't, but I think that then, at least, the question would have made no sense to him, as one may ask a psychologist (for instance), 'What is a psyche?' There isn't any answer because if there is, oh, even if it is merely considered, all the words are emptied of importance and with them their speaker. What was important to Lowry then, that moment, was the drink he was drinking and the dark little joint we were sharing, as drink is important only to writers and maybe painters who are so to speak pulling themselves up by their own bootstraps, who are each day making their world and turning the red blood their mothers poured into their veins into ink so that it may be used for words, a fantastic ambition and drive when harnessed to some un-God, some Nowhere.

He didn't have a job, and unlike an American made no apology for that. He had regular money from somewhere, enough for living and enough for liquor. At the rate he consumed it, even then, that was expensive, not as expensive as, say, heroin, but expensive and as insistent. The cost he never questioned, nor added up: literary drunks don't, not at least those I have known. I liked him but he was more literary than I. There was a slight shadow of Oxford[5] between us. I don't think he mentioned Oxford. But I was earning money at writing, which he wasn't, and of course I didn't mention that either. I don't know what I mean when I say that I felt he was Norwegian – but I felt that we were alike in something. We were friends at once.

After this encounter things happened to him, but I have forgot-ten what. He was published in highbrow magazines that I could not afford to write for and probably couldn't have 'made', either. Twenty years later I was back in Paris pursuing what Allan Ross Macdougal told me were ghosts (he was right) and one afternoon sitting on the terrace of Lipps, an artistic pansy, trailed by a furtive French punk, who had learned from tourists that he didn't have to run errands or lay bricks or whatever for a living, told me that a

4 Not true.
5 Lowry had of course been to Cambridge.

friend of mine named Lowry ('says he is a writer') lived in a small hotel back of the Deux Magots. I went to the dark, lower-class *zinc* of this hotel and there was my friend Malcolm Lowry. He waved at me. He always drank standing up and sweated as if he were swallowing some metallic poison that was even more alien to the human bloodstream than alcohol. He fought his liquor, as they say, but managed from time to time to smile about it.

We met as if there had been no years between, and he seemed no older. He named the exact place and date of our last meeting. He explained the Deux Magots no longer wanted him around and so he had retreated to this cave. He smiled and a clear, visible stream of sweat poured off his face. He raised his hands and said that this was where he spent his days. Not with friends but alone. I can't say that I understood Lowry. Who 'understands' an artist? He wasn't crazy, far from it, nor sick. When he went on the wagon, which he did occasionally, his natural muscular strength returned in a day or two as if he hadn't been abusing it, and he was again an athlete, although not a happy one. He poisoned himself on purpose. As he did so to stand alongside of him took more endurance than I had.

The part of this second encounter I think about when I read the beautiful and somehow faulty pages he left behind after finally doing himself in for good, and which are now being published, has its location on the rue de Cels up beyond the rue de Lambre where we had a tiny house and where my wife and Margerie (Mrs Lowry), who were friends by now, arranged a later afternoon tea or cocktail gathering in the second-floor 'living-room' (a measured ten feet by ten feet), but when she, Margerie, arrived it was to say that Malcolm had come only as far as our front doorstep and there decided that he could not just then meet strange people. He was not drunker than usual, but his need for solitude was uncontradictable, like some law of nature. Margerie, a little breathless and white with anxiety because she had left him alone, came up to our spiral doll-house stairway. In the hallway she whispered to my wife, Anna, that they had found a bistro in our block and that was where he was. Maybe I would join him? He is lonely, she said.

It was the kind of bistro that is scattered through France, a neighbourhood *zinc*. I had often passed it without seeing it. Malcolm had not only found it but recognised it. There was a tense, a dramatic situation in there as I entered. Madame, a thin and alas an ugly woman, dressed in old black, was controlling her hostility and her contempt with difficulty. Only she and Malcolm were there. She hated my friend for a number of reasons, because he was an 'American', because he drank rum as if it were water, mostly because he thought her bistro was funny. He certainly had not said he did but he had said when she had asked him why he was inspecting her café with such close interest that he found it 'uniquely interesting'. When the rum bottle was finished he asked for more and she brought a different brand, a terrible drink made in some cellar perhaps. He suggested nevertheless that he buy the whole bottle at once. She wouldn't have it. He showed her his money. She said No – it was her last bottle, she had other clients. He asked me to note the iron chairs, on the wall last year's calendar and a gilt-framed photograph of a group of 1914 conscripts, sad with youth and distance. He tiptoed to the back of the place where an arch was curtained across with folds of dark dusty cloth.

Madame, her bony face a white flame of hatred, stood behind her *zinc* wishing, I think, she could call the gendarmes to throw us out. Malcolm raised dust touching the curtains, making an opening, and dared me to look into the alcove behind, which was saved from utter dark by a small window, a bit of grey and dusty light in the back wall. In a corner, his relaxed feet two or three feet above the floor, a man, his black tongue showing, hung by his neck. I believed in it for a moment, while Malcolm watched my face, and then I saw it was an effigy, life-sized, fully dressed, some dismal fellow-Christian's idea of a joke. We went back to Madame for another of the dark harsh drink, the flavoured mixture she was selling us as rum.

Malcolm said, 'This place is like no other. It is complete. They even have an aquarium. Have you looked at it?' There was a square glass tank of water sentinelled by bottles of cheap apéritifs with strange unconvincing names. 'There is a fish in it.' There was, too, a creature too big for the tank. 'Tell me,' he whispered, 'is it or is it not a herring?' I said I thought it was a herring. 'But not a pickled one?'

'No,' I said, 'it is alive. It swims back and forth.' All he wanted was this corroboration.

'I find places like this,' he told me, 'dark small places with their own meaning, everywhere. I'm prone to them. Sometimes I think I first imagine them, see them in a nightmare and then find them actual and existent in the world. But the herring was special, wasn't it?'

We had at last left Madame and were standing outside her dingy doorway. As soon as we had closed the door behind us the lights had gone off, a sudden comment, like 'Good riddance.'

I don't know how much 'rum' or whatever other alcohol Malcolm had downed that day, a long day now drawing to a close, but he showed no signs of it except only the sweat of agony that dripped off his cheeks. I looked along the rue de Cels, treeless, grey, with sharp geometrical shadows on its housefronts; all its detail bulged out at me. The man and woman who passed, she shoving a kind of cart with handles to it, stared at us, and they were real and separate as ships far out at sea, real as ghosts, and fated, doomed, precisely like the rest of us, beginning with Malcolm Lowry and myself. The sky above Paris was alight with the last of the sun, the first of the night's electricity, and there was one long pink cloud. For a moment it seemed to me (but how would I know?) that I saw the world with Lowry's eyes, and I thought as I have thought this last week reading the static, staring clarity of his *Hear Us O Lord from Heaven Thy Dwelling Place*, in which he startles you with beauty, that if his world had been mine I, also, would have devised ways to avoid it for long whiles, if I could, but at the same time held desperately onto life.

My Friend Malcolm
Clarisse Francillon

Clarisse Francillon (dates unknown) was co-translator of the French edition of *Under the Volcano* and became Lowry's close friend, often taking him off Margerie's hands for stretches at a time to work on the French version of his book during their stay in France in 1948. Her account shows a man in a state of shocked withdrawal from the urban world he loathed into alcoholism. We see the lucid and compassionate Lowry transformed into 'the madman pursued by demons', locked inside a world of private obsessions, from which he emerged only intermittently.

The following (here translated by Suzanne Kim) first appeared in a longer version in *Les Lettres Nouvelles* (November 1957).

In 1948, the people living in the back streets off the Place Saint-Germain-des-Prés could see a strange figure passing: it was Lowry walking day after day with the same slow, regular stride; he was going as in a dream, seeming to look at nothing, nobody. His somewhat threadbare raglan overcoat, the colour of moss on a stone wall, opened on a tweed jacket and baggy trousers. The pupils of his eyes, the deep blue of underwater caves, his short arms almost like a child's, his chubby hands, we only noticed these later.

Paris did not interest him. Never during his stay here have I seen him look up to the top of a column, or wonder at an archivolt or at the grooves on a stone. One evening, as we were walking together down the rue de Babylone, he stopped for a long while to gaze up at clouds madly racing among the winter stars. That was all. Once or perhaps twice, he felt like going to the movies; we saw *Monsieur Verdoux* and also, I am afraid, *Le Diable Boîteux*, a very poor production. The poster of *The Grapes of Wrath*, whose opening scenes he had once admired, drew his attention. But we never got to the movie-house where they were showing this film by John Ford: in a town, there are uncountable stages on the road to drink.

Sun and trees, these he no longer knew how to appreciate. At the home of the English lady with whom the Lowrys were staying, he always disdained the garden with its closely cropped lawns and the delphinium beds in full bloom; he never looked out the window. Whether it was in this house or in mine, the ritual never changed. On emerging from an opaque sleep that lasted well on into the morning, he would, in a frenzy of impatience, slip on his grey woollen turtleneck sweater, thinking only of reaching the kitchen as soon as possible. The nervous trembling which shook his limbs only stopped once he had drunk the first glasses of red wine and water. This beverage was prepared for him in a small decanter, the stopper of which coming in contact with the neck punctuated the greater part of the day. In our worried minds, this clinking took on huge proportions, swelling to the clanging of an alarm-bell on a ship adrift in the mists. This lasted till Lowry would vanish eventually and, do or say what we would, escape from us.

He showed a marked preference for those dim taverns off the beaten track, little frequented unless by a handful of workmen in dungarees with a bag slung over their shoulder – rue Jacob, rue Gozlin, rue des Ciseaux, rue de l'Amiral-Mouchez. . . . As often as not, he stood at the bar for hours on end, ordering glasses of rum, fine beer, or else of heavy red wine, which, however, he thoroughly detested. He drank without haste, as if in a dream, treating to a glass the clients who happened to be standing next to him, some immediately recognised member of what he called the Great Brotherhood of Drunkards. In halting French, he would sometimes join in a ragged conversation; or he would snatch up a joke or a scrap of a story that interested him. To the proprietress of the Perroquet, whose sign was hanging near the Parc Montsouris, a lady he thought particularly open to pity, he expounded one evening the difficulties of translating into French the preposition 'under'. Should it be '*sous*', '*au-dessous*', or '*en dessous*'? The *patronne* gave her sober advice.

With hands which were beginning to suffer from the shakes again, how did he manage to get a few crumpled notes out of his pockets and lay them on the bar? And then, he would come quietly, letting himself be led away by one of us, unless the proprietors had to throw him out of the door, for it was often closing time when the floor had to be swept and the chairs piled up on to the table. Once in the street, he sometimes declared of a sudden: 'Just wait for me, I'll be back in a few minutes.' He never used to come back – we could search for him; we'd catch sight of him through the steamed-up windows of a neighbouring bar, his face flushed with a kind of glee at his release.

Only rarely did he give direct proof of his tremendous store of knowledge or his stupendous learning. No more than of his generosity, of that sympathy with his fellow-men, together with a quivering, agonising compassion. These could only be guessed at in flashes. But there was his book that bore witness to them abundantly. At the most, he would now and then explain a point of etymology or a cabbalistic symbol. I can also remember how, one evening, at dinner – he ate little as drink took away his appetite – and though he had more than crossed the frontiers into drunkenness, he was still able within two or three minutes to find a passage in the complete works of Shakespeare, and read to us some of Timon of Athens' magnificent curses. . . .

In most people, this type of memory, which I like to call culture, stands in contrast to that which I call the memory of things lived, and they go in inverse proportions. Just try an experiment: the more able a person is to quote, for example, such or such an aphorism by Nietzsche giving, if possible, an accurate reference of chapter or page, the less he will remember the shimmering of a slice of lemon floating in the glass over which you have one evening confessed to him your reasons for murdering the rich old lady next door. The same is also true the other way round. By what miracle did both types coexist equally in Lowry? The first memory vivifying the second, one supporting the other, made for an extraordinary verbal inspiration, not unlike that of Rabelais.

Who was the 'I', how to find this 'I', where had it got to? the Consul[6] asks, and similarly we can imagine Malcolm, always more

6 In *Under the Volcano*.

or less drunk, yet still coherent, a little mad but never altogether out of control, never having quite lost grip on himself, with the thought that the drunker a gentleman became, the more sober he should appear. To put it in Jacques Laruelle's[7] somewhat moralising words: an honest man in spite of all, and brave; who might have shown great capacity for good, an *hombre noble*: such was the Consul. . . .

To drink or not to drink, that *was* the question. On the one hand you had the most vigorous, lucid, sanest man that ever walked on earth, exceptional strength, an outstanding capacity for work going as far as asceticism; on the other, the maniac, the madman, a victim pursued by demons, the plaything of evil forces, who lets himself be driven out of the gardens of this world, to totter at the brink of the abyss outside. All his life, he had been that pendulum unceasingly and relentlessly impelled from one extreme to the other. Only Death put an end to this swinging back and forth. . . .

Under Under the Volcano
Arthur Calder-Marshall

Arthur Calder-Marshall, who first met Lowry in London in the early thirties, visited him in Mexico in 1937. They met for the last time in 1949. Lowry was returning to Vancouver from Paris and his plane was delayed for a day by bad weather. His old friend John Davenport arranged for some of his pre-war drinking cronies to meet him, including Calder-Marshall. Lowry told him he was now writing *Under Under the Volcano*, but his friend felt that he was in such poor condition he would probably write no more novels.

This is a further extract from the interview I conducted for the 1984 BBC radio programme, *The Lighthouse Invites the Storm*.

After the publication of Under the Volcano, *he wrote a poem saying that success was like some horrible disaster. He seems to have regretted success, yet you feel he did want to create a masterpiece.*
Well, I think, you see, *Under the Volcano* was created in a period of limited alcoholic intake in Canada. Also he had stayed in one place. Even when he was writing in Dollarton, you know, they had a limited amount of money and drink, whereas once he got some money and inherited money from his parents, he then got enough liberty to destroy himself, rather in the same way that successful

7 One of the four central characters in *Under the Volcano*.

American novelists like Thomas Wolfe, John O'Hara, Sinclair Lewis and God knows who else also succeeded in destroying themselves by alcohol.

Is that, do you think, why he didn't bring anything off after that? He didn't seem to complete much after Under the Volcano.

When he went back to Mexico with Margerie in 1945 and relived the thing, he unfortunately could not understand what was going on. It was quite plain that he hadn't got a clue as to what was happening when he was drunkenly down there with her. If Margerie had been with Malcolm in Cuernavaca in 1937 she could never have helped him write *Under the Volcano* in Dollarton later on. It was because she was at a stage removed – she was Number Two – that she could help him then. But when they went back, she was Number One, and there would have had to be wife Number Three in order to have now produced anything as good as *Under the Volcano* from that return trip.

When did you last see Malcolm?

They had a stopover in London en route from Paris to Canada in 1949. John Davenport rang me and said Malc was there. We met at Kensington Air Terminal in Kensington High Street. Malcolm was absolutely pissed, and there was only four hours to kill, so we crossed the road to a pub and ordered beer. Margerie felt beer would be all right. There was John, there was Margerie, a little, very, very much silent film-star woman, very worried. There was an old friend, John Green. Malcolm was very proud of the fact that he'd got the same trouble as the King and he pulled up his trouser leg and showed the most horrible sort of broken veins and ulcers, and he said, 'That's what King George has got.' But when I said, 'What are you doing after *Under the Volcano*?' he said, 'I'm writing *Under Under the Volcano.*' He kept on going to the lavatory so that he got away from Margerie, and when he went to the lavatory he produced a large bottle of brandy from his hip pocket. Margerie was watching every pint of bitter he drank and she knew that this was happening, and one could see that she was in fact under the most appalling stress. I don't know how she succeeded in going on living with him for so many years after that. I was very sorry for her. I didn't feel Malcolm would ever finish another book.

How close to reality do you think the Lowry myth is – the myth of the existentialist writer, suffering for his craft?

I think it would be true to say of Malcolm that he was a martyr to his genius, that he was a literary Antichrist, that he sacrificed the vision of heaven in order to reproduce the vision of hell as nobody had ever succeeded in doing – that particular alcoholic vision of hell. I think he knew that he was damning himself.

What would you say was his greatest quality as a writer?

Persistence. I think persistence was his greatest quality as a writer. The fact that he could go on and on writing and rewriting the same book without getting bored. I think any other writer would have been bored to extinction.

What do you think Lowry's deficiencies as a novelist were?

I think Lowry's deficiencies as a novelist were precisely the same as his virtues as a writer. I think he hadn't got any of the equipment that the ordinary secondary novelist has. I think telling a simple story, handling a situation, handling time – they provided problems for him which were absolutely insoluble unless he invented this peculiar form that he did, and, of course, he took a lot of the shape from *Ulysses* – the fact that it all takes place in one day, for example. He took an enormous amount of the style actually from film, especially from German Expressionist films of the 1920s . . . Malcolm is working from film images. He's describing the sort of thing one sees on films. He doesn't make a whole out of it – he just has a series of sequences.

Apart from his fascination with film images he was fascinated with words and making jokes out of words. Can you remember any examples of that?

Yes, the sort of example of cheerfulness breaking in was in the ending of that pathetic letter he wrote to John Davenport, pleading for money when he was in Oaxaca. He ended it 'Toulouse Lowry-Trek'.[8] He was capable of wonderful plays with words, which of course were Joycean in origin.

That's the kind of talent you might think would make a fine poet, and yet his poetry never seems to have really been much of an achievement, does it?

Well, he was too undisciplined. I think the trouble is that this mutual admiration with Conrad Aiken, which lasted a lifetime in fact, was a terrible detriment to Malcolm. I mean, he continued to say that he thought Conrad Aiken was one of the few great poets of our century right up until 1949. He hadn't grown out of Aiken. Whereas Aiken from my point of view, as a poet or a novelist or as an autobiographer, is not second-rate, he's third-rate. For Malcolm to model himself in imitation of a third-rate genius isn't good enough.

8 Conrad Aiken claims in a letter to *The Times Literary Supplement* that 'Toulouse Lowry-Trek' was his joke which Lowry 'borrowed'.

Malcolm Lowry Visits the Doctor
Dr C. G. McNeill

Despite a life of hard drinking and heavy smoking, and despite his various breakdowns, Lowry seemed to have remained in quite good physical condition. However, in Canada, at the shack, he had taken to working standing up, and had developed varicose veins. Early in 1949 he visited Dr C. G. McNeill (b. 1913) who had opened a consulting room at Deep Cove, not far from Burrard Inlet. The doctor's memory of that consultation indicates just how dependent Lowry had become on Margerie, or, perhaps, just how dependent he had been made to become. The doctor seems to have got his dates wrong. *The Volcano* was published in 1947, two years before he visited him.

This is an edited version of an article which first appeared in *American Review*, No. 17 (Spring 1973).

My acquaintance with Malcolm Lowry goes back to his days at Dollarton when he was writing *Under the Volcano*. I had just started in private practice and had opened up a branch office in Deep Cove, where there had previously been no physician.

He came to the office one morning accompanied as always by his wife Margerie. He was a short, sturdy, pink-faced man with an absent manner. His speech was clipped and slurred. There were frequent pauses as he stopped for the right word. During the course of the interview I asked him what he did.

'I am a writer,' he said. I wondered at the time if he wrote radio commercials, advertising copy, or did more serious writing but did not develop the point. . . .

I forget now what approach I used to elicit Malcolm Lowry's complaint but at any rate he was literate enough to tell me that it was the ache in his legs and that it was interfering with his work.

'I'm a writer,' he said, 'but I have to dictate. My wife takes down what I say.' Later I was to find that he had a mental block against holding a pen or pencil.

'Most embarrassing. Sometimes I have been in places where I was supposed to sign my name and when I pick up a pen my mind goes completely blank. My wife Margerie does all the business. This has even happened to me in the bank.'

'A saving block,' I interposed, 'if you were about to sign a check.'

'Malcolm dictates standing up,' said his wife. 'He leans with the back of his hands on the top of the desk. Sometimes he will stand that way for what seems an hour thinking for the proper word. At the end of the day his legs are all swollen and aching. Show him your hands, Malcolm.'

He held out his hands. They were short, stubby, muscular. On the backs of the knuckles and first joints of the fingers there were calluses.

'But these are anthropoid pads,' I exclaimed. 'The apes have these from leaning and dragging the backs of their hands on the ground. I have never seen calluses in this area before.' Nor was I ever to see them again.

Malcolm smiled. 'We have been trying to simplify our lives by living in this remote place away from everybody. Actually we are squatters in a house on the beach. But I did not know I had regressed as far back as the apes.' One could see that my comment had pleased him, and I believe that with the term 'anthropoid pads' I had established a rapport that was to bring him to me in the succeeding years. His wife also I was to look after, more particularly in the difficult period after his death when she was arranging his works for posthumous publication.

And I remember Malcolm and his numerous violences, his intense concentration and yet neglect of his own body's physiology. How one part of him could be in the room talking to you and yet the sensation was that part of him was outside looking in, watching critically, evaluating; words streaming forth but not emerging above his subconscious; his numerous 'hang-ups' and phobias; his fear of syphilis, rashes, and body distortion; his ruthlessness in condemning his own work when it did not come up to standards he himself had set.

I then asked him to strip for the physical examination. He was, as I have said, short and sturdy. He had a good-sized chest and I commented on his tan. His wife told me that he went swimming every day and was able to dive off their porch when the tide was right. Their house was built on piles partly over the water, and from it he could leap or dive directly into the sea.

'Malcolm swims like a fish,' his wife told me, 'but I have to keep an eye on him because he likes to float on his back and think. Sometimes he goes to sleep like this. Once on the Riviera he went to sleep under a blazing sun and slept for several hours, still floating. He had the most frightful burn on his face and chest. His eyelids were puffed closed, his lips all raw, and he was ill for days after.'

I finished my examination of his chest and abdomen. He seemed fit and I directed my attention to his legs. It was immediately apparent what his trouble was. Although still a young man, he had developed varicose veins from long periods of standing. Both legs were involved to above the knees. I explained to him that if he were to take the weight off his feet and dictate lying or sitting with his feet up his legs would stop aching – even walking around was preferable – or he could bandage his legs or wear an elastic-style stocking. None of these suggestions was an acceptable solution.

'It is not possible for me to dictate while walking about, or lying or sitting. The words will not come unless I am standing in just this position and leaning with the back of my hands on the desk.'

Surgery was then suggested, that of ligation and stripping to remove the varicose veins from the groin to the ankle. When he found that only a few days were required in hospital and that he would be able to resume his dictation in three to four weeks, both he and his wife thought this the only solution and asked me to arrange it.

While we had been talking Malcolm had dressed himself. All except his shoes and socks. These he now proceeded to put on. Sitting on the low stool that I had used in examining his legs, he reached out for his shoe and started to slip it over his toes.

'No, dear,' said his wife, 'put your sock on first.' He dropped his gaze momentarily, grunted and put on his right sock. Then the shoe. Then he reached out to the left side, groping, still talking to me. I was watching him fascinatedly and by golly he did it. He picked up the other shoe and started to put it on his bare left foot.

'No, dear,' said Margerie, 'you must put on the sock first.' Malcolm looked down, grunted, and did as he was told. Margerie and I looked at one another and both of us shook our heads. This was a man who needed a lot of looking after.

In due course of time a hospital bed became available. Malcolm went in and had his veins stripped. There were no complications and he was able to resume dictation. The book was finished and published. It was a sensation. Malcolm brought me a copy. He was very grateful.

'I should like to have autographed this for you, but unfortunately I have this mental block and am unable to sign my name. But look, give me a bit of paper and when the block passes I will write on it and you can paste it in the book.'

I tore off a blank from my prescription pad and he put it in his pocket. Two months later it came back to me in an envelope addressed by his wife. On my prescription blank was written in ink,

with affection   Malcolm Lowry.

'A Spree Drinker and . . . a Spree Writer'
Earle Birney

Earle Birney (b. 1904), the Canadian poet, former Professor of English at the University of British Columbia, met Lowry in May 1947, just three months after the publication of *Under the Volcano*. They became firm friends; Birney was a frequent visitor to the shack at Dollarton, and encouraged Lowry to send off some of his poems for publication. After Lowry's death Birney edited his *Selected Poems*, and, together with Margerie, he helped 'piece together' the novella *Lunar Caustic* from two earlier, unpublished versions, *The Last Address* and *Swinging the Maelstrom*.

The following passage is extracted from the 1967 BBC TV *New Release* programme, *Rough Passage*.

The shack was about twenty feet square – that was about all. It was quite small and it was divided . . . into two lengthwise so that you had a long reach of front room, kitchen plus living-room, with panelled windows looking right down into the water. The water kept coming up under the panels all around you. The other part was the bedroom, and it had no windows at all, as I remember, and no furniture – simply a big double mattress on the floor and blankets. The front room had very simple furniture. He used a couple of apple boxes up-ended for bookcases, and he had an old broken-down iron stove with a little chimney coming up which you had to watch because it could catch fire very easily. But it was a wooden shack without any lining particularly, and when the weather got cold, in the middle of the winter, the Lowrys would always go into town and rent a flat for a month or six weeks.

He was a man who was a spree drinker and he was a spree writer, too. He did things in great bursts of activity of one sort or another, and he would build up a head of steam. He would start – he wasn't an early riser particularly, most of the time – he'd get up about the middle of the morning and first thing off he might go for a swim. And then he would do a little reading, and the reading would start getting him thinking, and he'd begin to turn that reading into something he was writing. And he would start [writing], and he might go on then right throughout the evening and right on through the night, and he might still be working the next day. And if he ran out of paper he would use anything in sight, and if there was nothing left, just because it was coming out of him, he would start writing over sideways on top of what he had already written, until he would stop out of sheer exhaustion. Or he would get a blockage and then he would take a drink and then he might pass from writing to drinking.

'He Hated Literary People'
William McConnell

After the publication of *Under the Volcano* Lowry acquired a few Canadian literary friends, among whom were the poet Earle Birney (see p. 161) and William McConnell (b. 1917), a young Vancouver lawyer and editor. When McConnell writes that Lowry hated literary people he is clearly referring to those who cultivate the literary scene, and in whose company he had been so ill at ease in New York. Lowry's prodigious memory to which he refers is widely attested, but the claim that he was obsessed with accuracy is strongly challenged elsewhere in this volume by Russell Lowry and Arthur Calder-Marshall. Also the story that the manuscript of *Under the Volcano* was destroyed in a fire is almost certainly another one of Lowry's inventions. However, his love of natural beauty, his struggle with alcohol and his terror of being evicted from his Canadian paradise are well portrayed. The impression McConnell got of Margerie and the marriage, while supported by David Markson, is challenged by Harvey and Dorothy Burt (see Part 7).

The following is an edited version of McConnell's 'Recollections of Malcolm Lowry', which first appeared in *Canadian Literature*, No. 6 (Autumn 1960).

. . . He hated literary people; to the same degree he accepted and loved those he felt were dedicated to literature. Quite often this blind acceptance caused him self-hurt and disappointment, but more often it created deep friendship. . . .

Most of his life from the time he left university until he discovered Dollarton was spent in physical activity in odd corners of the globe, but, like the scattered notes which he wrote on bus transfers, cigarette papers or any other chance piece of paper, all of his life was lived for metamorphosis into short story, poem or novel. He could discard nothing and, consequently, writing to him was not the usual casting for idea, figure of speech, or character portrayal, but rather a painful, tortuous process of selection and arrangement.

He had that rare (and rather frightening) gift of near total recall. I saw him sometimes after intervals of several months. For the first five minutes he would stare contemplatively across Burrard Inlet at the evening outline of Burnaby Mountain, then reflectively at a gull sweeping low over the water, then finally at me. Out of the air with magic, it seemed to one like myself who had little memory whatever, he would recount word-perfect an argument we had had on our previous meeting. He would review exactly what each of us had said, then quietly announce that he had been (or I had been, it doesn't matter) in error in a particular statement. Accuracy, even on trivial matters, was an obsession. . . . A deep observer, he believed nothing was or could be wasted in nature and that death itself was necessary for creation.

Was this knowledge, perhaps, the reason for Lowry's bouts of alcoholism? Unlike most of his friends I never saw him during such times. He did discuss everything but the reason for them with me candidly and simply (there was no false pride, no pantomiming of excuse, but simple direct statement). On several occasions I know his fear of groups triggered him off. Once he arrived at an august tea party staggering and all but speechless, wanting to hammer ragtime on the piano instead of being listened to with respect and awe. There were other occasions when he was alone and his loneliness simply could not be borne. I suspect that sometimes the creativity which constantly welled up from within himself could not be channelled as he wished it and had to be deadened by some anodyne. He didn't possess the routine and familiar antidotes with which the majority of us are equipped. During these frightening periods his understanding and devoted wife and the few friends, such as Einar and Muriel Neilson of Bowen Island, to whom he turned like a child, carried him through and, more important, beyond, during the even more bitter period of contriteness.

He told me one day that during the long months when he had written *Under the Volcano* he had not taken a drink even of wine, though he had been staying with a friend who had vineyards and made wine while he wrote. I mentioned earlier how every tag end of event was of importance to him, and somehow incorporated into his writing. This was true even of his attempts at forgetfulness, his wild occasional descents to escape the unbidden imagery he could not momentarily harness. . . .

Many are generous, as he was, with material possessions, but few extend the intellectual generosity he was capable of. It mattered not to Malcolm whether someone was famous or unknown, skilled in the craft of writing or a fumbling tyro. He, who knew how difficult it was to piece together common words so they sang and wreathed in rich meaning, gave consideration, time, advice (but never didactically, always subjectively) and encouragement to all who asked for it. He not only loved language and the individual warp and woof rendered by a writer, but revered it. He, a master, considered himself a tyro and anyone who tackled the same task with love he viewed as a potential genius.

Malcolm's relationship with his wife was far more than the customary one. They were partners in everything they did, sharing the successes or the periods of actual want with equal zest. He was proud of her attractive gaiety and her theatrical (she had been an actress) manner. More important, he was as concerned with her writing as he was with his own – and as proud of it. Margerie's opinion was constantly sought and considered. Equally, her concern and consideration for his welfare, her honest and penetrating appraisals of his work, supplied Malcolm with a reserve of strength and stimulation which always carried him through the bleak non-productive periods every writer encounters. Margerie possessed that rare quality – intellectual honesty and forthrightness. They admired and respected as well as loved each other.

I recall Malcolm's delight when I introduced him to T. E. Lawrence's *Seven Pillars of Wisdom*. I was a bit taken aback at his enthusiasm until I realised Lawrence's writing resembled his own in its rare concern with metaphysics. . . .

His last novel (unfortunately the middle section was taken out and never replaced) was typical of this.[9] For several years there had been recurrent rumours that the waterfront shacks, including his own, were to be bulldozed and the occupant squatters forced out of the beach strip. This had a terrible effect upon him. Here, as I said, he had found his uneasy peace. For a month he and Margerie had searched the Gulf Islands and Vancouver Island for an alternative home. The novel was, on the surface, about the search for a home and dispossession, but the recurrent symbolism of many facets raced through it contrapuntally. Just as *Under the Volcano* had been written and rewritten four times (once completely rewritten in a month when the previous draft had perished in a fire), so did this final and tremendous work undergo many changes and alterations.

One afternoon – early, about 2.30 – he started to read the first draft of his last novel to myself, Margerie and my wife. The typescript was interlineated with his spidery written additions and changes. He would finish a page and, without dropping a word, walk into the bedroom to pick up a scrap of waste paper on which

9 *October Ferry to Gabriola.*

was an inserted paragraph. We had brought a bottle of gin. As it was a festive and important occasion he had bought two himself. Margerie, my wife and I had several drinks, but were spellbound after that by his resonant voice and the wonder of his prose. He read on and on, drinking in sips of straight gin, without slurring a syllable or slighting a word. Finally, at 2.30 in the morning, he finished the last paragraph, the three bottles empty. My wife and I were terribly exhausted, but elated. When we got up to leave Malcolm was immersed in a paragraph he wanted to rewrite again, but rose to light our way up the trail with warmness and thanks, as if it had been we who had performed the favour. 'God bless you,' he would always say, instead of 'Goodbye'. This is the Malcolm we'll remember, and the one to be seen in his verse and prose.

Last month we drove by on the cliff road overlooking the former Dollarton shacks. Bulldozers were matting the underbrush to make way for a park. The squatters' shacks, Malcolm's included, had long since disappeared. We were sad and spoke retrospectively, then brightened, remembering the seagull dead from oil, the dropped needles which made the forest floor. He surpassed all of these, Malcolm did, for during his lifetime, not after it, he created life from his own.

The Family and its Black Sheep
Russell Lowry

While younger brother Malcolm was wandering around living the life of a Bohemian writer at his family's expense, Russell was in business in Liverpool. After his father's death early in 1945 his eldest brother, Stuart, took over the responsibility for Malcolm. It was Stuart, therefore, who had to cope with the difficulties into which Malcolm got himself on a disaster-ridden visit to Europe in 1948.

The following is a further extract from the interview he gave me on 2 September 1983.

Over the years, what was the family opinion of Malcolm, this rather distant young man who kept getting into scrapes and asking for money?
Two words: bloody nuisance!
You really didn't want to know anything about him?
... We were all very sorry that he'd got into such a mess. He always seemed to be in prison, or trouble, at least, and somebody had to get him out. And by this time there was a war on.

Were you surprised that Malcolm didn't join up, or do you think that he wouldn't have made much of a soldier?

It was no concern of mine whether he did or not. He was in Canada or Mexico or wherever it was by then, and he himself made a splendid excuse for not joining up: because he'd got a wounded knee. The incident happened when he fell off his bicycle as a child, but he attributed it to a gun battle in Singapore, which was nonsense.

You were aware, of course, that he married twice. What did you think of that?

Nothing.

Now after the War he came to Europe, and he got himself into some difficulties on the Continent, didn't he? Can you tell us a bit about that, because you got involved partly?

Well, he came to Europe, yes. And word came, I think from John Davenport, that he was in very bad physical shape. Stuart went on a self-imposed mission to try and sort Malcolm out. This was extremely difficult in a post-war world where there were no travel allowances, or next to none, and currency was controlled out of existence. There was a suggestion to get Malcolm to Dr Jung's clinic. It was quite unrealistic. I saw the correspondence. One, it involved Swiss currency, which was unobtainable, and anyhow it involved amounts which were far too big to be worthwhile in a cause already lost. Malcolm by then was rotten with alcohol. Nothing could have rescued him.

However, Stuart went off to Cassis with his wife Margot, who spoke better French than Stuart, and they had a very distressing experience indeed. Stuart was a completely realistic man; he knew all about the drink, and so there were no 'attitudes' about it at all. Malcolm was in serious difficulty; he was liable to be stuck in an asylum permanently by the French authorities for making a public nuisance of himself, breaking up furniture, setting fire to the curtains and being generally obstreperous. Stuart managed to organise things and get him away from Cassis and up to the American Hospital in Paris, out of which Malcolm eventually discharged himself. . . .

When he'd published Under the Volcano *in 1947, were you aware that he'd published a book at the time?*

Well, it wasn't a very important matter as far as I was concerned. Yes, I was aware that it was published, but I don't think it was published at the same time in this country, so we couldn't get hold of it. One of Malcolm's bitternesses was that none of his brothers showed any signs of recognition about this book being published.

One, we couldn't get the book because it was published in America, and then, two, it does raise the question, if you come to think of it: 'How does a man write to congratulate his young brother on drinking himself to death?' It just can't be done. So *The Volcano* was not a pleasurable event as far as we were concerned.

7 Canada: Obscure Endeavour, 1950–4

In April 1950 Dylan Thomas, an old friend from Lowry's Fitzrovia days, arrived in Vancouver on a reading tour of North America. Lowry turned up for a Thomas performance and the two spent the evening drinking and reminiscing. But such encounters were rare for Lowry. He had lost touch with the prevailing literary climate in post-war Britain, where fiction had moved into a decidedly realistic and parochial phase, and the kind of cosmopolitan experimentalism that Lowry represented was eclipsed. In fact the Dark Ages for modernism had probably descended a decade earlier, which is why writers like Samuel Beckett, Lawrence Durrell and Lowry were driven abroad.

The film script of *Tender is the Night*, now complete, was sent to MGM. It was well received but considered impracticable. However, Lowry was heartened by a generous letter of appreciation from Christopher Isherwood, who had been given it to read in Hollywood. For the rest of 1950 he returned to fiction-writing, producing more stories based on the European trip and turning his Canadian story, 'October Ferry to Gabriola', into a novel. The technique of producing short stories from notebooks kept during his travels and then expanding them into novels had become Lowry's characteristic method of working, since *Ultramarine*.

His work was also becoming more and more experimental, anticipating in many ways the French *nouveaux romans* of Alain Robbe-Grillet and Nathalie Sarraute. But he was ahead of his time and his agent was unable to get his work published.

In December 1950 his mother died intestate. There was now the prospect of an end to financial worries, though for most of 1951 his monthly cheque and $200 from his publishers was his sole income.

Around the middle of 1951 Lowry began to develop a scheme which would incorporate all his fiction into a master design. In 1946 he had already proposed a trilogy based on Dante's *Divine Comedy*, to be called *The Voyage That Never Ends*, with *Under the*

Volcano representing the *Inferno, Lunar Caustic* as *Purgatorio* and *In Ballast to the White Sea* as *Paradiso*. Now he produced something more ambitious under the same title, but headed *Work in Progress*. It was a plan for a whole series of novels, stories and poems, with *The Volcano* at the centre, and representing life as a voyage of self-discovery, a cyclical pattern of initiation and struggle, the struggle of life 'to give delirium a form'. In April 1952 Albert Erskine, now at Random House, found the project impressive enough to persuade the firm to give him a contract and salary for three years in return for two novels and a book of short stories.

It was shortly after this that he was visited by David Markson, a young American postgraduate and the first of a long line of students to produce theses on *Under the Volcano*. Lowry seems to have 'adopted' Markson. Perhaps, having outgrown a series of surrogate fathers, he had now acquired a surrogate son. Markson here presents a far more generous picture of the Lowrys' relationship than do their neighbours, Harvey and Dorothy Burt, who felt there was little love left between them and found Margerie over-dramatic and insincere. But Malcolm had become entirely dependent on her and she appears to have still nurtured the belief that her husband was destined for greatness.

The threat of eviction now hung over them and, when Lowry failed to produce anything which Erskine felt worth publishing, he broke off the contract. This was a blow from which Lowry never fully recovered.

The years since the appearance of *The Volcano* had not been entirely unproductive, however, and although the several novels he had worked on remained in various states of incompletion, he had managed to have two short stories, a book review and an essay published as well as a couple of dozen poems. But Lowry probably needed a far more sympathetic publisher, one who would have appreciated the experimental thrust of his fiction rather than one who kept looking for the next best-seller. To that extent, the success of *Under the Volcano* was probably more of a disaster for him than even he believed at the time, and yet, without that masterpiece, he would almost certainly have remained unrecognised.

On 11 August 1954 Lowry left Canada with Margerie for the last time, bound for Italy where they hoped to settle. Margerie, at least, had had her fill of the primitive life; she wanted a wider stage on which to play wife to the great writer. They broke their journey in New York and there Lowry had his last meeting with Conrad

Aiken – a sad, drunken and miserable encounter, from David Markson's account.

Europe, as before, threatened to become Lowry's undoing. When Dorothy Burt visited the couple in Taormina in November he appeared to be hallucinating and, for most of the time, incapable. But he had lost none of his power to charm and to make the most improbable stories sound convincing.

Malcolm Lowry: A Reminiscence
David Markson

In 1951 David Markson (b. 1927), the American critic and novelist, wrote to Lowry asking for advice on a thesis he was writing on *Under the Volcano*. Lowry responded with kind generosity, as is evident from *The Selected Letters of Malcolm Lowry*, and even seems to have adopted him as a kind of 'spiritual son'. A year later Markson spent time with the Lowrys at Dollarton, where Lowry claimed to him that he had once met James Joyce in Paris and that they had spent the day together. In 1954, on the eve of their departure for Italy, the Lowrys stayed with Markson in his New York flat where, despite attempts to conceal all available booze from him, Lowry found something alcoholic to drink, and later on disgraced himself at a party where he met Conrad Aiken for the last time.

This passage is from David Markson's book, *Malcolm Lowry's Volcano: Myth, Symbol, Meaning*, Times Books (New York 1978).

For seven or eight days, in the summer of 1952, I visited with Malcolm Lowry in the squatter's shack on the beach beyond Vancouver where he had written most of *Under the Volcano*. In September 1954, while awaiting the departure of a freighter to Italy, he and his wife Margerie lived for two weeks in my New York apartment. The duration of both visits seems greater in retrospect, since time spent with Lowry was somehow concentrated, or *distilled*. Speaking of Dylan Thomas, Lowry told me once, 'You know, I never saw him when he wasn't drunk.' I have to begin with the same qualification about Lowry.

The man could not shave himself. In lieu of a belt, he knotted a rope or a discarded necktie about his waist. Mornings, he needed two or three ounces of gin in his orange juice if he was to steady his hand to eat the breakfast that would very likely prove his only meal of the day. Thereafter a diminishing yellow tint in the glass might belie for a time the fact that now he was drinking the gin neat, which he did for as many hours as it took him to collapse – sometimes sensible enough of his condition to lurch toward a bed, though more often he would crash down into a chair, and once it was across my phonograph. Then he would hack and sputter through the night like some great defective machine breaking apart.

Yet what one remembers is somehow less the excess than Lowry's own attitude toward it, a remarkable impression he conveyed that he could never take any of it quite seriously. He had an acute sense of his own dissolution, eternally chagrined at being a nuisance, apologising hourly after small disasters, but what he sensed equally was the underlying absurdity in it all: the very idea, a grown man and that is the third burning cigarette I have misplaced tonight. So he laughed; and most often, one felt, with the delight of a naughty child who has 'gotten away' with something.

One afternoon in New York Margerie and I had to leave him alone for a time, though at his promise that he would remain 'safely' within the apartment. Because a party was being given for him that night, Margerie had done her best to establish what Lowry termed her 'tyranny of five o'clock', a prohibition against hard liquor before then. Such gin as I had was hidden, and we left him with six or eight cans of beer. I was the first to return, about three hours later. Within moments, Lowry had commenced to giggle. Sheepish, but no less transparently gleeful, he glanced about furtively before he confessed: 'I have a funny story to tell you, about something that happened when you were out.' Something had 'happened', as opposed to being done. A day or two before, I had bought fresh shaving lotion. I did not ask what it had used to dilute itself.

One jokes because Lowry joked: this was mischief only. Though the mischief was somehow cosmic too, as if ordained. In his autobiographical narrative *Ushant*, Conrad Aiken remembers a younger Lowry as 'visibly and happily alight with genius', and the phrase means exactly what it says. Lowry *looked* like a genius, there was a gleam not within but *behind* his eyes that seemed to transcend any ordinary alertness or mirth. The notion will prove more provocative if one recalls the Consul's 'demons' in *Under the Volcano*, and how often those demons are 'in possession' – though I am still aware that I risk exaggeration.

A typical instance comes to mind. Lowry is in the midst of a conversation. Making some point or other, he prefaces it thus: 'As old Stendhal might say, if he were here. . . .' Abruptly he pauses.

That 'look' is there, far more than speculative, as he considers a vacant chair, perhaps even a window ledge. 'And probably he *is*. . . .' When he glances back he is full of merriment again. There is even a hint of self-mockery in it – or would be, if the observer did not endure the unsettling feeling that it was he himself for whom the allowances were being made.

Lowry had 'Norse' eyes, with a certain whiteness in the pigmentation of the lids that complemented that demonic glitter. But his upper teeth protruded slightly, suggesting a grin whether one was intended or not – though one generally was – in the end making of him a roguishly improbable Faustus at best.

He was really too 'bookish' for the role too, even if there was a distinct manner in which he cared less about the written word than about the shade of the man who had put it down. A novel became a kind of introduction, for Lowry, to the author personally, and it would follow that an insight likened to one of Stendhal's, say – or Kafka's or Melville's – would often be one that the latter had never anywhere expressed, but that only he among writers might have. Lowry could be uncanny in this regard.

Then again his 'familiars' were not necessarily always his peers. During another New York conversation, and after another unpredicated pause, the talk had been taken up again for some ten or fifteen minutes before Lowry announced, 'Incidentally, there was an owl perched outside there just now. You saw it, of course?'

An owl. On West 113th Street. Well, it was not impossible. Anyway it more than suited the general run of Lowry's conversation, which, again like the Consul's, was wholly unpredictable, wholly implausible, if not to say so full of involution and subordination that even the most simple statement was rarely completed: every owl reminded Lowry of twelve other owls. One afternoon, drinking with friends, he began an anecdote about a French hospital where, apparently, several kindly but ill-advised nuns had supplied him with litre after litre of red wine. The story also seemed to have something to do with his Cambridge friend John Davenport, the English critic. It was started at least eight times. But after digressions about the China Sea, and Mexican jails, and the reading habits of James Joyce, and certain Manx fishing customs, it spiralled finally into absolute incoherence:

'Malc, will you for heaven's sake tell us what you are talking about?'

'Well, it's difficult. But you have to listen. It's . . . *contrapuntal!*' (Expresses delight as he fixes upon the word.)

'And there *was* an owl!' – this also a typical Lowryism,

declaimed not on the night of the bird's alleged visitation, but a week later perhaps, and apropos of nothing in the new conversation save that same unreadable, *reflexive* consciousness.

The story of the Davenport visit was told, in so far as it was, in a midtown hotel, under circumstances that were themselves characteristic. Lowry was to meet his agent there about noon. After various confusions he arrived at approximately four, wearing baggy denim trousers, a boyish sports shirt without a necktie, and a zippered denim jacket of the sort one might golf in, but hardly designed to gain admittance into an exclusive British enclave on Manhattan's East Side. In fact he was in the process of being turned away, until another member of the party was recognised by the doorman – though Lord Peter Churchill's[1] status at the hotel has presumably been in question since.

A point should be made that such situations did not arise because of the drink alone, though they had nothing to do with anything like Bohemian protest either; rather there was a kind of naïveté in the man, and a considerable innocence. Lowry simply did not *think* about such things as neckties. But too, he had lived in removal from normal society for so long, in Cuernavaca and in British Columbia, that it was rarely necessary for him to be anything other than himself. In the Dollarton woods, where the Lowrys had neither electricity nor plumbing, an 'appointment' meant a casual invitation to drop in for seafood at the shack of some fellow squatter a hundred yards down a stony beach.

As it happens, Lowry and I did take a more 'formal' excursion up there one day, or what began as such. The Dollarton house was situated on one of the deep-water inlets east of Vancouver Island, which is to say off the Strait of Georgia, which is really to say off the Pacific. Somewhere to the south, though out of sight beyond a thrust of headland, lay a town called Port Moody that Lowry decided we might inspect. It was 'just around the bend', and we could be there in thirty minutes. In bathing trunks, carrying our clothes, we set out via dinghy: 'Around the Horn to Valparaiso!'

The latter was more like it. We were an hour making the bend itself, in that case because there were flora and fauna to be investigated along the wooded shoreline. But even then, no Port Moody; instead we were next evidently in the great Strait itself, banging about amid currents, inspecting the looming, rusted underbellies of freighters at anchor a mile or more from any docks, absurd

---

1 Viscount (Peter) Churchill, the husband of Joan Black, a friend of the Lowrys from their days in France in 1948.

though maybe intrepid too in our tiny craft. Only after four hours did we make fast, our tour of Port Moody now to be taken in twilight – save that we were able to venture no farther than to the first dockside tavern. Somehow, en route, Lowry had lost his pants over the side.

Undaunted, we had the required drinks. Yet even after some hours Lowry was reluctant to depart, and again for other than the ordinary Lowry reasons. Now what held him was a special flavour of the tavern itself, of the sea at its door and of men who followed the sea. More often than literature, or Mexico, the sea coloured Lowry's talk, recollections of his one long boyhood voyage to the East, of other passages thereafter, and for all his remoteness from it now, it lured him still. This stocky, clumsy, shy little man, just turned forty-three, unkempt hair spilling into his eyes, without a cent in his pockets – for that matter without pockets – appearing on the threshold and grinning ingenuously, yet timidly too, which was characteristic of him among strangers . . . and yet within a moment being grinned at in turn, his obvious pleasure infectious and winning. Men lifted their glasses, they called hello. There is a line in one of the stories: 'The very sight of that old bastard makes me happy for five days. No bloody fooling.' Long after recording it, Lowry remained too pleased to admit that he had overheard it being said about himself.

But at last departure: water, mountains on every hand, a starless night sky. Once Port Moody was behind us, and the random night lamps of the freighters drifting at mooring had faded to port, the darkness was absolute. 'Now listen, Malc, do you recognise this inlet?' 'Oh, it's near, it's near.' He, himself, all but invisible in the stern, sprawling, dragging one arm or another in our wake. 'There are whales here now and then, have I told you?' Shadows loom and disappear, we have lost all landmarks now, and were I not pulling at the oars I would be shivering from the cold. Then from somewhere in the hills the eerie 'Zinnnnng! Zinnnnng!' of a sawmill running through the night. 'Ha! There is old Kafka, leading his orchestra. He must have been a splendid fellow, Kafka. I prayed to him once, and he answered my prayer. Incidentally, that could very well be a whale just off to starboard, the shadow that glistens that way –'

It is well past midnight when we locate the solitary dim gleam in the distance. Still, we may be rowing an additional half-mile out of the way. But no, it is the shack, Margerie has left a kerosene lamp in the window. She has been asleep for hours. 'Oh, I knew you chaps would have some adventure or other.' To which, Odysseus:

'I say, you do have the decency to offer us a drink?'

In Dollarton, and evidently in Sicily too, before the last trip to England, Lowry swam for half an hour or more each morning, whatever the weather. It may have saved him, certainly it postponed the inevitable. He was all chest, though in that ageing athlete's way of going to fat so that chest and stomach become one, stumplike. He had short arms that often seemed to flop about ineptly, like the appendages of some beached sea thing.

Yet he had been handsome, and, as the photos show, with his beard the face expressed a kind of gravity and wisdom in the last days. But at this time he was weathered, and turning fleshy. Interestingly, the older Errol Flynn, cast as the boozy Mike in *The Sun Also Rises*, took on a look almost precisely like Lowry's.

I have said there was something naïve or ingenuous about him. On another level it was simply honesty – one was convinced he had never in his life been motivated by pettiness. But he was also able to talk about love, in an essentially masculine, Platonic sense, without being accused of mawkishness, or something more extreme. A case in point involves Aiken, who had filled an *in loco parentis* role for him in his youth, and whom he had not seen for nineteen years before the New York visit.

Aiken was on Cape Cod when the Lowrys arrived, and Margerie sent a telegram. After two decades, and though he was sixty-five then himself, Aiken still knew his man. It was he who took a train.

Unfortunately, his arrival coincided with the aforementioned party. For some years Aiken had maintained a cold-water flat in the East 30s, and a meeting was planned there first. It was five or six. Lowry was still in fair shape outwardly, the after-shave 'bracer' to the contrary. (He had this faculty: musing, perplexed by unmentioned private visions, he could be teetering at the edge of the abyss and for a time not seem drunk at all, merely abstracted. Eventually, of course, he would come back to reality like a bridge collapsing.) At Aiken's, the fare was martinis. Lowry had been elated for days over the prospect of seeing the man again, but here too he was initially shy, and there were false starts. Finally Aiken asked Lowry what he had been writing. In rough form at the moment was the novel, *October Ferry to Gabriola*. For some minutes Lowry endeavoured to summarise its nonexistent plot, after which: 'Well, nothing happens. Nothing should, in a novel.' Whereupon Aiken, whose *Blue Voyage* Lowry readily acknowledged as the critical influence on his own concept of fictional subjectivity: 'No. No *incidents*.'

Lowry talked a good deal about his condition of the moment also, laying it in part to his distress at having to leave Dollarton, where the squatters faced eviction. 'I have to slide through this time of crisis on my unconscious,' was a statement repeated more than once. During the conversation he was beset by the shakes, and discussed this 'professionally' also. (Shortly after his arrival in New York, having to sign a paper before a notary, he had been unable to write his name. Three martinis had remedied the difficulty, though he had spilled the first and the second had had to be held for him.)

Margerie had gotten him into a tie and jacket for the evening, and I had shaved him – one relived portions of *Under the Volcano* with his presence – so at the party itself his appearance may again have been briefly deceptive. Present were his friends James Stern and James Agee, his former editors Albert Erskine and Frank Taylor, and two or three wives. The night was exceptionally hot; Agee, apparently already ill himself, stood through most of it in a pool of sweat that had literally dripped from his chin to the floor. Almost at once, Lowry drifted into a kind of rapt silence, likewise sweating profusely, gazing at nothing; perhaps an hour passed in which he spoke to no one at all, nor did he move from his chair. Then, suddenly, cupping his hands to his mouth, he commenced to make sounds that can only be described as 'beeps' – though one who knew could infer jazz, more specifically tunes associated with Bix Beiderbecke: 'Singin' the Blues', 'I'm Comin', Virginia', 'In a Mist'. For half an hour at least, even more absolutely lost to the rest of us now, the man rendered the Dixieland he had loved as a youth. ('I learned to write listening to Beiderbecke,' he had remarked in Dollarton, meaning something about a kind of 'controlled' freedom. He owned an ancient, hand-cranked phonograph and a collection of scarred recordings to which he could listen for hours. 'Oh, what pure art!' he might cry, or, 'Ah, the discipline!' When he heard some of the same pieces in New York, from reissued LP pressings, he immediately noticed elisions in several 'breaks' – nor did it take seconds for him to perceive that my turntable revolved too slowly.)

The private recital ceased only when Aiken announced his departure: 'Good night, disgrace.' Then, however, Lowry insisted upon seeing him home – this with no idea where Aiken was headed, and, chances were, with no money in his possession either, since Margerie normally handled all cash. Once again Aiken knew what he was up against. In the street, in jest but in sadness, the two began to wrestle as a taxi drew up. Breaking

Lowry's hold, Aiken tumbled to the floor as the vehicle took him off.

Those next moments, gazing into the empty street where only now a small rain, like a mist, had begun to fall, Lowry could not have appeared more sober. 'He is an old man,' he said. 'And now I will never see him again.' He was right enough, if for a wrong reason; and for a time he wept.

By morning, the twinkle had returned. Aiken had spoken of a nine o'clock train, and Lowry did not begin to function until well past that hour. 'Listen,' he insisted none the less, 'I know Conrad, he won't have made that train. Let's go see him off.' And again: 'After all, he is my father, and I haven't seen him in fifty-eight years. How can you keep me from him?' And yet again: 'Of course, I would have gone to Massachusetts myself if I had to, even on all fours.' In the end he settled for a telegram: WAS ON DECK 7 A.M. TO SEE YOU OFF WEDNESDAY BUT WAS OFFSET BY HURRICANE AM GOING TO ENCOUNTER MONDAY AFTERNOON OFF CAPE HATTERAS. . . . (There was in fact a hurricane along the coast that week, called 'Edna', which Lowry talked about incessantly, and which he insisted he had 'invoked'.)

At the same time he was able to regret what he determined had been 'rudeness' at the party, apologising too for the mounting havoc in my apartment: glasses broken, books and bottles and half-smoked cigarettes scattered everywhere, if not to mention the sheaf of manuscript poems reposing for days now beneath the kitchen sink, or the blood that had mysteriously appeared on his blanket. Conversely: 'You simply do not understand at all' – this should anyone suggest he postpone the next drink.

Meanwhile, a year before my Dollarton visit, I had written a master's essay on *Under the Volcano* which led to frequent repetition of another sort of admonition altogether: 'Whatever a writer does, he must make notes.' Those that follow I revise as form demands, but they appear in essence as recorded in 1952 and 1954.

Dollarton

He and Margerie bicker, insignificant household disagreements. Always, Lowry cuts it short with a word: 'I love you, do you know?' Or: 'My God, you are beautiful.'

Jimmy Craige, an old Manx boatbuilder, stops by one evening, bearing a gift of live sea crabs. The man is rough hewn, essentially unlettered – and a cherished friend in this wilderness. Gossiping, radiating affection, Lowry communicates with him totally, Irish songs are sung, then sea chanties and hymns. The man tells an anecdote about a stranger in the area, 'a Greek fellow'. To which Lowry: 'Like Aristotle.'

Lowry talks of having known 'a poet' of seventeen or so, in London – 'a wild boy who insisted he was already dying, smashing glasses after each drink, that sort of thing'. Some years later he had begun to admire the work of 'one' Dylan Thomas, whom Margerie then met during a visit to London without Lowry. 'And how is ruddy Malc?' – this with Margerie certain Lowry did not know the man. Nor could Lowry himself make the connection until a new Thomas volume appeared with the Augustus John portrait as a frontispiece.

He is overwhelmed, even almost ill, when I extend the good wishes of a reader of *Under the Volcano* whose comment had been, 'Tell him I'm glad he's alive.' 'Oh, my God,' Lowry sobs.

The jazz figures he names most often, after Beiderbecke: Django Reinhardt, Stephane Grappelli, Eddie Lang, Joe Venuti, Frankie Trumbauer.

On types of authors: 'You cannot trust the ones who are too careful. As writers or drinkers. Old Goethe cannot have been so good a man as Keats or Chatterton. Or Rimbaud. The ones that burn.'

A private myth: 'I arrived in America with one football boot and a copy of *Moby Dick*.' He claims, too, that seeking out Aiken in Boston for the first time, confused over currency and arguing with a cab driver, he stopped a passer-by for assistance – and the passer-by was Aiken.

O'Neill and Conrad 'sent me to sea', he declares, though both finally 'wrote from the bridge', which is to say they did not know the stokehold. With the exception of Melville's, the best sea novel is Nordahl Grieg's *The Ship Sails On*.

Grieg is a second writer with whom Lowry 'identified' – his word – as a youth. Several times, he speaks of occult 'correspondences' involving the man. To have written a novel (*In Ballast to the White Sea*, a manuscript destroyed by fire) about a boy who loves a book, and who composes imaginary letters to its author, and then to seek out that author in reality and find him living *exactly* as in the book you yourself have conceived. Or to have changed the name of a ship that figures in Grieg's novel, and to discover that one's substitution is identical with the name of the actual vessel used by Grieg as a model. Or, immediately after the fire in which one's manuscript is lost, to move in with a friend who that day has been assigned to write Grieg's obituary.

More of the same. One morning at the shack, he says, a bird

twice plummeted from a tree to crash against a window. Horrified, but assuming it drawn by some sort of reflection, Lowry threw open the glass. Yet the bird came on one more time, now to enter the house, circle, and at last depart. The question to be asked at Margerie's return, for Lowry, was self-evident: 'Is there mail? Someone is trying to get in touch with me.' It is almost redundant that Margerie carried a letter from a complete stranger, the last line of which read: 'You have got to write to me.' [No one who knew Lowry made light of any of this. In New York, Thomas had once started to scribble a note that he asked I pass along to Dollarton. In it, he mentioned a James Travers, a Cambridge friend of Lowry's who had burned to death in a tank in North Africa. On second thoughts, Thomas tore up the sheet. 'Christ, no, the old boy will have nightmares.' As evidently Lowry had, *before* learning of Travers's death.]

One evening, Margerie reads aloud the unpublished manuscript of 'The Forest Path to the Spring', which, if a beatification, captures their life here in absolute detail. With water slapping at the pilings beneath the house, branches scraping at the roof, gulls wheeling over the inlet in the twilight, I endure the curious sensation that I am somehow 'inside' the story as I listen. Lowry himself remains diligently absorbed through it all, feigning 'thoughtfulness' – though here and there unable to disguise the self-conscious grin of approbation.

Lines from the novels, or from stories in progress, are often repeated in conversation, though in their original context. A favourite, voiced by a local fisherman in outrage at the sightseeing ferry that had almost run him down: 'What's the matter with you? You look as though you'd swallowed Pat Murphy's goat and the horns were sticking out of your arse!'

Hart Crane, Lowry comments, 'must have been a wretched sort of man'. Also: 'I don't think the bridge is a good sort of symbol.' When pressed, he cannot explain, seeming to mean it static. Yet there is a way to read the full poem as 'genuine tragedy'.

Proudly, he tells of once having recognised Joyce – 'smiling' – in the Luxembourg Gardens. He insists they spent the day together. But details are lost to the usual digressions.

'Every French writer I ever met was a homosexual. Most of them were not good people either, except for Gide.'

On the night before my departure, Lowry surreptitiously presses into my hand a tiny medal, his own from Mexico, from the church of 'the Virgin for those who have nobody with'. But I am not to tell Margerie. 'She'll be sure something might happen to me if I no longer have it.' And when I protest: 'Believe me, it is all right to *give*.'

New York

He borrows a copy of *The Confessions of Zeno* from James Stern, a book he has not read. He contrives to spend two full hours describing its plot, however. 'And I am going to learn from it, a method of treating the consciousness.'

Whenever he leaves the apartment, the generous impulse: 'Here, here, let me pay.' Then the hand at the pocket, the sigh of frustration. 'Well, later, Margie has money.' Neither will he forget, ultimately demanding that she contribute 'my share, at least', to an accounting not worth the notice.

Much of his wit plays on alcohol itself. Someone quotes a line about the ghost in *Hamlet*: 'What, has this thing appear'd again tonight?' 'You know what that is, of course? – that is old Will's way of presenting the d.t.s.' Or again, in reference to virtually anyone's masterpiece: 'Naturally you understand he was tight as a tick when he wrote it?' Yet in all seriousness he cannot seem to comprehend the notion of working for a living; one morning, when a friend is already hours late, he commences a 'note' to the latter's employer explaining the delinquency. 'Here, we can take care of all that.'

Amid the baggage is a ukulele. A string is missing, however.

'I never quite understood that,' he says of opera, as recordings are played. 'I mean, I never really got it.'

Only one evening does he face up to the complications of a meal at a respectable restaurant. He allows Margerie to order for him, then eats only a few peas – one or two at a time.

Like the Consul, he himself is hardly unaware of the extent to which, finally, he can become a trial. One night when he has been making no sense whatsoever for hours, but has refused short of physical force to return to the apartment, in a 4 a.m. explosion of ruptured patience I deliberately smash a full bottle of gin against a kerb. Perhaps four days pass before a word about this is spoken, and then only: 'That was wasteful, do you know?' After which the gleam: 'Ha! Because I had already crossed the street you thought I was too drunk to see!'

One night we lose him completely, a check of every bar in the neighbourhood proving fruitless. Then at dawn I discover him asleep in a chair outside my apartment door. 'Well, after all, I didn't want to wake Margerie.' (The story unfolds only some days after this. By chance, he had run into a woman to whom I had introduced him earlier, who in turn had taken him home to meet her husband, an admirer of *Under the Volcano*, but who in his own turn had misinterpreted the entire situation – and had thrown Lowry out before his name had been mentioned. Evidently Lowry had slept in *that* corridor first.)

'But I will pull out of all this in Sicily. Under Etna, wait and see.'

They are to sail, via an Italian line, from Brooklyn. With great glee, he proclaims that the ship is certain to carry high explosives.

He thinks *The Hamlet* 'a great book', Ike Snopes and the cow 'tragic'. Parts of *A Farewell to Arms* are 'Homeric', but most of Hemingway is 'not much'. He shakes his head wistfully over a copy of *Finnegans Wake*: 'I did not give this as much time as I should have.'

Ushant – 'You Shall Not, by God!' – is a 'further manifestation of Aiken's genius'. But he admits to annoyance at the portrait of himself, apparently over certain ultimate privacies intruded upon; nor will he permit Margerie to read the book. [Lowry appears as 'Hambo' in the work; only in an edition republished after Lowry's death did Aiken append an identification.]

Other recently read fiction that has impressed him: *Demian*, *The Barkeep of Blemont*, *The Wild Palms*, *Oblomov*, and Dostoevsky's short novels, particularly *The Gambler*. Also De Assis and Broch.

His *big* books, however, would at the moment remain these: *Moby Dick*, *Blue Voyage*, the Grieg, *Madame Bovary*, Conrad (particularly *The Secret Agent*), O'Neill, Kafka, much of Poe, Rimbaud, and of course Joyce and Shakespeare. *The Enormous Room* is a favourite, as is *Nightwood*. Kierkegaard and Swedenborg are the philosophers most mentioned, and in another area William James and Ouspensky. Also Strindberg, Gogol, Tolstoy.

Lifting a Maupassant from a shelf (nothing has been said of the man before this): 'He is a better writer than you think.'

Of Djuna Barnes: 'I was in the same room with her once, and wanted to rush up and scold her for not writing more.'

En route to the docks, on the morning of departure, he is much taken with the Brooklyn Bridge, is 'almost tempted' to revise his judgement on Crane. He comments, too, on the 'drama' of the New York skyline as seen from the cab. Ever loyal, he reminds me that I must read the stories of Jimmy Stern, which are 'brilliant', and Agee's *Let Us Now Praise Famous Men*. Likewise Aiken's *Great Circle* – 'Though I did not write that. The only one I wrote in another life was *Blue Voyage*.' And throughout the drive he repeats a line, cum spurious Mississippi accent, that he attributes to Faulkner: 'Ah can stand anything. Ain't nothin' wrong with me that a good bour-bon won't cure.'

In fact he stands the first few hours well. At breakfast the shakes are extreme, but he acknowledges without argument that he must be shaved. And he achieves the freighter in relative sobriety, again in jacket and tie, visibly excited, with passport in hand. But the sailing will be seven or eight hours delayed, by which time he will be semi-conscious in his bunk.

'I must see the skipper. If he is not a company man, this will be a happy ship.' Meanwhile he impresses upon Margerie the urgency of tipping the steward at once: 'Italian ships have holds *full* of Chianti.'

The final words which will perhaps be allowed in a reminiscence of this sort: 'I'm a pretty bad man, but you should really come to Sicily with us. We love you, you know, but not so that you have to shove a cork up your arse, old man.'

In my apartment, a carton full of empty bottles. Abandoned across a chair, a torn shirt. There is blood on the collar.

Three years and intermittent letters later, the cablegram: MALCOLM SUDDENLY DEAD – MARGERIE.

And *vale* – since words do not recapture him anyway. One was convinced, at last, that the demons were real; but what one remembers is the innocence withal, the mirth, the sheer *abundance*.

'. . . for I loved the man, and do honour his memory, on this side idolatry, as much as any.'

The Neighbours from the Shack Next Door
Harvey Burt, Dorothy Templeton Burt

Canadian ex-teacher of English Harvey Burt (b. 1920) and his wife Dorothy (b. 1908) were looking for a weekend cottage at Dollarton in 1950 when they first met the Lowrys. They took the next shack along the beach and became close friends of their unusual neighbours. Harvey and Dorothy each developed strong opinions about the relationship between Malcolm and Margerie, and were witnesses to Lowry's slow slide into obscurity after the enormous success of *Under the Volcano*. They were later to be close to the Lowrys during the final years in Italy and England.

The following is an extract from an interview given to me in August 1982.

Dorothy, what did you make of Margerie, because she played quite an important part in Malcolm's life, didn't she, and she was to become your neighbour?

D.T.B.: Oh, she was very dramatic, terribly dramatic, always posing.

She'd been a child star in Hollywood, hadn't she?

D.T.B.: Yes, that's what she said. She said she had, and she also wrote books herself, she wrote mysteries. . . . But you couldn't really believe anything Margerie said. She just exaggerated everything, and one day it would be one story, and the other it would be something else, so we never really knew what to make of Margerie.

But they were both writers and you'd think that two writers living together would make a great team. Harvey, was that your impression? Do you think they made a team?

H.B.: Malcolm was totally dependent on Margerie and I find it now difficult to understand why Margerie stayed with Malcolm under the circumstance of living in the shack. I suppose one could say love, but it may be other than that. Maybe she saw the potential in Malcolm's writing and was devoted to the artist rather than the man. But she did serve him; she looked after him, she cut wood for him, she did the shopping, got library books, supplied gin when it was necessary, and did all his typing and much of his pre-submission editorial work. What Malcolm did for Margerie is difficult to say. I don't think that we ever heard Malcolm criticising any of Margerie's work, although we heard Margerie criticising, commenting on Malcolm's work. But they stayed together many years after that even. As a team I don't know, but they were together.

What was the impression you got of how he worked? Did you have an opportunity to see that?

H.B.: Not directly. I remember when we first got there, Margerie said to us, 'I don't want you fellows,' as she always called us, 'to come over in the morning because Malcolm is working, and if you want to borrow the boat take it for God's sake, but don't disturb Malcolm.' So this we did, and we followed that for evermore. It was during this time that Malcolm was writing, or working on, *October Ferry to Gabriola*. He was behind schedule. I don't think he was producing very much, because we did hear the same passages a couple of times. I don't think that he was writing very effectively. He didn't say ever that he was doing well, although he seemed to be writing; he seemed to be working and we obeyed that command . . . in fact we didn't ever interfere with them. We were always sought out. We did use the boat, but we never went to see them.

Malcolm came to us a couple of times, but Margerie used to come to visit us most of the time.

He seems to have been a pretty shy chap in a lot of ways.

D.T.B.: Yes, he was, he was quite shy. I think he was very shy really, but we thought really very friendly. He was very shy at the beginning, but then he never seemed to be after that, was he?

H.B.: No, and furthermore he was terribly sensitive to our moods, if you remember, because we were going through a kind of a difficult spell in our own lives and we would come down there and he would say, 'Oh what's wrong? There's something amiss.' He knew this, and even then he would be half drunk, but he was aware that we were having problems and he was looking out for us to a certain extent.

Did he undergo a transformation when he drank?

H.B.: I really can't say that I ever noticed it. He would ultimately undergo a transformation; he would literally go from consciousness to unconsciousness, or he would apparently pass out. But no, I think that he spoke about the same speed . . . with the same clarity, the same kind of witticism or seriousness. But there was a point when he was obviously drunk. He did repeat himself when he was drunk, as we all do, and then at a certain point he would sort of pass out. But then he would come to; he would know what else was going on. He didn't pass out in the fullest sense; he simply retired from the scene; he refreshed himself and then there was a kind of a renaissance. He would come back in the midst of a sentence almost, or in the midst of a conversation, and he wouldn't have missed anything. In fact you've seen that recorded before, but it's true that he would be conscious, listening, thinking, but absolutely dormant or inanimate until that moment of resurrection, if you like, and then. . . .

Did he talk to you much about what he was writing? And did he read to you ever?

D.T.B.: Oh yes, they kept reading *Gabriola* all the time. There were some very funny parts in it, but we heard that too many times, you know. . . .

Was he good at reading his own work?

D.T.B.: Yes, he was.

Did he dramatise it? Did he speak in different voices and so forth?

D.T.B.: No, Margerie was better at that than Malcolm.

H.B.: At the same time, though, Malcolm was very good at seizing attention; he would make good pregnant pauses and look up and grin and then gesture and then come back to the punchline. He was good at that; he was a real ham that way. He didn't read particularly well, but he – what shall I say – he enlivened the thing extremely well. He might have been an actor, he could have been an actor maybe, I don't know. He didn't have much flexibility, but still, he had a good sense of timing in that respect. Maybe that's because of the music, who knows?

Do you think he really would have preferred to have been known as a poet rather than as a novelist? Did you get that sense that he had a feel for language when he read his work?

H.B.: Yes, not only when he read his work, but just ordinarily when he was speaking, no matter how drunk he was. One thing that strikes me about . . . the prose he wrote is the way he spoke. He thought and spoke in parentheses and between dashes, and he would remove himself from what he was saying and get such a complicated structure, and then he'd come down to the point he'd started with. And, you know, so many times when I read his work I think, 'Oh God! That is Malcolm! That is Malcolm speaking.'

Was he happy here in British Columbia?

H.B.: He hated anywhere but Dollarton; that's the only place in the world where he felt at ease, because he felt that he was striding like a colossus between the great wild ocean and civilised land. He was there, he was living in both worlds, the hell and heaven. I mean he could literally see 'HELL' written across the inlet. It shone out in red lights – 'HELL'. It was the SHELL sign – the big 'S' had gone out, and there it was, this huge refinery, 'HELL', and it looked like hell too. But he saw himself, I think, as a kind of equaliser between these two great worlds and he understood them both in a sense. He understood the world of hell; he lived in it most of the time. He lived physically in the heaven of Dollarton and spiritually in hell, so he was at peace there, stabilised. But anywhere else he was miserable.

Somewhere he wrote about a great trail of bottles that he'd left behind him in his life. Even when he was going through a relatively sober period, alcohol must have been an ever-present fact in that cabin. Were you aware of that, too?

D.T.B.: Oh yes, there was always alcohol, certainly.

H.B.: Somehow they would always be able to produce – one or other would be able to produce – a bottle which they'd hidden from the other person. It would be down amongst the empty bottles, for example, or it would be in the brush up near the out-house, or it would be somewhere, but they could always drag out a bottle if there was somebody that they wanted to give a drink to. They were forever sniping at each other, keeping the bottle from Margerie or Malcolm, but there was a time when it would become desperate – they would have to produce one for themselves, so they would go out into the darkness and come in holding up a bottle of light, as it were.

There's some suggestion in some of the things he wrote that he saw alcohol as some source of inspiration.

D.T.B.: I think that was an excuse. I think that Malcolm would just say that it was, but I don't believe that, I don't. He was very inclined to excuse himself and use that, but I don't think he ever really felt . . . well, I don't know, I just don't think that that's so.

Have you got any ideas about why he drank?

D.T.B.: No, I haven't. He was just so afraid of things. He just couldn't have managed anywhere alone. I don't think I've ever met anybody that liked Margerie, but he couldn't have got along without her. That book never would have been published without Margerie.

Did he love her, do you think?

D.T.B.: No. I don't think there's any doubt about that.

H.B.: There's no doubt about it. Any sort of overt sign of affection that one would see would be from Margerie to Malcolm, but it would be for public consumption. She would put her arms around him occasionally and hug him and kiss him, but it wasn't any genuine feeling of warmth, I don't think. Not to be unfair to Margerie, but she was given to acting . . . she was acting for Malcolm. She kept Malcolm believing (a) that she was totally confident in his ability, (b) that she loved him and (c) that he was the greatest writer who ever lived. She did that, and I mean that was acting, because that wasn't true at the time. She may have believed it, but it hadn't been proven, and yet she did that, she looked after him, she prepared meals, she made him eat. She couldn't stop him drinking. She drank herself – to protect herself from the misery, perhaps. But she did look after him very well indeed, I think.

The Disappointed Editor
Albert Erskine

Albert Erskine (dates unknown) was Lowry's New York editor, first with Reynal and Hitchcock and later with Random House. In 1947 he was responsible for the promotion and publication of *Under the Volcano*, and met the Lowrys when they arrived in New York by Greyhound bus on the very morning of the book's publication, 19 February. Unlike Margerie and the biographer Douglas

Day, Erskine did not think that the success of the book upset and dismayed Lowry so very much. Erskine felt Reynal and Hitchcock were not sufficiently enthusiastic about *The Volcano* and took Lowry with him when he moved to Random House. Then in April 1952 he gave their new author a three-year contract, with an advance to be paid as a monthly allowance. Lowry sent his novel *October Ferry to Gabriola* to Erskine in sections, but the editor found it tedious and tried to keep the manuscript back from his senior editor, Robert Haas. Finally Erskine had to pass the material over, and as a result Lowry's contract was terminated on 6 January 1954. The writer took the news badly, and some commentators date his final downward slide from this disastrous turn in his fortunes. He sent a bitter letter to Erskine accusing him of betrayal, but later wrote to apologise and repair their friendship.

This is an edited version of an interview given for the National Film Board of Canada's 1976 documentary feature, *Volcano*.

Could you tell us about your first contact with Lowry and The Volcano, *how it came about and your reaction to it?*
Well, it came, as you know, to Reynal and Hitchcock after having made quite a round of publishers, and the first reader and assistant editor said he thought we ought to have more readings of it. So I read it, and Curtis Hitchcock read it, and we immediately decided to do it. And all of my contacts with Malcolm were by mail for quite a long time until the actual publication date, which was February 1947.
Your immediate reaction was to go ahead?
Yes. We had considerable correspondence about details and trying to get the Spanish corrected. I remember it was quite a thing, because we sent it to a teacher of Spanish at New York University to correct the Spanish and he came back with the news that I would have to find out what Malcolm thought this meant, so that he could put it into Spanish, because he couldn't even tell from what was on the page. . . . For the promotion we did an edition of about a hundred paper-bound copies which we printed from type before we made the plates. I wanted to get these into the hands of people who might ask *The New York Times* and other journals for the privilege of reviewing it, and to get some good quotes to put on the back of the jacket.

We were very successful in doing that, and I think it launched the book in a way that would not have been possible otherwise.
Were you surprised at the reviews?
No, I knew about them ahead of time.

Your first meeting, then, would be in February 1947 when Malcolm showed up in New York?
If I remember, it was 17 February that we published the book, but I'm not sure of that now.[2] I went to meet them at the Greyhound Station and then took them to their hotel. He went immediately to the bar.

Did you meet what you expected to meet, or was it a surprise?
It was a surprise.

Could you describe that meeting to us?
It was a cold and ugly day and everything seemed to be a little bit off-key to me for some reason. I don't know if he'd been drinking all day or not; I never really had a conversation with him under complete sobriety. It made me drink more than I normally do, too, just trying to keep up. . . . They were here for about ten days or two weeks, and he was supposed to be coming into the office to see Reynal but he didn't show up. That is the story that has been told over and over again, about Margerie and me looking for him in bars and, having exhausted Third Avenue, finally finding him in one on Lexington, and he walking in while we were there and saying, 'I knew you'd be here.'

Were you aware of his drinking before you met him?
I assumed from his book that he had had some experience, but I thought that maybe he'd stopped. The book seems to disapprove of it.

I get the impression from Margerie and others that he just couldn't cope with massive success or the crowd that he had to deal with. Do you feel that?
I don't. Doug Day implies that, too, I think, but I don't know if that's true or not. I think he was amazed by the degree of success, but I can't believe that he was dismayed by it. Jimmy Stern gave him a big party one night and Frank Taylor had a party one night, and I would help take him home afterwards.

Did he behave normally?
Pretty much so until he had too many drinks. We had to carry him home from Jimmy Stern's, as I recall.

Did you find that you liked him?
I liked him more through the mail than I did face to face, I think. I just didn't know how to cope with him and, when we met briefly the following year in Paris, I got along with him better than I expected. In fact I looked forward to that. We were supposed to meet in Rome, but our letters got crossed up. He used some of

2 It was 19 February, according to Douglas Day.

them in his story 'Elephant and Colosseum', I think. But it was fated, you see, that everything would go wrong.

Later the letter-writing to you was very profuse; you got an awful lot of letters. Is there something ominous when an editor, dealing with a writer, all of a sudden gets lots and lots of letters but not too many books?

No, the letters came mainly while we were preparing the book for publication. But then I got a lot more letters after I moved into Random House, because we were trying to get him out of his contract with Reynal and Hitchcock, and it turned out they were not too reluctant after reading some of the short stories.

But eventually there seemed to be a great number of his letters to you – innumerable excuses for non-delivery of manuscripts – but we don't have too many of your replies.

I have never been a very long letter writer. I would probably say, 'Don't worry about it, Malcolm. Just do it at your own pace.' Something like that.

But eventually this must have become a source of some exasperation to you, the continual non-delivery and the excuses.

Not too much. At the time I was really worried that he was not going to get that allowance from Random House and, of course, after that stopped, I had no hold on him for the delivery of anything else.

You finally cut off his contract in January 1954.

Oh, is that when it was?

This was after receiving, I think, 150–200 pages of October Ferry to Gabriola.

I think we'd given $3600 in advance, payable $100 a month over three years, but that it could be cut off if the book didn't seem to be going well. Well, I had received several instalments and I knew that as soon as Bob Haas read any of this *October Ferry* that the money would be cut off. So I didn't tell him I had it until he kept asking, 'What about Lowry?' It got to be every week he would ask me, so finally I came in one day with all that I had accumulated and said, 'Here's what we have now.' And the reaction was what I had feared. Of course, I wasn't too pleased with it myself. I found it just about as tedious as anything I'd ever read, and, coming after the other book, I couldn't understand it.

I had the feeling it had been written by somebody else. Why do you think it was as bad as it was?

I think he was going to pieces really. . . .

Did you feel hurt when he wrote to you giving the impression that you had deserted him, when in fact you had backed him to the hilt as far as you could?

I think I was more angry than hurt, but only briefly. And he wrote me a following letter – I don't remember how much later on – more or less apologising for the attitude he'd taken. And then any other correspondence was as friendly as it had been. It was a sort of loss of face for him at that stage, I think. He felt insulted by this breaking of the contract.

Did you get more letters from him than from your other writers?
Sometimes they were pretty difficult to read. I don't know whether you saw the transcription of a penny postcard that my secretary, using a reading glass, typed up? It was one and a half pages of type-written copy – all on the side of a postcard. Mostly about birds.

When was the last time you saw him?
I think it was during the last visit to New York[3] when Markson had a party that Conrad Aiken walked out of. They never came back to this country after that, I'm sure. But, during that time, Markson and Margerie conspired with me. They felt that I ought to have one conversation with Malcolm early in the morning, before he'd had anything to drink, so that he would be coherent. They told me about this plan . . . and I was coming up at nine in the morning. Then, just in order that he would not have had a drink, all of the liquor had been removed and put in a neighbouring apartment. And when I arrived he was high as a kite. They had forgotten about a new 8-oz bottle of shaving lotion that he had left in the bathroom and that had gone right down the drain. So we never had our conversation.

Do you remember him as a sorrowful figure or do you remember him as a guy who created a work of genius?
Both. Even towards the end he could be both amusing and highly irritating at the same time. I remember when I went to see them off on the ship – they had to stay on that freighter all day, they didn't know when it was leaving. I don't think we went over in the cab together, but I went over in the afternoon. Malcolm was in a pair of slacks with no shirt on and we walked out on deck where dockmen were loading cargo. And his old experiences of seamen came out, and he started saying things in a vocabulary and style that these men were not very appreciative of, and I saw the expression on their faces and thought, 'He's going to be lucky if he makes it to the other side if he keeps this up.' It was amusing and pitiful at the same time. He was being quite funny, but they were not very appreciative, and he didn't seem to be aware of that.

3 In September 1954.

8 The Final Years, 1954–7

In June 1955 the Lowrys arrived in London. Malcolm was now drinking constantly and had become so dependent on Margerie that he was even incapable, it seems, of lighting a cigarette. They lived for a time in flats in Earls Court and then in Richmond, where they were eventually evicted for causing drunken disturbances. Margerie, who had not been a heavy drinker when she met Malcolm, was by this time close to being an alcoholic herself. She was due to go into hospital for a gall bladder operation, and Lowry planned to move into John Davenport's flat in Chelsea. However, on 12 September he was admitted to the Brook General Hospital in Woolwich, and Margerie followed him in for her operation shortly afterwards. She later claimed that a doctor at the Brook suggested that Lowry have a brain operation which would render him docile, and that he had meekly agreed to it. Despite his poor condition, however, he was able to write coherent and witty letters to his friends in North America, and by the end of October seemed to have improved. Margerie, now recovered, was annoyed to find that he had not received psychiatric treatment, although he had been kept well away from the drink. Then one day the patient took off with a friend to a pub and was promptly discharged.

The Lowrys moved to a hotel in the Cromwell Road, and the heavy drinking began again. An old friend, Ralph Case, recommended a consultant psychiatrist, Sir Paul Mallinson, and through him Lowry was admitted to the Atkinson Morley Hospital in Wimbledon on 28 November. He arrived drunk, as Dr Michael Raymond, then the senior registrar at the hospital, recalls. John Davenport, who had brought him along with Margerie, had spent the afternoon with him in a local pub, and he was settled in with some difficulty.

Dr Raymond found him not only alcoholic but also so dependent on Margerie that he could not even tie his own shoelaces. Although Lowry was initially uncommunicative, the doctor soon found it impossible to stop him talking. He seemed to enjoy being the centre of attention and took the opportunity to trot out all the tall stories he had invented about his childhood. He also gave the doctor his version of the Paul Fitte suicide as well as confessing to some less well-publicised sexual fantasies. Of course, this could have been him living out the scenario he had spent a lifetime writing for himself – an oddly Freudian one in many ways – simply for the benefit of the psychiatrist. Certainly it makes dramatic reading, with expressions of terror and self-loathing as well as of hatred of Margerie.

He was subjected to aversion therapy and, not surprisingly perhaps, ceased to romanticise alcohol as he had done to begin with. Interestingly, Lowry's complaint about being constipated as a child is borne out by the doctor's findings. This could also explain the old obsession with bodily hygiene, which Hugh Sykes Davies had observed in the early thirties and which now resurfaced. The doctor observed Lowry's tendency to let his imagination flow freely – something Aiken had thought important for a writer to cultivate – and to appear to be operating on several different levels at once, reminiscent of his narrative technique in *Under the Volcano*. As well as aversion therapy, Lowry had been given drugs and electro-shock treatment before being released on 7 February 1956.

Margerie had found a cottage in the secluded village of Ripe in Sussex, and the couple settled there for a comparatively sober and productive sixteen months. Lowry's output of short stories, poems and letters was as prolific as it had ever been, broken only by one drunken spree on a visit to London and a short spell of further treatment under Dr Raymond. The Burts, over from Canada, arrived for a visit. He learned that the pier at the Dollarton shack had been swept away by a storm, and he wrote movingly in a letter about the sense of the lost paradise which the news had evoked. At the Atkinson Morley he expressed great resentment against Margerie for treating him like the child she had always wanted and for meddling with his writing. Margerie herself had a breakdown and spent several days under sedation in a London hospital.

In March 1957 they went to the Lake District, a landscape reminiscent of Dollarton, where Lowry swam and indulged his passion for bird-watching, something he had long expressed in both his poetry and his prose. However, photographs taken at the time show him looking withdrawn, exhausted and resigned.

Back at Ripe on the night of 26 June, the Lowrys returned from a local pub with a bottle of gin which Malcolm half consumed. In the bedroom there was a struggle during which it was smashed. Lowry threatened to attack Margerie, who fled next door and spent that night with their landlady, Mrs Mason. The following morning she returned to find him dead at the foot of the bed, a half-eaten meal scattered across the floor. That was the story which Margerie told at the inquest, and that was the story which was accepted. The coroner's verdict was 'Death by misadventure' and no precise cause of death was determined. The death certificate mentions consumption of large quantities of alcohol, barbiturate poisoning and the inhalation of stomach contents. He was buried in the churchyard at Ripe on 5 July 1957 with a small number of friends present: brother Stuart, Ralph Case, John Davenport, Harvey and Dorothy Burt and Mrs Mason. He had died a month short of his forty-eighth birthday; none of his work was in print in his own language.

Margerie spent the next twenty-two years working to establish her husband's reputation. She managed to have published *Hear Us O Lord from Heaven Thy Dwelling Place* (1961) and his *Selected Poems* (1962), and herself helped edit *Lunar Caustic* (1963), his *Selected Letters* (1965), *Dark as the Grave Wherein my Friend is Laid* (1968) and *October Ferry to Gabriola* (1970). *Malcolm Lowry: Psalms and Songs*, which includes some previously unpublished stories, appeared in America in 1975. Still to be published are Lowry's collected poems, *The Lighthouse Invites the Storm*, the film script of *Tender is the Night* and a variety of stories and letters. In 1983 *Under the Volcano* was filmed in Mexico by John Huston, with Albert Finney as the Consul. Lowry himself had hoped to write the screenplay of his great book, but, although the film rights were taken up before his death, no production was ever launched. It took the abortive efforts of over a hundred writers and a galaxy of talented directors before the film was finally made. Tragically, Margerie suffered a stroke in November 1979, and, though taken to see the film when it appeared, was unable to communicate her reactions to it.

Aversion Therapy
Dr Michael Raymond

Dr Michael Raymond (b. 1922) was first assistant to Sir Paul Mallinson, consultant psychiatrist at the Atkinson Morley Hospital, Wimbledon, to which Lowry was first admitted on 25 November 1955. At their first meeting Dr Raymond found his new patient drunk and 'thoroughly objectionable'. Later, during analysis, he found him very demanding, and reluctant to let him go even after more than five hours. Lowry paraded all his old stories about childhood illness and abuse at the hands of nursemaids and about his father being repressive. He spoke frankly about his attitudes to sex and to alcohol. He was subjected to aversion therapy and on one occasion went 'absent without leave' in the company of another alcoholic patient, returning drunk and causing a disturbance. He was released in February 1956 and shortly afterwards went to live at Ripe. After five months he was readmitted on 30 June 1956, and then discharged on 11 August.

This is an edited extract from an interview given for the National Film Board of Canada's 1976 documentary feature, *Volcano*.

When you first met Malcolm Lowry, what sort of person was he at that first encounter? Was he an easy patient?
Well, of course, he was drunk when I first met him and thoroughly objectionable, without any sort of communication at all. One would have had to give him some sort of physical examination as well as try to make an assessment of his mental state, but this was just impossible. He just said, 'Yeah, that's right,' to everything I asked him, and nodded and looked rather as though he was sharing a secret which he didn't intend to divulge. He was difficult, but then, when we put him to bed, I didn't find any problem at all. The only problem was that he was so demanding. I mean, there was one occasion on which one of our interviews went on I think from half past one until seven o'clock in the evening. I was absolutely flaked out, and then, when I broke it off, he said, 'Well you know, this is nothing short of spiritual coitus interruptus.' He could never have enough attention. That was a difficulty, certainly. Mark you, most of the interviews weren't as long as that, but that was one I shall remember for the rest of my days.
What was wrong with him?
It is always difficult to pin a label to people; to pin a label to Lowry I think would be rather absurd. He was, of course, an alcoholic, and he was subject to recurring bouts of depression. But, by the time I saw him, he had become, as we should say nowadays, institutionalised. Now that may surprise you. It's the sort of thing, as you know, which you see in patients who have been for too long in an institution, such as a psychiatric hospital, and when you come to rehabilitate them you are up against the problems of absolute dependence. Well, then we try treating in the community, letting them learn to stand on their own feet. But some people can become institutionalised in the community . . . in the

family. Now this is what had happened to Lowry; he had become institutionalised. He was incapable of doing up his shoe-laces, he was incapable of opening his mail, he was incapable of making a telephone call, he was incapable of deciding when to have a bath or when to change his clothes. He was utterly dependent upon Margerie, his wife, so that this was another facet that one had to deal with.

Then there was the extraordinary ruminative process, the almost obsessive rumination of his thinking which, coupled with depressive retardation, made him at times almost inarticulate. His speech was slow, hesitant, halting. It took him a long time to say things and he told me that in the same way it took him a very long time to write anything because it had to be revised and polished, subjected to further revision – and in fact writing for him was a travail.

And then, of course, he was haunted, you know, by a sense of guilt and sin, much of which one could and did trace back to earlier instances of his life. But predominantly he was a depressive. Now whether he was a *manic* depressive is a little difficult to be sure about. I never obtained a clear history of wild manic swings, but his lifelong friend, John Davenport, told me that since his Cambridge days he had been the subject of periods of black depression and, if I remember his words right, periods of 'exuberant satiability'. Well, he may have had this manic depressive temperament. Certainly there was evidence of recurrent depression, but, as far as I was concerned, no clear evidence of manic swings.

What was the sense of sin and guilt due to?
Well, first of all, when he was a boy he had a period of four years when it was thought he might go blind ... this was the story I heard. He had, as I understood it, some sort of corneal ulcerations. Well now, during this period he was looked after by a nurse or a nanny who was very repressive and to whom he attributed his very strong super-ego. He was obsessed with his super-ego.

Then his father was a very strict, puritanical, repressive individual. There was a link, as he told me of it, between the nanny who had always smacked him when he played with his penis, which he did quite frequently, and the subsequent threats of blindness if he masturbated, which he did very frequently, too. He had a great sense of guilt about this because he was a highly sexed individual, there was little doubt about that.

Then later on, when he went up to Cambridge, a fellow undergraduate had tried to have a homosexual relationship with him.

Lowry thought this was extremely funny. He thought it was a great joke, and when the young man said that if this were not possible he would commit suicide, Malcolm Lowry told me that he said, 'That's a good idea. Why don't you go ahead? You will probably be much happier and better off there than here.' The next morning the young man was found to have committed suicide. Now this haunted him for the rest of his days, and at one time, you know, he became a spiritualist. Eventually he discarded most of that, but he had a very strong belief that it did not matter what one did with one's body and it didn't matter much what one did with one's mind. But there was in one a spirit which one should not tamper with. He saw suicide as releasing this spirit, and this is why his suicide surprised me. He was, in a way, religiously opposed to it. He often expressed these views to me.

Was he in fact a homosexual?

This is a routine question. His categoric reply was 'No! Never!' And indeed his fantasies were entirely heterosexual. Now . . . I had an opportunity to give him methedrine, during which time, I have little doubt, he spoke the truth. A lot of the time he didn't speak the truth, and a lot of what he said was pure fantasy, and he had a tremendous number of fantasies about the women in his life. . . . Eventually he said, 'Well this, of course, is all fantasy, and I have always enjoyed giving the impression that I was a Don Juan.' But this is entirely traceable to his inferiority about his penis. Now when he first went to school, his life was made absolute hell, particularly on bath night, because he was held to be such a curiosity with this very, very small penis; and it led to his experimenting, not very successfully, with prostitutes, even during his schooldays. But he was always geared towards heterosexual activity and not homosexual activity. And he was, he said, beautifully seduced by a frustrated lady in a cottage on [Dartmoor][1] and after that he didn't look back for a while, though of course his sexual relations with his first wife were not good for one reason or another. His sexual relations with his second wife were, from her account and his, entirely satisfactory until the last two or three years before he came to England for treatment. So, in summary, I would state categorically that, no matter what view you take of homosexuals and latent homosexuality and the underlying pathology of alcoholism always being homosexual, Malcolm Lowry was not homosexual.

---

1 This is not clear from the transcript, which reads, '. . . in a cottage on D——'. Dartmoor seems likely, as Lowry did spend part of Easter 1932 in Devon, However, the episode sounds like another Lowry 'story'.

Is alcoholism a sort of weakness that comes from certain types of inner problem?

Well, of course, there are so many underlying pathologies, but one of the common ones is depression. Quite often you get a periodic drinking pattern in manic depressives, but certain people who suffer from depression treat it with alcohol, and not very successfully.

Didn't you give him aversion therapy?

Yes.

Would you explain exactly what that is and how a psychiatrist can use it?

Well, in those days it was based entirely on Pavlovian principles with strict regard as to timing. One gave an injection of apomorphine, which one knew perfectly well would produce nausea and vomiting in about ten minutes, although it varied with the individual. Having done that, and having determined what was the nausea time, one then gave alcohol just before the nausea ensued. And, without any doubt at all, it is relatively easy to produce a conditioned aversion to alcohol. Now I never took the view that this was all that was required and that this was likely to be durable for all times. My view then – and I eventually modified my technique very considerably – was that if you could establish, even temporarily, this conditioned aversion, it would give a chance for re-evaluation of alcohol and the alcohol problem. And in fact we did achieve a change in Malcolm Lowry's attitude to alcohol. When he embarked on this treatment he saw alcohol as a very romantic thing, but he subsequently changed his attitude, though he was always frank and said, 'I cannot believe that there is no middle road of moderation for me.' He said furthermore that he could envisage giving up the hard liquor, but he would never be able to give up beer. This is an interesting point, as far as his lying is concerned, because alcoholics will always rationalise. Some of their rationalisation for drinking is really quite fantastic.

But he said, 'I could never give up beer because I would be so terribly constipated.' And he was serious about this. So I discussed it with him and he told me that, during the period when he was finishing *The Volcano*, he'd had two years off alcohol, and he said this constipation had been a terrible problem. He said, 'There is something wrong with my bowels, you know.'

And I said, 'All right, if that is so we will investigate it,' and I had a special barium meal study made of his bowels. And he was absolutely right. He had the most enormous megacolon, no doubt about it, and this had existed probably since his childhood, I think. But I am not suggesting for one moment that this was the cause of his alcoholism.

Anyway, he needed to drink large quantities of fluid, and I was interested, after he went down to Ripe, that he had periods when he was not drinking.[2] I visited him, and he would be writing at his desk, and there, lined up, were four or five glass jugs full of orange squash or lemonade, and a couple of tumblers, and he would drink continually and say, 'Well, I do need a lot of fluid.' So this was an example of where he was in fact telling the truth, when he spoke of his constipation.

There were other odd sidelines to him. He had a horror of stinking, and when he was in hospital his bedside locker would be packed with deodorants. Now during this aversion treatment, which was only a fairly minor part of his treatment at Atkinson Morley's, we used, in those days, to withhold fluid. The only fluid that the patients had was alcohol. During a lull at the end of one of these sessions he was taking some milk. And now he was very thirsty. But he first used the milk to scrub his fingernails and wash his hands, and then he drank. Well now, this was perhaps bravado, but none the less it was very striking.

It has been reported that the aversion therapy lasted a good deal longer than usual: two sessions, one for ten days and one for twenty-one days. Was that correct?

Well, one session was for ten days, but there was a mid-session break of two days, so that it wasn't a continuous ten days. Certainly he didn't last longer than the majority of patients. Rather the reverse, in fact, because during the second session, and in the light of what he had told me after being given methedrine, it was very clear that this man was never going to stop drinking beer at any rate – and probably wine. It appeared much more important to rehabilitate him, to make him more independent, and most of his second period of hospitalisation was devoted just to that.

Didn't he go absent without leave at one point?

Oh, frequently, yes. But not for very long periods. He formed an alliance with another patient who was also an alcoholic, and they used to disappear off across the Common[3] and when they returned they made a nuisance of themselves – so much so, in fact, that after his second admission he was not to have been readmitted to the Atkinson Morley. What I did, however, was to make arrangements, if necessary, to admit him somewhere else down in Surrey. But certainly they had had quite enough of him at Atkinson Morley.

2 I.e. alcohol.
3 Wimbledon Common.

Was the question of a leucotomy ever seriously considered as a treatment for Lowry?

Now that's an interesting point, because my memory is that we had never considered it at Atkinson Morley Hospital. I was working there as a first assistant and I had responsibility for the day-to-day treatment of Lowry. Originally he had been referred to one of the consultants, but it wasn't in order to consider leucotomy. I looked at my notes about this, and what happened was that Lowry had been in Sicily with Margerie before they came over here, and I think it was John Davenport who introduced him to a surgeon who had been at Cambridge with them. This man was a neurosurgeon and he admitted both Margerie and Malcolm to his hospital for a while. Then apparently he made the suggestion that Margerie should go off to the country and Malcolm should stay with friends and write. But she resisted this very strongly, and so he washed his hands of the whole matter.

Well now, after Malcolm had been admitted to Atkinson Morley, I had a telephone call from this surgeon who told me that he felt I should know that Margerie was very jealous of Malcolm because his book had been acclaimed and hers had not made the grade, and that she had suggested leucotomy effectively to stop him writing again. Now this was actually said, and I recorded it at the time. Next day I put this to Margerie Lowry and she was absolutely horrified, and she said that in fact she had been entirely opposed, that the suggestion had been made by the surgeon and she had said that no stone must be left unturned to have him treated in some other way. Two days later I had a letter from Mrs Templeton, who was a friend they had known in British Columbia. She wrote and said, 'Well, I dislike Margerie Lowry intensely and she is an awful liar, but one thing you should know and that is in the matter of Malcolm's health she has been quite wonderful, and certainly she did not want him leucotomised.' Two days later, John Davenport came to see me and told me exactly the same thing, so that, whoever suggested the leucotomy, it was certainly not Margerie Lowry and certainly it was no one at Atkinson Morley Hospital. It wasn't ever considered there.

It has become another Lowry myth.

Yes.

When was the last time you saw him? Was it close to his death?

I haven't an accurate note of this, but I think it would be about May 1957. He died, I think, in July.

Had he shown much change in his condition? Was he much different?

Well, yes. After his first stay in hospital I saw him as an outpatient, and Margerie said, 'Well, he is quite changed. He is so much more considerate. He's grateful for what's been done for him, etc.' And this attitude rather led to his relapse, I think, because I saw him on 31 May of that year, which was, I think, 1956, and he had to be readmitted within a month. He told me that what had happened was that Peter Churchill[4] had visited them, and Churchill and Margerie had sat there drinking and saying to Malcolm, 'You know, it's absolutely splendid that you're off this stuff. You are a much better chap; you're a much better personality; you're much more considerate.' And he just couldn't take it, so he went right back and joined in the drinking. But he had changed in so far as, after I visited him at Ripe, I had letters from him and he would say things like, 'I actually went to buy some postage stamps. I actually went to take some books from the library.' Formerly he had been unable to get out, let alone make any sort of transaction, so that he had changed in that respect. I think that his attitude to alcohol had changed; he no longer saw it as a romantic and desirable medium of escape. He saw it as thoroughly undesirable, but something over which he had no power. Yes, there had been changes.

Had you read Under the Volcano?

No, I hadn't.

When you read it, did you recognise it as Lowry's work?

Oh, not really, no. I think not, except that he was capable, you know, of two or three conversations at a time, particularly if he had had alcohol. And to begin with one thought that he was talking complete gibberish, until one realised that he could be on two or three entirely different planes. He would talk about the most mundane matters and then he would talk about spiritual matters; he would talk about writing and his friends in his literary world. I suppose one could describe it as a flight of ideas or a circumlocution. But, if you were prepared to wait long enough, all three skeins would come out and become intelligible. To that extent I think one recognised some of the passages in *The Volcano*.

'He Was There in a Heap'
Edwina Mason

Mrs Edwina Mason (dates unknown) was the owner of the White Cottage at Ripe in Sussex and the Lowrys' landlady for the last sixteen months of Malcolm's life. She obviously liked both her

---

4 See footnote 1, page 173.

tenants and admired Lowry, whom she regarded as a gentleman and a scholar, even if he did have the occasional attack of alcoholic dementia. It was to her other house, next door to the White Cottage, that Margerie ran on the night of 26 June 1957, claiming that Malcolm had attacked her with a broken gin bottle. Next morning the two women found him dead. Mrs Mason, a pious woman, was extremely relieved when the coroner's verdict proved to be 'Death by misadventure', because it meant that Lowry could be buried in consecrated ground.

The following are two versions she gave of the death. The first is taken from the 1967 BBC TV documentary, *Rough Passage*, and the second from the BBC radio programme of the same year, *A Portrait of Malcolm Lowry*.

Malcolm used to start working towards the evening and work late into the night, and, as Margerie was a light sleeper, over and over again she slept in the bedroom to the left. And he would get a meal at about two o'clock in the morning, and that was what happened that last night. She was not sleeping in the room with him and obviously he went down and prepared a meal. Next morning she came in and said, 'Malcolm's gone!'

And I said, 'Where?'

And she said, 'Oh, he's gone. He's dead!'

And then we both rushed up and obviously he had prepared a meal and gone upstairs again. In my opinion it was heart and nothing else. And he was there in a heap, in a huddle at the foot of the bed and a broken plate and broken meat spread all over the room and that's where we found him in the morning. . . . Beyond that I'm a bit hazy because I phoned the doctor straightaway and then the house seemed to have been full of people wanting to know this, that and the other – questions which I couldn't answer and she was in no state to answer.

They had words because presently Margerie came in to me and said, 'I'm frightened. Can I sleep here?' . . . We were pretty intimate when we did meet.

And I said, 'Yes.'

And in the morning she said, 'Well, I suppose I must go and get poor old Malcolm a cup of tea, but I've decided what I'm going to do. I'm going up to Liverpool to see if I can get powers of attorney to hold over him when he has these rare attacks.' So she went, and came dashing back in a few minutes. 'Oh, Winnie,' she said, 'he's gone.'

And I stupidly said, 'Where? Liverpool?'

And she said, 'No, he's dead.'

And after the inquest the Revd Talbot Baines, who was a great saint, came and said to me, 'It's all right. I can give him Christian burial.'

'Malcolm's Dead!'
Dr Ralph Case, Adrienne Case

Dr Ralph Case (b. 1908) had known Lowry in his student days and then in London during the early thirties when they played jazz together around the pubs in Fitzrovia. They met again when Malcolm returned to England in 1955, and Case was responsible for referring him to Sir Paul Mallinson at the Atkinson Morley Hospital. He visited the cottage at Ripe in Sussex, and on hearing the news of his old friend's death travelled down there to help Margerie.

Mrs Adrienne Case (b. 1930) met the Lowrys for the first time in London in 1955. She remembers clearly Margerie's reaction to Malcolm's death and her apparent anxiety to conceal the somewhat sordid nature of their last evening together.

This is an edited extract from an interview the Cases gave me on 12 August 1984.

Do you remember that meeting in 1955 when Malcolm came back to England?

R.C.: Yes, I do.

How was he?

R.C.: He was drinking rather a lot. I don't wish to imply that I remember him as being sozzled each time I met him. It wasn't true at all, but I did gather both from Margerie and one or two other friends that Margerie was rather worried about him, and in fact I think I was instrumental in getting him to see Sir Paul Mallinson, and I sent him along to see him in Harley Street and Mallinson got him into the Atkinson Morley, which was a hospital at which he was the leading psychiatrist and they had a few beds for alcoholics – not very many. And Mallinson said it might be a month or four or five weeks before they could get him in, and Malcolm said, 'Oh, good, that will give me time to enjoy myself before going in there.' He went in eventually.

Did you visit him there?

R.C.: Yes.

What sort of treatment was he getting?

R.C.: He got what they called aversion therapy and for a time he was improving, and then one night he and another patient 'scrammed' from the hospital. They left the hospital and they went to a local pub. I've forgotten how long they stayed but they came back eventually . . . he'd had a few drinks, as you can imagine. I think soon after that they had to discharge him from Atkinson Morley Hospital.

Wasn't there a doctor called Dr Raymond who looked after him there? I thought there was some suggestion that they might do a leucotomy on him.

R.C.: That's true.

How was it when you went to see him at Ripe? Did he seem as if he was improving?

R.C.: Yes, because I think that the first time I went to see him he was on the wagon. He had previously drunk to some extent at the pub near Ripe two or three miles away,[5] but then he was drinking in the local pub at Ripe and he started drinking alcohol-free cider, Cydrax, or something. At that time he was not drinking. . . .

Could you say a bit about Margerie, because this was the first time you'd met her, wasn't it? What did you make of Margerie?

R.C.: I liked Margerie. She was very fond of Malcolm, as indeed he was of her. There were times, of course, that his behaviour was not at all conducive to a happy relationship, but on the whole they were, I thought, rather suited and they loved each other, even though he upset her at times. . . .

Can you remember how you heard about Malcolm's death?

R.C.: Yes, Margerie rang me up. I'd been down to Ripe shortly before, and I remember her ringing, and I said, 'How's Malcolm?' and I remember her saying, 'Oh, Malcolm's dead.' That's the first I knew of it, and that was a day or so after this episode when he threw a whisky bottle or something at the wall, I think. It broke and then he picked it up, and Margerie was obviously terrified because a chap with a broken whisky bottle, you never know what will happen, so she cleared out of the house and went to the woman next door, Mrs Mason, and she wouldn't go back till the next morning and she found him dead, and that was the morning – I think it was either that day or next day – that she rang me up. Of course I hadn't heard about this and she said, 'Malcolm's dead.' . . . I went down to Ripe.

What did you find when you got there?

R.C.: I didn't find Malcolm, because he'd been removed already. I

5 At Chalvington.

found Margerie lying on her bed and weeping most of the time, and having an occasional drink, because *she* would sometimes drink a fair amount, you know. She was clearly very upset.

But then do you remember going to the funeral?

R.C.: Yes, I think I did go, but I can't remember the details of it.

What version did she give you of Malcolm's death when she came to see you?

A.C.: Oh, I think she told us on the telephone actually. . . . She wanted him to be buried in church, and so therefore she wanted to avoid anyone thinking he maybe had tried to commit suicide, because everyone knew he was drinking, so that was nothing new. But she did want to know what had happened, and I think up to a point she did blame herself because she hadn't returned. You know she went away to stay with the landlady and the landlady said, 'Oh don't worry dear, he'll be all right tomorrow. You can sleep here.' So she slept in the landlady's cottage. She didn't go back, you see, and the next day when she went back about nine o'clock Malcolm was dead, and she felt that maybe if she'd returned or hadn't gone that would not have happened.

But I don't think she blamed herself that much – I mean I don't think she had a guilt feeling about it. But obviously she was terribly upset and I think she felt that she was alone – you know, there was no longer anybody around and he had been so much part of her life that she suddenly found she was there and what was she going to do? Was she going back to America? And she was very, very anxious about Malcolm. You know, she said, 'Malcolm is one of the greatest writers that ever lived.' I remember her in my kitchen stating that with a gesture . . . and so I think she was very anxious to protect his memory. You know, she didn't want people to know about that sordid thing which happened just before he died.

The fight?

A.C.: Yes, the fight and the broken bottle and the drinking and so on . . . and that was not something she wanted people to know, or maybe even to remember herself. So she was terribly anxious that at the inquest none of that would come out, and I don't think much did, because after all there were no witnesses – you know, the landlady only knew that she'd come there, and she didn't really know much what happened before – maybe she didn't want to tell, either. . . . In such circumstances you don't go and blurt it all out in the coroner's court.[6]

---

6 A report of the inquest in the Brighton *Argus* seems to suggest that the story of the fight did, in fact, come out.

Isn't it extraordinary – the energy and the determination that Margerie had to promote him and get him established as the great writer she always claimed him to be?

A.C.: I think she made it her life's work, actually. She was absolutely committed, you know, to making him known and remembered and so on. . . . And I remember she said, 'There's a full trunk of writing.' I also remember Martin[7] saying, 'Yes, I know she's going to get a lot of things out – letters, novelettes and so on – and I hope to goodness she doesn't tamper with them and put in paragraphs which are missing and this kind of thing.' You know, sort of write some of the bits maybe Malcolm hadn't finished. I remember Martin saying, 'I hope she's not going to mix her writing with his,' because she had been a writer. . . . I remember once after he was dead she said, 'Well, after all, thanks to me he wrote *The Volcano*, he finished *The Volcano*,' so I don't know whether she put in bits. But what is certain, I think, is that she pressed on until he finished all his revision, all his rewriting and so on and published it, and I think she considered that it was thanks to her that *Volcano* was published, and it's probably true.

The Visitors from Canada
Harvey Burt, Dorothy Templeton Burt

Harvey and Dorothy Burt had been the Lowrys' neighbours at Dollarton. When Malcolm and Margerie went to Italy in 1954 Dorothy visited them. She was struck by Lowry's wretched condition, yet fascinated and horrified by the stories he told and the obsessions which haunted him. Later, in England, the Burts stayed at the Lowrys' cottage at Ripe, and it was here that Harvey told Malcolm that the pier he had built at his shack in Dollarton, and to which he seemed to attach a highly personal significance, had been destroyed. Douglas Day claimed that this had been one of the final blows which shattered Lowry's fragile stability, a claim hotly contested by Burt. Lowry did not die until almost a year later. The couple were also among the very few to attend Lowry's modest funeral on 5 July 1957.

The following is a further extract from the interview given to me in August 1982.

---

7 Martin Case, a friend of Lowry's from his Cambridge days and brother of Ralph.

When they left Canada in 1954 they went originally to Italy, and Dorothy, I believe you visited them in Sicily, didn't you?

D.T.B.: I stayed with them for a while, and it was pretty grim. He wouldn't get up till noon, and he *couldn't* get up until he had a drink, and then we'd sit for two hours watching him try to get through a piece of bread and a piece of cheese. It was just – oh, it was just agony. . . .

He never went out except when he went to the dentist. He was very impressed with the dentist because the lights went out, and he thought he was simply wonderful because he was able to fill his teeth in the dark. So he decided he was a very clever dentist – which certainly seemed very odd, to think that that's what would make him a good dentist. But then he told a story about a girl eating a live bird with the feathers on, and he described this bird, he described her eating the bird and I believed every word of it. And he just saw it in his head somehow; it was the most fantastic thing. He went all through how she was chewing it, and how the feathers were falling out. The description was absolutely ghastly, and I believed every word of it. But he'd just made it up.

Was he telling this with his tongue in his cheek, or did he believe it?

D.T.B.: No, no, I think he believed it, because he didn't smile at all. He was terribly serious and he just stared at me. . . .

Was he hallucinating, do you think?

D.T.B.: I think he might have been . . . I don't know.

After Sicily, he went to London with Margerie, didn't he, for a while?

D.T.B.: Yes, they both went into a sanatorium. He went in to get over his drunkenness, and then he went to this psychiatrist, Dr Michael Raymond.

Dorothy, you visited them at Ripe. What was the set-up there?

D.T.B.: Well, Malcolm wasn't doing very much writing. He would make an attempt now and again, but I wrote back to Harvey and said, 'I don't think he'll ever write again.' He had really gone downhill. He didn't go out very much. He'd go out for the odd walk, and always . . . he'd get something to drink when he was out. I don't remember him doing very much.

Wasn't he drinking Lucozade at that time?

D.T.B.: Yes, but he would go to the pub and get something as well as the Lucozade, and they seemed to be fighting quite a bit, but that wasn't particularly unusual. I don't remember having any real fun the way we had at the shack. He was, I think, more morose.

There seems to be some sense that once he left Dollarton he was no longer in the environment he loved, and do you think that moving away from here was in some ways a tragic break for him?

D.T.B.: Yes, I certainly do. I think he'd probably be alive if it weren't for that, because he was simply miserable once he got away; he didn't really seem to enjoy anything. He would sit and write, and then he'd get up, move around. He didn't seem to eat very much, he didn't seem to enjoy anything – I can't think of him enjoying anything. We must have had some good times, but I can't really remember having any there.

Was he mentally ill? Because at the end he did go to a psychiatrist, didn't he, and there was some suggestion that he might even have a leucotomy, I think, at one point?

D.T.B.: Well, that was Margerie's story – I don't know whether that was ever really contemplated. I mean I met two psychiatrists who looked after him, but I never heard anything about the leucotomy thing. . . .

Were you surprised when he died?

H.B.: It was an absolute shock – absolute shock, no indication. They had been in the Lake District just a couple of weeks before . . . and we had received cards and a letter. As a matter of fact I received a letter on the Wednesday morning, when I got home from school in Metz,[8] and I got a call from Dorothy the next day, a phone call that she'd received the wire from Margerie that Malcolm had died that night. So I received the letter at the same time that he had died – it was uncanny.

But then you went to England and there was an autopsy that had to be performed and a coroner's inquest. Did you think they came to the right decision about him?

H.B.: Well, it's difficult to know. I suppose that, whatever happened to him, it *was* misadventure and that he had died in his own vomit. But the fact is that we found it very difficult to believe that Malcolm, who was so incompetent when he was sober and worse when he was drunk, could open a bottle of sleeping pills, or two bottles of sleeping pills, and swallow them down. It defies belief that a man who couldn't take a cigarette out of a package, or could scarcely open the package, could have this kind of fine muscle control to open a couple of bottles of sleeping pills. But yes, I suppose the verdict was acceptable and it was misadventure.

You were at the inquest. There wasn't a very impressive attendance, was there?

H.B.: Margerie had said, 'Oh, you've got to come with me.[9] I don't want to go down there alone. There'll be people from all over the world.' She talked about *The New York Times*, and various other

8 A summer school he was attending in France.
9 To the inquest.

journals, but the only people there were, I think, two reporters from the *Eastbourne Review* or whatever the paper was. It wasn't covered at all. And she had the same apprehension about the funeral, but when it occurred there were about eight or nine people. There were Stuart Lowry and Win[10] and there was Davenport, and I can't remember if Jimmy Stern was there, but anyway there were only some eight people or so. It was a very small funeral indeed, and nobody from the press as far as I'm aware. It's just ironic that this great expectation should be so disappointed.

Is the fact that Lowry has subsequently come to be judged a great writer a surprise to you, or do you think that that was to be expected?

H.B.: Well, it came to me as a bit of a surprise, because I think he's been sold largely by his widow, who has done some unkind things in publishing material that Lowry didn't himself publish. That's not to detract from *Under the Volcano*, which, however, would have stood by itself. But he has been well advertised. There has been a Lowry industry; there is in fact a Lowry industry now, and it stems largely from Margerie's efforts to get Malcolm recognised. Perhaps that's not the right word – to get Malcolm 'famous', because it's selling the books that's important; that's what makes people famous, I suppose. But I don't know. I think we'll have to let history judge whether or not the stuff that was published after *The Volcano* merits the kind of credit that he still gets for his work.

'Such a Waste and Such a Loss'
Jan Gabrial

Jan Gabrial, Lowry's first wife, did not see him again after she began divorce proceedings in 1939. For a long time she knew nothing of his whereabouts, but frequently reflected on their young and stormy marriage together. In 1947, with the successful publication of *Under the Volcano*, not only did she learn that Malcolm was still alive and living in Canada, but she received confirmation that the man she had married in Paris in 1934 was, after all, the 'genius' she had first thought he was. She was particularly incensed by accounts of herself and of her relationship with Lowry which appeared in Douglas Day's *Malcolm Lowry: A Biography*, as well as those which had previously appeared in the writings of Conrad Aiken, notably in *Ushant*. Her last thoughts of Lowry stand as a fitting epitaph.

10 Edwina Mason.

This is a further extract from the interview conducted in 1975 by the Canadian film producer, Robert Duncan.

When Under the Volcano *came out and you read it, what did you think? Did you recognise Yvonne as yourself?*

I didn't really think that Yvonne was me. She was a composite. I didn't find it an offensive portrait. I thought it was rather an interesting quirk that she was killed by the stallion at the end. That seemed to have an interesting little bit of Freudian something or other in it. I didn't find it offensive, but it wasn't me. She was far more assured, probably a far more successful, far more emotionally self-sufficient woman than I was at that time. Had I read any of the Conrad Aiken things, which I really never cared to do because my relationships with him were always so inimical and there was such a sense of dislike on his part for me always, I probably would have found that Yvonne was a glowing portrait compared with what Conrad envisioned.

Did you recognise Malc as the Consul?

Yes, in a way. There was much of Malc in that – a great deal, especially the wit. . . . When he was sober or maybe just wondering, Malc had a strange mellowness and a richness flavoured with this very delightful humour which the Consul had. And then, of course, there's the doomed quality which was so absolutely a part of Malc.

Were there any other characters in the book which you particularly recognised?

No, I think he took bits and pieces from people that we had met, you know, but he wove them in his own way. And don't forget that, over the time that he wrote it and finally worked out the final draft, he had probably made such composites of things that it was hard to tell where imagination came in and where reality left off.

So Under the Volcano *was a big surprise to you, because that was the first time you realised he was still alive.*

The first time that I – well, of course I didn't know *where* he had been. Now I knew (a) that he was alive, (b) that he'd got the book out finally, (c) that he was married, and (d) that he was an overnight sensation.

And then what happened? He sort of disappeared again?

No, then I kept following very closely, because I knew he was writing and I was waiting to see what else would come out. Then I read three books that Margerie had written; I got them out of the library. I think they were thrillers. And there was a fourth, *Horse in the Sky*, which I couldn't finish. It's a bitchy remark, but I really couldn't. And I watched to see what else would come out from Malcolm. I think, if I remember, there was just an occasional short story or poem or something, and then, after we moved down here in '55, I heard very little more about him.

Where were you living before that?

In the Los Angeles area, near Beverly Hills, but not in it. Then I picked up *The New York Times Book Review* one day and read of his stuff. And then I read another article which said that he had died choking on his own vomit, which seemed to me so awful. . . . I tried to relate it to the Malcolm I had known and I remembered scenes like where, in Taxco at night, he would be drunk and lie down in the street with pigs rooting around, and I wondered whether it was something like that; I couldn't imagine. Now I know a little bit more about it. I realise that if you take a lot of alcohol and a lot of sleeping tablets and drugs, that this can happen to you. You do regurgitate and . . . if you're drunk enough, presumably choke on your own vomit. . . . But that seemed to me so awful. I couldn't get over it; I couldn't get the picture out of my mind for a long time. Of course I didn't know what had happened, and then I didn't know about the Douglas Day book. I got away. I let *The New York Times Book Review* slide and got away from the whole picture. . . . I had been meaning to get the Day book, but perhaps I had been consciously putting it off because I didn't want to read somebody else's interpretation of what had happened. Then a friend wrote and told me that she had heard something on *Bookbeat*[11] which had outraged her, because she said the picture of me was so unfair and wasn't at all like what I was. So I went out and bought the book, and I was hurt and angry that somebody would write the details of conversations and activities without ever trying to track down the person, and who had just made them up.

Malc's death, of course, is still a little bit confusing to most people.

Well, I know this. In the years that I was married to Malc we had quarrels, obviously. We were both highly strung; marriage was a new thing for both of us; neither one of us was used to that kind of restraint, and it was a question of feeling our way and neither one of us was very skilful about it. But we developed. I don't know how much in love we were at the time we were married. We were fascinated by each other when we married, but our relationship grew. There was a very deep love that developed between us. But everything was on a very intense scale. When things were going well, they went well intensely. We were together; we couldn't envisage

11 Probably an American radio or television programme.

not being together. It was in everything we did. We would write for a time; we'd go for walks in town; we would take trips to nearby villages; we made up songs in the street and sang them to each other. It was all very charming and very innocent, sort of like the early morning of one's life. And when we quarrelled, it was equally intense and very often alcohol-inspired, and we would shout at each other. It was not physical violence, but we would say anything that we could that would hurt the other person, except as far as the work was concerned. That was sacred. I would never have dreamed of attacking Malc's work and he never attacked mine. Anything else was fair game.

What sort of things did you fight about mostly?

Oh, nonsensical things. The spats would come up out of nothing. I can remember one idiotic occasion: we were walking through Chicago and I think I wanted to go to one museum and Malc wanted to go to another, or something like that, and all of a sudden everything flared up and we were shouting at each other. And I'm not proud of myself, but I remember that I kicked him in the ankle, which was not kind. His ankle swelled up for about four days. By the way, that's the only actual physical violence that I can remember on either part.

But when we had quarrels they didn't last very long. They might last a day or they might last overnight, but they generally didn't last. . . . When Malc came over from Europe to join me after our marriage, we went to Provincetown and we had a marvellous sexual week. I can't remember the name of the hotel, but it was in Martha's Vineyard, and this attempt was a particularly marvellous night for us, so we decided we would use 10 August as our watchword, and if we had a quarrel and we couldn't get it terminated one of us would say '10 August' and that would terminate it.

But what I'm getting at . . . is that during this time there were times (I found the letters later – well, at least one that Malc had written) when he was contemplating suicide. But he wrote the details of what he wanted. You know, 'You can have my books, and Jan is to have this and that and the other', and he was very explicit, and of course everything with Malc went down on paper, everything. You went into a restaurant with him – he would have four pages of notes before he was out of the restaurant. . . . His own experiences, his own actions fascinated him as much as anyone else's. So everything went down. So . . . there is no way that I can conceive of Malc committing suicide without there being . . . copious notes, letters, something to indicate why. He was not a man to slip away quietly into the night. There's no way. He was far too rumbustious and far too colourful, unless he had just been absolutely drained to a peapod, which I doubt.

But, as I say, when I first heard of the death and the choking, I was so saddened and so worried as to what had really happened and what could have happened and what was the story and what was the picture. I had a great sense of loss because really at that point the only great book he had come out with was *Under the Volcano*, and I thought he was capable of many others. He was very, very young, you know. Shaw once said, 'I think talent is a matter of longevity.' Forty-seven isn't very old, and here you have another forty-seven years to go to be as old as Shaw and to really produce, and it seemed to me such a waste and such a loss.

Bibliography

Lowry's Own Work

'Port Swettenham', *Experiment*, 3 (February 1930), pp. 22–6.

'Goya the Obscure', *The Venture*, 6 (June 1930), pp. 270–8.

'Punctum Indifferens Skibet Gaar Videre', *Experiment*, 7 (Spring 1931), pp. 62–75.

Ultramarine, Jonathan Cape (London 1933); rev. ed. Lippincott (Philadelphia 1962); Jonathan Cape (London 1963); Penguin (London 1974).

'On Board the West Hardaway', *Story* III, 15 (October 1933), pp. 12–22.

'In Le Havre', *Life and Letters* (July 1934), pp. 462–6.

'Hotel Room in Chartres', *Story* V, 26 (September 1934), pp. 53–8.

Under the Volcano, Reynal and Hitchcock (New York 1947); Jonathan Cape (London 1947); Vintage–Random House (New York 1958); Penguin (London 1962); Lippincott (Philadelphia 1965); Signet (New York 1965).

'Economic Conference 1934', *Arena*, 2 (Autumn 1949), pp. 49–57.

Hear Us O Lord from Heaven Thy Dwelling Place, Lippincott (Philadelphia 1961); Jonathan Cape (London 1962); Penguin (London 1969).

Letters between Malcolm Lowry and Jonathan Cape about 'Under the Volcano', Jonathan Cape (London 1962).

Selected Poems of Malcolm Lowry (ed. Earle Birney), City Lights (San Francisco 1962).

Lunar Caustic (ed. Earle Birney and Margerie Lowry), *Paris Review*, 29 (Winter/Spring 1963), pp. 15–72; Jonathan Cape (London 1968).

'Bulls of the Resurrection', *Prism International*, 5 (Summer 1965), pp. 5–11.

The Selected Letters of Malcolm Lowry (ed. Harvey Breit and Margerie Lowry), Lippincott (Philadelphia 1965); Jonathan Cape (London 1967).

Dark as the Grave Wherein my Friend is Laid, New American

Library (New York 1968); Jonathan Cape (London 1969); Penguin (London 1972).
October Ferry to Gabriola, World (New York 1970); Jonathan Cape (London 1971); Penguin (London 1979).
'Ghostkeeper', *American Review*, 17 (May 1973), pp. 1–34.
Malcolm Lowry: Psalms and Songs (ed. Margerie Lowry), New American Library (New York 1975).

Most of Lowry's original manuscripts are in the collection at the Library of the University of British Columbia in Vancouver. Some of the manuscripts of the main texts are on microfilm at the Senate House Library of the University of London.

Biography and Criticism: A Select Bibliography

Ackerley, Chris, and Clipper, Lawrence, J., *A Companion to Under the Volcano*, UBC Press (Vancouver 1984).
Binns, Ronald, *Malcolm Lowry*, Methuen (London and New York 1984).
Bradbrook, M.C., *Malcolm Lowry: His Art and Early Life*, Cambridge University Library (London 1974).
Costa, Richard Hauer, *Malcolm Lowry*, Twayne (New York 1972).
Cross, Richard K., *Malcolm Lowry: A Preface to His Fiction*, University of Chicago Press (1980); Athlone Press (London 1980).
Day, Douglas, *Malcolm Lowry: A Biography*, Oxford University Press (New York 1973; London 1974).
Grace, Sherrill, *The Voyage That Never Ends: Malcolm Lowry's Fiction*, UBC Press (Vancouver 1982).
Knickerbocker, Conrad, 'Swinging the Paradise Street Blues: Malcolm Lowry in England', *The Paris Review*, Vol. 10, No. 38 (Summer 1966), pp. 13–38.
Lorenz, Clarissa, 'Call It Misadventure', *Atlantic Monthly* (June 1970).
McConnell, William, 'Recollections of Malcolm Lowry', *Canadian Literature*, 6 (Autumn 1960).
Markson, David, *Malcolm Lowry's Volcano: Myth, Symbol, Meaning*, Times Books (New York 1978).
Noxon, Gerald, 'Malcolm Lowry: 1930', *Prairie Schooner* (Winter 1963–4).
Smith, Anne (ed.), *The Art of Malcolm Lowry*, Barnes and Noble (New York 1978); Vision Press (London 1978).
Stern, James, 'Malcolm Lowry: A First Impression', *Encounter*, XXIX (September 1967), pp. 58–68.

Wood, Barry (ed.), *Malcolm Lowry: The Writer and His Critics*, Tecumseh Press (Ottawa 1980).

Woodcock, George (ed.), *Malcolm Lowry: The Man and His Work*, UBC Press (Vancouver 1971).

Woolmer, J. Howard, *Malcolm Lowry: A Bibliography*, Woolmer/ Brotherson (Revere, Penn. 1983).

The Malcolm Lowry Review (formerly *The Malcolm Lowry Newsletter*) is published twice a year by the Department of English, Wilfrid Laurier University, Waterloo, Ontario, Canada.

Index